The Princeton Review

Verbal Workout for the New
GRE

Fourth Edition

Yung-Yee Wu

PrincetonReview.com

Random House, Inc. New York

The Princeton Review, Inc.
111 Speen Street, Suite 550
Framingham, MA 01701
E-mail: editorialsupport@review.com

ISBN: 978-0-375-42821-0
ISSN: 1559-8640

Permission has been granted to reprint portions of the following:

"The Self-Reproducing Inflationary Universe," by Andrei Linde.
Scientific American, Nov. 1994, pp. 48–49.

Compulsive Beauty, by Hal Foster. MIT Press, Cambridge, MA,
© 1993 Massachusetts Institute of Technology, pp. xi–xiii.

Death Comes to the Maiden: Sex and Execution, 1731–1933, by
Camille Naish. Routledge, a division of Routledge, Chapman and
Hall Inc., NY, © 1991, pp. 5–6.

*Free Soil, Free Labor, Free Men: The Ideology of the Republican
Party Before the Civil War*, by Eric Foner. Oxford University Press,
NY, © 1970, pp. 2–4.

The Perils of Humanism, by Frederick C. Crews. Princeton
University Press, Princeton, NJ, © 1962, pp. 3–6.

*Gender Differences at Work: Women and Men in Nontraditional
Occupations*, by Christine L. Williams. University of California
Press, Berkeley and Los Angeles, CA, © 1989, pp. 3–6.

"Cerebral Meningitis Epidemics," by Patrick S. Moore and Claire V.
Broome. *Scientific American*, Nov. 1994, pp. 44–45.

City of Women: Sex and Class in New York, 1789–1860, by
Christine Stansell. University of Illinois Press, Chicago, IL, © 1982,
pp. xi–xiii.

California Indian Shamonism, edited by Lowell John Bean. Ballena
Press, Menlo Park, CA, pp. 15–16.

Editor: Selena Coppock
Production Editor: Michael Breslosky

Printed in the United States of America on partially recycled paper.

10 9 8 7 6 5 4 3 2 1

Fourth Edition

Editorial
Robert Franek, VP Test Prep Books, Publisher
Seamus Mullarkey, Associate Publisher
Laura Braswell, Senior Editor
Selena Coppock, Editor
Heather Brady, Editor

Random House Publishing Group
Tom Russell, Publisher
Nicole Benhabib, Publishing Manager
Ellen L. Reed, Production Manager
Alison Stoltzfus, Associate Managing Editor

ACKNOWLEDGMENTS

My first thank you must go to the people at The Princeton Review who helped me put together this tome. Thank you, Jeannie Yoon, for helping me and for always listening. Thank you, Amy Zavatto, for providing me with critical feedback and for actually reading every word.

Finally, thank you to Fritz Faerber for feeding me while I wrote. Thank you, thank you, thank you, Lin, Shi-yu, Yung-Hsing, and Mie-Mie for keeping me sane. And last, but not least, thank you, Woobie, for being you.

—*Yung Yee Wu*

Special thanks to Adam Robinson, who conceived of and perfected the Joe Bloggs approach to standardized tests and many of the other successful techniques used by The Princeton Review.

The editorial team would like to thank all of the TPR tutors and teachers who helped us revise many books for the new GRE. This includes Elizabeth Aamot, Jennifer Amerkhanov, Michael Chapian, Vanessa Coggshall, Loren Dunn, Peter Hanink, Karen Hoover, Alison Howard, Michael Levy, Lisa Mayo, Jerome J. O'Neill, Elizabeth Owens, Debbi Reynolds, Tim Ricchuiti, Lisa Rothstein, David Stoll, Scott Thompson, and particularly Curtis Retherford, Neill Seltzer, Jennifer Downey, and Liz Rutzel.

ABOUT THE AUTHORS

Yung-Yee Wu joined The Princeton Review in 1993. She began as an instructor and later worked in research and development as the director of high school, graduate, and international courses.

CONTENTS

Introduction 1

Chapters

1 Strategies 7

2 Text Completions 17

3 Reading Comprehension 55

4 Sentence Equivalence 115

5 Analytical Writing 149

6 Vocabulary 187

7 Mixed Drills 239

Introduction

THE GRE AND YOU

So you've finally decided what to do with your post-college life. You're not going to pursue the vaunted M.D., nor are you going to chase the lucrative J.D. Rather, the initials you desire to follow your name are M.A., M.S., or Ph.D. In short, you want to go to graduate school. However, since you can't simply sign up for grad school, you're going to have to tackle the application process. That means writing essays, soliciting recommendations, gathering transcripts, and taking the Graduate Record Examination, otherwise known as the GRE. Nearly all graduate programs require the GRE, so no matter what field you intend to pursue, the GRE probably lies in your future. The GRE is written by the Educational Testing Service (ETS), the same folks who inflicted the SAT upon you during your high school days.

WHAT DOES THE GRE MEASURE?

That's an excellent question. According to ETS the GRE measures "analytical writing, verbal, and quantitative skills that have been acquired over a long period of time and that are not related to any specific field of study." Let's think about that for a moment. What seems to be missing from this statement? If you said, "Something directly related to how successful I will be as a grad student," you're on the right track. Notice that even ETS doesn't claim that the GRE measures how well you'll perform in a program of anthropology, or psychology, or religious studies, or art history, or physics. The GRE is not a test of intelligence or of your aptitude for graduate study. Despite this, graduate schools use it because it gives them an objective way to compare applicants whose other qualifications are often quite subjective.

SO WHAT DOES THE GRE *REALLY* MEASURE?

The GRE tests how well you solve GRE problems. It's true that in order to do that, you need some basic math skills, basic reading skills, basic writing skills, and a good vocabulary, but, perhaps most important, you need good test-taking skills. Many people (including those at ETS) view the GRE as some kind of general assessment of your ability. They believe that you either have what it takes, or you don't. But in reality the GRE tests very specific information and skills. You can learn that information and you can develop those skills. The key is to approach the GRE as a *specific* task, like learning to play the piano or hitting a golf ball. The same two things that will help you become a better piano player will help you become a better GRE test taker: 1) Instruction, and 2) Practice. And both of those are what you will get with this book.

REGISTERING FOR THE TEST

The GRE is a computer-based test that you will take in a designated testing center. You can take the test year-round, on almost any day, morning or afternoon, weekday or weekend, subject to the availability of test appointments at the test center you want to use. The earlier you register, the more likely you are to get your preferred appointment. You can only take the GRE once per calendar month, and a maximum of five times in any 12-month period. In order to schedule a test, call 1-800-GRE-CALL. If you're taking the test in the U.S., Puerto Rico, or most U.S. territories, the GRE currently costs $130, and you have to pay by credit card. The test costs $160 from most other locations. There's a $40 fee if you need to reschedule. These prices may change, so for up-to-date information, visit **www.gre.org**.

HOW IMPORTANT IS THE GRE?

The definitive answer to this important question is: It depends. How much weight the GRE is given will vary from school to school, and from program to program. Some schools consider the GRE very important, while others tend to view it as a formality. Some don't use it at all for admissions, but only in awarding scholarships. Schools may also give different weight to the different sections of the GRE. If you're applying to a masters program in English Literature, for example, they might not care too much about your Math score, and focus instead on your Verbal and Analytical Writing scores. The best way to find out how important your GRE score will be is to contact the schools you're interested in and ask them. Most graduate programs are happy to talk about the application process and can let you know how they evaluate GRE scores.

In any case, there is always much more to a graduate school application than GRE scores. Your grades, undergraduate institution, recommendations, personal statement, research or work experience, and interview are all part of the process. The GRE can be important, but it's never the whole story.

THE STRUCTURE OF THE GRE

Let's take a moment to review the basic structure of the GRE.

THE SCORED SECTIONS

The GRE contains five scored sections:

- One 60-minute Analytical Writing section, which contains two essay questions
- Two 30-minute Verbal sections, which contain approximately 20 questions each
- Two 30-minute Math sections, which contain approximately 20 questions each

The first section will always be the Analytical Writing section, followed by the Math and Verbal sections, which can appear in any order. All of the Verbal questions are multiple-choice. The Math questions are mostly multiple-choice with some Numeric Entry questions which require typing in an answer.

You will be able to see your Verbal and Math scores immediately upon completion of the test, but you will have to wait about two weeks before your Analytical Writing section is scored.

You will get a 1-minute break, enough time to close your eyes and catch a breath, between each section. You will also get a full 10-minute break after the third section. Be sure to use it to visit the bathroom, take a drink of water, refresh your mind, and get ready for the rest of the exam.

THE EXPERIMENTAL SECTION

In addition to the five scored sections listed above, you will also have an unscored experimental section. This section is almost always a Math or Verbal section. It will look exactly like the other Math or Verbal sections, but it won't count at all toward your score. ETS administers the experimental section to gather data on questions before they appear on real GREs.

Thus, after your Analytical Writing section you will actually see five multiple-choice sections: either three Verbal and two Math, or two Verbal and three Math, depending on whether you get a Verbal or Math experimental section. These sections can come in any order. You will have no way of knowing which section is experimental, so you need to do your best on all of them. Don't waste time worrying about which sections count and which section does not.

Here is how a typical GRE might look:

Analytical Writing – 60 minutes
Math – 30 minutes
10-minute break
Verbal – 30 minutes
Verbal – 30 minutes
Math – 30 minutes
Verbal – 30 minutes

Remember, the Analytical Writing section will always be first, and it will never be experimental. In the above example, the two Math sections were scored, but out of the three Verbal sections only two of them were scored. One of the three was an experimental section, but we don't know which one. Of course, on your GRE you might see three Math sections instead of three Verbal sections, and they may come in any order. Be flexible, and you'll be ready for the test no matter what order the sections come in. In fact, they may not even include an experimental section! If so, count your lucky stars that you didn't have to waste your time on a meaningless section.

RESEARCH SECTION

The GRE will occasionally include an optional research section. This section will always be the final section of the test and will be clearly identified. ETS uses this section to test out new oddball questions. Nothing you do on the research section will change your score in any way.

HOW IS THE GRE SCORED?

You receive three separate scores for the GRE, corresponding to the three scored sections:

- A Verbal score from 130–170, in 1-point increments
- A Math score from 130–170, in 1-point increments
- An Analytical Writing score from 0 to 6, in half-point increments

THE GRE VERBAL SECTION UNMASKED

Let's look in more detail at the Verbal section. As we said before, the two scored Verbal sections contain approximately 20 questions each. You are given 30 minutes for each section.

The GRE Verbal section contains three types of questions:

- Reading Comprehension
- Text Completion
- Sentence Equivalence

These questions will not appear in any particular order. There will be about the same number of each question type. Some questions will come in different varieties, such as Reading Comprehension questions which require choosing all the answers that apply, or require selecting a sentence from the passage.

Within each section, you will be able to answer the questions in whatever order is easiest for you. Any question you feel like doing later, just hit Next and you can return to that question anytime within the 30 minutes.

Once you have finished a section, however, you can't return to it. The GRE will use your results from the first Verbal section you complete to determine which questions to give you on your next Verbal section. If you do well on the first section, you'll get harder questions. If you don't do as well, you'll get easier questions.

How does this affect you? It doesn't. You should still try your best on every single section, whether it's the first or second section of that type. In fact, when you get to the second Verbal section, don't try and guess whether or not it's easier than the first one. People are incredibly bad at guessing how hard questions are for other people, and if you're focusing on anything but how to answer the question in front of you, you're wasting your time. Ignore the fact that the GRE is adaptive, and instead focus on the section you're currently working on, not the section you already finished. Every question is worth the same amount of points, so focus on answering questions correctly.

THE ANALYTICAL WRITING SECTION DEMYSTIFIED

In the Analytical Writing chapter, you'll learn all you need to know about writing high-scoring essays. But in the meantime, we'll examine a few of the basics of this section.

The Analytical Writing section requires you to write two essays:

- One Issue essay in 30 minutes
- One Argument essay in 30 minutes

You are given two prompts for the Issue essay, and you must choose one. For the Argument essay you are only given one prompt.

HOW THE ESSAYS ARE SCORED

Each essay will receive two scores from 0 to 6. The two scores are averaged for each essay, and then the scores for the two essays are averaged and rounded to the nearest half-point.

The only number that schools ever see is the final score. They don't see how you scored on the individual essays. However, ETS plans to eventually make the individual essays themselves available to schools, so that they could read them if they choose.

ANALYTICAL WRITING PERCENTILES

Essay Score	Percentile
6	96
5.5	87
5	71
4.5	52
4	32
3.5	17
3	7
2.5	2
2	1
1.5	0
1	0
.5	0
0	0

These are the most recent percentiles ETS has published, however the current percentiles may be slightly higher or lower.

HOW TO USE THIS BOOK

There are probably two categories of people who have purchased this book. See if you belong in one of these.

1. People who have also bought a book that covers the whole GRE (such as, perhaps, the excellent *Cracking the New GRE*) and are simply looking for some more verbal practice.

2. People who are very comfortable with the math on the GRE and want to focus their preparation mostly or exclusively on the Verbal section.

If you fit into the first category, then you will already know much of the information in this book. However, it's still worth reading all of it. First, doing so will reinforce the points and techniques that you've already studied. Also, the material is presented in a slightly different way in this book, and you will benefit from seeing the same techniques described in different words.

If you fit into the second category, then you obviously will want to study all the material carefully to learn how to approach each type of question. Make sure to practice the techniques when you do the practice sets, and read the explanations carefully to ensure that you pick up both the big picture and the details of our methods.

If you fit into a third category, well, we're sure you'll be able to figure out how to use the book to your advantage.

Whatever your situation, one thing you definitely must do is obtain as much real GRE material as you can to practice on. The most important book to get a hold of is *The Official Guide to the GRE revised General Test*. This book is published by ETS, and contains questions for every single question type, Math and Verbal, and practice essay prompts. You can buy it (or order it online) at any large bookstore or directly from ETS at **www.ets.org/gre**.

Included on a CD-ROM inside every copy of *The Official Guide to the GRE revised General Test* is a copy of the GRE *POWERPREP II*® software. *POWERPREP II* contains a computer-based GRE, sample writing topics, sample essays with commentary, a math review, and some tutorials. The most important part is the practice tests. The GRE is a computer-based test, so part of your preparation must include practice on a computer. By taking the *POWERPREP II* computer test, you'll become familiar with the layout of the buttons and the feel of the computer format, and have the opportunity to practice our techniques in a realistic setting. We recommend taking the computer test only after you've completed all the material in this book. You can also download *POWERPREP II* for free from the GRE website at **www.ets.org/gre**.

The most important thing you need to do is work hard. No GRE book can help you if you don't put in the time to learn the techniques, practice the techniques, and then use the techniques on the actual exam. As in many other situations, the results you get out of your GRE preparation will be largely determined by the amount of effort you put into it.

So let's get to work!

1

Strategies

STRATEGIZE

Before we get into the specific techniques for tackling the verbal questions, we need to discuss some of the overall strategies that are important on the GRE. Some of these will make perfect sense, but others may seem counterintuitive. Trust us that everything we recommend here has been tested, refined, and proven through a great deal of experience. Stick with it, and practice until it all becomes automatic and second-nature.

We'll have a lot to say about the computer shortly, but before looking at that, we're going to discuss a few things that are crucial to scoring your best on the Verbal section.

BE METHODICAL

One reason many people particularly despise the Verbal section of the GRE is that there is a specific disadvantage to verbal questions that doesn't exist on math questions. Math questions always have answers that are exact and provable, whereas the answers to verbal questions are always debatable. They involve shades of meaning and nuance that you simply don't have to deal with in math questions. When $x = 7$, you just look for the 7 in the answer choices, but you can never have the same certainty that the answer you choose for a verbal question is correct.

Unfortunately, what many people take from this is the idea that answering verbal questions is a matter of groping your way toward the right answer and picking the one that smells/tastes/feels right. If that's the way you approach verbal questions, it's going to be hard for you to improve. The key to becoming better at solving verbal questions is to adopt a systematic approach. You need a step-by-step method for attacking each part of the Verbal section, and you need to apply that method consistently. Not surprisingly, we will be showing you these techniques in the subsequent chapters.

MEET YOUR NEW BEST FRIEND: POE

This POE is not related to Edgar Allan, but is rather the Process of Elimination. You should use the Process of Elimination on every question in the Verbal section. To understand why POE is so important, we need to look at several elements of the GRE. The first is that the GRE is a multiple-choice test. All the correct answers are given to you on the GRE Verbal section, but each one is surrounded by several incorrect answers. Because there are more wrong answers on the Verbal section than right ones, the wrong ones are easier to spot. And when we spot them and eliminate them, we narrow the range of options we have to choose from, even if we end up guessing.

Another important reason is based on the nature of verbal questions themselves. As we mentioned above, the correct answer to a verbal question is never correct in an absolute, mathematical sense. It's correct because it's the best of the available options. This is why ETS refers to the right answer as the "credited response." Even ETS doesn't claim that one answer is "correct," merely that there's one answer for which you get credit. The point you need to take from this is that the right answer to a verbal question will sometimes be pretty bad. Nevertheless, it will be the least bad of your options. Therefore, what you're really looking for on verbal questions is not an answer choice you like. You're looking for the least objectionable answer, the one that stinks less than all the others.

It's important to understand that POE is not just a matter of crossing off answer choices as you go. It's not simply a physical process. Rather, it's an active mental process that evaluates answer choices by looking for flaws, looking for reasons to get rid of them. Nothing is more frustrating than looking at a few answer choices and not liking any of them, or liking more than one and being unable to decide between them. Get in the habit of making the best case you can *against* each answer choice, and you'll be much more successful.

WATCH OUT FOR TRAPS

ETS has given the GRE to hundreds of thousands of students, and because of all this data and experience you can believe one thing: They know how you think. Don't feel bad about this. They know how you think because most of us think in very similar ways. We all share many of the same associations and tendencies. It's simply part of our nature. ETS has learned how to take advantage of this by writing trap answers, sometimes called "distractors," because they distract you from the right answer. For example, on a tough Text Completion or Sentence Equivalence question, ETS loves to include an answer choice that contains words that remind you of the original sentence, but don't actually fit. Say you get a sentence like "Vincent approached each canvas ------- , carefully considering the perfect location for his next brush stroke." ETS knows that if they put an answer choice such as *artistic*, many people will choose it because Vincent is an artist, and it seems like the best thing they can find. Don't fall for it. If the answer could be found that way, it wouldn't be a hard question.

SCRATCH PAPER

The GRE is a computer-based test, so you can't write on the problems themselves. (The test center employees get very unhappy if you write on their computer screens.) All your work must be done on scratch paper. For Verbal questions, there are between 3 and 6 answer choices. If you have a Sentence Equivalence question, which requires choosing two out of the six answer choices that could fit into a sentence, then you don't want to waste time trying to remember which answers worked and which didn't. This is exactly what the scratch paper is for. As soon as you see the question, start writing.

Later on in the book, we'll discuss exactly what to write for each particular question type, but for every single question type you'll write down a letter for each answer choices. For a Sentence Equivalence question, since there are six answer choices, you'll write A B C D E F vertically on your scratch paper. As you work on the problem, you'll cross off answers that you know are wrong. After that, you can focus on figuring out which of the answers you have left are correct.

Get used to using a simple notation on your scratch paper to tell you which answers are still possible. If an answer is clearly wrong, cross it off. If an answer seems like it could work, put a check mark next to it. If an answer contains a word you don't know, then put a question mark next to it. You may need to look at the answer choices you haven't crossed off or question marked a couple times until you've crossed off all the wrong answers.

Your scratch paper for a Text Completion question could look something like this:

2. A̶
    B ✓
    C̶
    D̶
    E ?

There's a bit more you'd write for this type of question, but for now let's focus on the answers. Even without the question or answer choices, which answer should you pick here? Pick (B). Although you put a question mark next to (E) because you didn't know the word, it doesn't matter what that word means if you knew what (B) was, and that word works with the sentence.

Notice that we wrote down the question number? Since you can skip questions and return to them later, you may end up selecting one answer for now and returning to this question later if you have time. If you do return to this question, you don't want to have to redo all that nice writing you did on your scratch paper. If you've numbered each question's answer choices on your scratch paper, then returning to half-completed problems is much easier.

What if your scratch paper looks like this? Which answer choice would you pick?

4.   ~~A~~
      ~~B~~
      C
      ~~D~~
      ~~E~~

That may seem like an obvious question, and it is. Pick (C), because it's the only answer left. Clearly (C) wasn't a very good answer, otherwise it would have gotten a checkmark. But it wasn't clearly wrong, so you moved on and looked at the other answer choices. Remember what we said about POE: Sometimes the correct answer is not very good.

There are three major advantages to using your scratch paper on every single problem. The first is that, as already mentioned, you don't want to have to waste time and brainpower remembering which answers worked and which didn't. If you have all that information written down, you can let your weary brain focus on moving forward, rather than remember what you already did.

The second is that you are more likely to know when it's time to guess on a problem. Say you've got this on your scratch paper:

5.   A ?
      ~~B~~
      C ?
      D ?
      ~~E~~

You've crossed off two answers, but have question marks next to the other three answer choices. That means have three words on the screen that you don't know. At that point, it's a better use of your time to guess one of those three mystery words and work on other questions than it is to sit and stare at those words, hoping that you magically remember one of the definitions.

The last reason to use your scratch paper is so that you don't have to redo your work when you return to problems. If you've already crossed off three answers on a Reading Comprehension question and decided to move on, then when you come back to that question you don't want to waste time rereading the answer choices you already know are wrong.

This book, of course, is not a computer screen, and you may be tempted to just cross off answers in the book, rather than writing on your scratch paper (or in the margins) your answer choices. Resist that temptation. As much as possible, set up your scratch paper while doing practice problems in this book in the exact same way you will eventually set it up while doing the actual test. Using your scratch paper should become an automatic response to seeing a GRE question, and if you don't start right now, then you'll be in for a shock when you get to the testing center and you're not used to looking down at your scratch paper to know which answers you have left.

At the test center you'll be given about six sheets of scratch paper. If you need more you can request it, but the proctor will take away all your old paper at the same time. Also, if you run out of paper in the middle of a section, you'll need to put your hand in the air and wait for a proctor to notice, collect the paper, and bring it in to you. You don't want to waste your precious time waiting for the proctor to attend to you. Time is ticking away! So even though your scratch paper is technically unlimited, don't be extravagant. Try to make it last. Use your 10-minute break to get more paper.

VOCABULARY

It might seem odd to think of vocabulary as a strategy, but learning vocabulary is one of the most important things you must do to maximize your score on the GRE Verbal section. The Text Completion and Sentence Equivalence sections are hugely vocabulary-dependent. Only the reading comprehension questions give you a partial respite from this vocabulary obsession.

This means that you have to tackle the vocabulary issue directly. The techniques we'll be showing you are strong, but at some point vocabulary will put a ceiling on your score. The more words you know, the higher that ceiling is. Studying words is unquestionably dull, but you'll know how serious you really are about raising your GRE Verbal score by how diligently you work to expand your vocabulary.

To assist you with this, we have included Chapter 6, which contains lists of words that commonly appear on the GRE. This chapter contains the GRE Hit Parade (which also appears in *Cracking the New GRE*) and additional word lists (that do not). Furthermore, there are drills, quizzes, sample questions, and advice for building your vocabulary. Study these words assiduously, and you'll give yourself a big advantage on test day. But don't wait until you've worked through the rest of the book to turn to the vocabulary chapter. Start working on vocabulary from the very beginning. You need to spread it out over the whole period of your GRE preparation for it to be effective.

Ultimately, the most successful way to a higher GRE Verbal score is the combination of better technique and better vocabulary. Either one alone will help raise your score, but truly high scores and stellar improvements require both.

COMPUTER STRATEGIES

Now we're ready to tackle the computer. Taking a test on a computer is strange. If you haven't taken one before, you'll probably discover that it's stranger than you anticipated. This is one reason why it's so important to take the *POWERPREP II* tests mentioned in the previous chapter. You will not be comfortable taking the real GRE unless you have some experience with the computer format.

In addition to experience, however, you need to have knowledge about how the computer test works and strategies that take advantage of it. Here we'll be looking at the details of the computer format. Let's start with a look at the computer screen itself and a quick explanation of what the various buttons do.

BASIC FORMAT

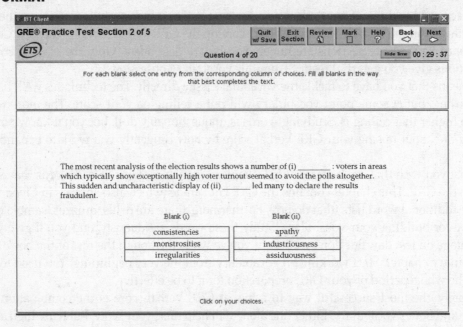

As you can see, the question will be in the middle of the screen, and the answers will be below the question. There are several ways that the GRE can present answer choices, each of which affects how you will select answers and how you will use your scratch paper.

The answers to Text Completion questions will have words inside a table, like this:

exacerbate
plummet
mitigate
rescind
allege

If the question is a sentence with one blank, then there will be five words. You will have to choose 1 of the words.

Blank (i)	Blank (ii)
querulous	preoccupation with
abysmal	affection for
diffident	predilection for

For some Text Completion questions, you will be presented with a sentence which contains 2 or 3 blanks. For each blank, you will have to choose 1 of the three words given. If you don't choose the correct answer for both (or all three) blanks, you get zero points for that question.

For some Reading Comprehension questions, you will be asked a question followed by 5 answer choices, each of which has a circular bubble next to it.

○ refute an erroneous theory
○ assert a controversial claim
○ describe a possible flaw
○ contradict an earlier statement
○ highlight a relevant notion

Whenever you see circular bubbles, you will have to choose 1 correct answer.

For Sentence Equivalence questions and certain Reading Comprehension questions, each answer choice will follow an empty box, like so:

☐ ubiquitous
☐ specious
☐ ephemeral
☐ orthodox
☐ universal
☐ conventional

Whenever you see square bubbles, you will have to choose *all* the answers that apply. For Sentence Equivalence questions, there will always be 2 answers that work, and you must choose both correct answers to get any points for that question. For Reading Comprehension questions with square bubbles, 1, 2, or all 3 of the given answers could be correct, and you must select every correct answer to receive any points for that question. At least one of the 3 answers choices will be correct.

To sum up: If you see words in a table, select one word from each column. If you see circular bubbles, choose one answer. If you see square bubbles, choose all the answers that work.

Once you've selected an answer or answers, you must click the Next button to go the next question. Now that we know how the answer choices work, let's turn our attention to the screen itself.

The top of the screen contains the following buttons, from left to right:

- **Quit Test**: This button will end your test. Don't use it unless you're so ill you have to leave the test center. Otherwise, even if you decide that you're going to cancel your score at the end of the test, continue taking the test if you can. You may change your mind at the end, and even if you don't the extra practice and experience will be helpful.

- **Exit Section**: Clicking this button will allow you to exit the section you're working on and move on to the next one. Don't use it unless you've answered every single question in the section and reviewed the questions you weren't sure about.

- **Review**: This button will show you a list of all the questions in the section, by question number. Whether or not you've answered each question is listed next to each question number. Use this button to return to questions you had skipped.

- **Mark**: Clicking this button will mark the current question. This mark will appear on the Review screen, allowing you to easily see which questions you wanted to return to.

- **Help**: Clicking this button will bring up a screen with directions for the current question type. Don't waste your time with this on the actual test. It won't help you solve problems, and you should already know how the buttons and questions work by the time you take the real test.

- **Back:** This button will bring you to the previous question. Any answer you selected for the current question will be saved.

- **Next**: This button will bring you to the next question. You must click this button to move to the next question after selecting an answer. You do not need to pick an answer to move on to the next question.

- **Hide Time**: This button hides the onscreen timer. Ignore this button. Seeing how much time you have left in the section will help with your pacing (more on that in a bit), and without the timer you may answer questions too quickly or too slowly. However, some people find that they just can't concentrate with the timer counting down in front of them, and they need to hide the timer in order to focus on the questions. In any case, when the section is almost over, the timer reappears (if it was hidden) and you can't hide it any longer.

KEEP MOVING

You've got 20 questions to answer in 30 minutes. If a tough question comes up, and you're not sure how to solve it, what should you do? Sit and stare at it until time runs out? Of course not. Remember that Mark button we mentioned earlier? Use it. Click the Mark button so that you know to return to that question when you've completed everything else in the section.

Get used to completing each section in two passes. On the first pass, you're going to get most of your points answering questions that you know how to do. They may not be easy or straightforward questions, but they're questions you know how to solve within a reasonable amount of time. As soon as a question gives you trouble, run away. Flee. Click Mark, then click Next, and forget about that tough question for now. Focus on the question that's currently in front of you. Read it carefully. Do you know how to get started? Do you know what to start writing on your scratch paper? If so, give it a try. If not, then run away. Next question.

Your first pass should be a confidence builder. As you begin to study for the GRE, the first pass may not inspire much confidence, but as you get to know the different question types better you'll find that there are a certain number of questions in any given section that you can answer without too much trouble. Your goal on your first pass is to answer those questions.

Once you click Next on question 20, the GRE will remind you that you can return to any previous questions. Click on Review and look at which questions you left unanswered or marked to come back to. Take a look at the timer. How much time do you have left? How many questions? Out of the questions you have left, choose the easiest. Work on that one. If you still can't answer it, guess and move on.

IBT Client

GRE® Practice Test Section 2 of 5

ETS

Question 16 of 20

Return | Go To Question

Hide Time | 00 : 28 : 15

Below is the list of questions in the current section. The question you were on is highlighted. Questions you have seen are labeled **Answered**, **Incomplete**, or **Not Answered**. A question is labeled **Incomplete** if the question requires you to select a certain number of answer choices and you have selected more or fewer than that number. Questions you have marked are indicated with a ✔

To return to the question you were on, click **Return**.

To go to a different question, click on that question to highlight it, then click **Go To Question**.

Question Number	Status	Marked
1	Answered	
2	Answered	
3	Not Answered	✔
4	Answered	
5	Incomplete	
6	Answered	
7	Not Answered	✔
8	Answered	
9	Answered	
10	Answered	

Question Number	Status	Marked
11	Answered	
12	Answered	
13	Answered	
14	Not Answered	✔
15	Answered	
16	Not Answered	
17	Not seen	
18	Not seen	
19	Not seen	
20	Not seen	

PACING

Two of the most important skills for the GRE are how to use you scratch paper, which we've discussed, and pacing. Pacing does not mean rushing, it means knowing how much time to spend on each question. How each person paces himself or herself will change depending on that person's skills, so this is when practice, such as with GRE's *POWERPREP II* software, is key.

However, everyone will follow the same basic timeframe. On your first pass, you shouldn't spend too much time on any one question. Reading Comprehension questions may take some time here, because you'll need to parse the passage, but other than that no single question should take too long. You're not rushing here; you're choosing the easy battles.

On your second pass, take into account how much time and how many questions you have left. You're not going to rush through all these questions. Instead you're going to choose the best questions of what's left, answer those to the best of your ability, and if you don't have time for some other questions, you'll guess. If you have 3 minutes and 5 questions, you may only have time to work on 2 or 3 of those remaining questions. That's fine. It's better to take your time on those questions you know how to do, and get some of them correct (and quickly guess on the others), than it is to rush through all five questions and get almost all of them incorrect.

GUESSING

Don't be afraid to guess. In fact, get used to it. The GRE is designed using tough vocabulary and dense passages. Let's say you've got two answer choices left: perorate and adumbrate. You know you're looking for a word that means to deliver a big fancy speech, so you crossed off the other answer choices, but now you're down to these two words you've never seen before. In that case, guess and move on. Remember that you've got other questions you can spend that time on, and you have to answer every single question. So congratulate yourself on crossing off so many incorrect answers, pick one of the answers left, and worry about some other questions. (By the way, perorate means to orate either formally or for a long time.)

Guessing is not great, but it's a basic part of taking the GRE. Once your only options on a question are "Guess and move on," or "Stare at the question and the timer until you have a nervous breakdown," then guess. Remind yourself that you're doing what a smart test taker should do by not letting one question ruin both your score and your confidence.

The last important thing to know is that you must answer every single question on the test. Do not leave any questions blank. Depending on your particular pacing, you may not have time to work on every question, which means there may be some questions at the end that you have to guess on. That's fine. If you did the questions that you spent time on correctly, then guessing on a couple questions at the end is not going to affect your score in any major way.

A Final Note about the Computer

One final feature of the computer-based GRE is that you'll get your Math and Verbal scores immediately at the end of the test (the essays still need to be read, so you'll receive your Analytical Writing score in about two weeks along with your official score report). Once you've completed the multiple-choice sections, the computer will give you the option to accept or cancel your scores. Of course you have to make that decision before learning what they are. If you choose to cancel, you will never find out how you did. If you accept, you can't cancel them later. Unless you were ill or there was a major distraction during the test (e.g., the person seated next to you had a seizure and was hauled away by paramedics), you should accept your scores. There's no reliable way to know how you did except by seeing the scores. Remember, the test is supposed to be hard for everyone.

2

Text Completions

TC

THE GOAL: FILL IN THE BLANK

Your job on any given text completion question is to pick the answer choice that best completes the sentence by filling in the blank or blanks. Not too hard, right? Well, not too hard if you know what *not* to do.

What not to do is "plug and chug," which (unfortunately) is probably the most common thing people do when they hit a text completion. Here's a typical question:

> Most of Newton's biographers refer to the _____ story of the apple tree and the discovery of gravity, despite the story's lack of verifiable sources.

humorous
empirical
baffling
apocryphal
comprehensible

And here's what those poor people who decide to plug and chug do:

(A) Most of Newton's biographers refer to the *humorous* story of the apple tree and the discovery of gravity, despite the story's lack of verifiable sources. *(Was the story humorous? What happened in that story again? Something about being hit in the head by a snake with an apple, right? I'm not sure about this answer.)*

(B) Most of Newton's biographers refer to the *empirical* story of the apple tree and the discovery of gravity, despite the story's lack of verifiable sources. *(Empirical? What's that mean? Something about an empire? Maybe the Roman empire? Does it mean that he wore a toga? Did Newton wear a toga? I don't think so, so this answer is probably wrong.)*

(C) Most of Newton's biographers refer to the *baffling* story of the apple tree and the discovery of gravity, despite the story's lack of verifiable sources. *(I'm baffled about the story, so this makes sense to me.)*

(D) Most of Newton's biographers refer to the *apocryphal* story of the apple tree and the discovery of gravity, despite the story's lack of verifiable sources. *(Is apocryphal related to apocalypse? Did Newton's discovery of gravity almost cause the world to end? Not sure...better ignore this answer choice.)*

(E) Most of Newton's biographers refer to the *comprehensible* story of the apple tree and the discovery of gravity, despite the story's lack of verifiable sources. *(Stories can be comprehensible. Sure. That makes sense.)*

In other words, when you plug and chug, you just take an answer choice and pop it back into the blank or blanks. How effective is this? Not very. People tend to plug and chug because they think it's the fastest way to answer a text completion, but guess what? It's not. In fact, it's the slowest way, because when you plug and chug, too many answer choices *sound* good. That is, more than one answer choice may seem as if it could work.

A Better Approach

Rather that rereading the same sentence or paragraph over and over again, here's a better way. The first thing you should do, as with all GRE questions, is start writing stuff down. For Text Completion questions, down A B C D E vertically on your paper. (We're just going to talk about 1 blank Text Completion questions, with 5 answer choices, for now. Later in the chapter, we'll explain what more of to do with Text Completion questions with 2 or 3 blanks in which there are 3 answers per blank. Of course, the first thing will be to write A B C and D E F for 2 blank Text Completions, and A B C, D E F, and G H I for 3 blank completions.) Once you've got your letters on the paper, you're all set up to do some Process of Elimination, so let's figure out what we need to eliminate.

Read the sentence. Do not read the answer choices. The answer choices are there to sound nice, and to sound as if they fit nicely in the sentence, which is exactly why ETS put them there. We don't care how good a word sounds in sentence. We only care if a word means exactly what we know the blank has to mean. As you read the sentence, try to see if there's a word or phrase that you think would fit in the blank. This word or phrase doesn't have to be a fancypants GRE word, it just has to mean what you know the blank has to mean. Simple words are fine.

Once you have your own word or phrase for the blank, write that word or phrase down on your scratch paper, right next to your A B C D E. Now it's time do some Process of Elimination. We'll use the same POE marks we talked about in Chapter 1: If an answer choice kind of matches the word or phrase you wrote down, put a check mark. If an answer choice does not match the word or phrase you wrote down, cross off that answer choice. And, last but not least, if an answer choice contains a word you don't know, put a question mark next to it, and do not cross it off.

That's it. After you've gone through the five answers, hopefully you have at least one check mark. If not, guess one of the answers you put a question mark next to, and move on. Notice that although we'll spend more time than you're used to at the beginning of the question, trying to think of and write down your own word or phrase, we more than make up for that time when we do POE. Think of all the time you'll save over the "(A) Most of Newton's....(B) Most of Newton's....(C) Most of Newton's" method of rereading the same question over and over again and seeing what word sounds right.

To summarize:

- Write down letters for each answer choice: A B C D E

- Read the sentence, but not the answers.

- Come up with your own word or phrase for the blank.

- Find the answer choice that matches your word or phrase.

- *Never* eliminate an answer choice if you don't know what a word means.

It's Your Word

Let's take a look at an example. Remember, the first thing to do is to ignore the answer choices.

The actress, though portrayed by the media as an arrogant prima donna, was, in fact, both charming and _____.

improvident
gracious
enthusiastic
exceptional
lithesome

What word might fit into the blank? *Nice, modest, delightful.* Anything in that vein. Now that you have your own word, go to the answer choices and pick the one that most closely matches your word. The best match doesn't have to be your word exactly—it doesn't even have to be a synonym of your word. It just needs to get across the same idea or feeling.

To go back to the above example: You want to find a word that matches *nice.* Don't cross out (A) if you don't know what *improvident* means. Put a ? next to (A) on your scratch paper, and move on. Don't start playing the word association "what does this word sound like?" game. What about (B)? Does it work? Sure, *gracious* is a good match for *nice.* Put a check mark next to (B) on your scratch paper, and check the next answer. For (C), *enthusiastic* doesn't mean nice. Although someone who is *enthusiastic* COULD be nice, they could also be mean. Cross off (C) on your scratch paper. Same goes for (D), because *exceptional* doesn't match *nice.* If you don't know what *lithesome* means, then put a ? next to (E). Your scratch paper should look something like this:

A ?
B ✓
C̶
D̶
E ?

Even though we didn't know what *improvident* or *lithesome* meant, you should know which answer to choose just by looking at your scratch paper. Since (B) got a check mark, then (B) is the answer.

Note that in working through this example, we went through each and every answer choice. On any text completion—on any verbal question—you *have* to do this. You must. Why? Because Verbal is about finding the *best* answer, not the right answer. That means you may come across an answer choice that seems to work, but another answer choice further down the road works even better. The lesson: Always, always look at every single answer choice. Let's try another text completion.

Although perfumes were first created from the natural oils of plants, chemists have, since the early nineteenth century, produced thousands that contain _____ ingredients.

uncultivated
piquant
synthetic
aromatic
variable

Did you remember to ignore the answer choices? What word did you fill in for the blank? Probably something along the lines of *man-made*. (A) doesn't match your word, so eliminate it. (B) is a slightly hard word. If you don't know what *piquant* means, then you have to leave it in. (C) looks good—*synthetic* is a good match for *man-made*—still, don't forget to check out (D) and (E). *Aromatic* and *variable* aren't close to *man-made* at all. So you're left with (B) and (C). Since (B) has a ? and (C) has a ✓, pick (C).

QUICK QUIZ #1

In the following questions, come up with your own word for the blank. The answers are on page 43.

1. The kidnapping of the son of Charles A. Lindbergh in 1932 so _____ the public that laws were soon adopted with severe penalties for the offense.

   exault 吓住

2. Though, in his lifetime, Mark Twain received much (i) _____, today's critics esteem him to such a degree that they (ii) _____ him.

   appraise 赞美

   崇拜 教书神

3. By (i) _____ all of the genes on the human chromosomes, the Human Genome Project, established in 1990, hopes to gain (ii) _____ into human evolution and study the genetic similarities (iii) _____ by all species.

   analysing
   progress
   carried

4. Even with the (i) _____ of the battering ram and catapult, which reduced the effectiveness of large-scale fortifications, castles during the Middle Ages still remained (ii) _____.

   expanding 所应、壳发

   lush 繁盛

5. Mosses, though limited to (i) _____ habitats because they require water for fertilization and lack a vascular system for absorbing water, are considered (ii) _____ plants due to their resilience.

   water 水生植物

   desert 沙漠

6. The _____ sources that Fahey drew upon extensively in the mid-1960s can be clearly heard in compositions such as the motley "Stomping Tonight," which incorporates elements from the classical music of Vaughan Williams, a Gregorian chant, and the blues of Skip James.

   varied 多样化

7. The judge did not wish to _____ the tensions between the feuding parties by seeming to favor one side over the other.

   extend 加重

A CLUE, A CLUE, A CLUE

Let's take a look at a text completion that you'll never see on the real GRE.

ETS is _____ company.

a nonprofit
a wealthy
a devious
a cautious
an enormous

How should you always approach a text completion? By ignoring the answer choices and coming up with your own word for the blank. But if you do that for this particular question, guess what? Anything could go in the blank. (A) through (E) could all be right.

This particular question would never show up on the real GRE because there is no right answer—any of the five answer choices could work. But what if we changed the question a little so that it looked like the following:

ETS, which earns over four million dollars
each year, is _____ company.

a nonprofit
a wealthy
a devious
a cautious
an enormous

What's the answer now? (B), right? How do you know (B) is correct? You know the answer is (B) because of the clause "which earns over four million dollars each year." That clause gave you a clue as to what belonged in the blank. Let's change the question again.

ETS, which likes to trick test takers on
hard questions, is _____ company.

a nonprofit
a wealthy
a devious
a cautious
an enormous

The answer now is (C). What tells you the answer is (C)? The clue "which likes to trick test takers on hard questions."

On every single text completion, there must be a clue that tells you what belongs in the blank. Without a clue, there would be no right answer. So, anytime you're coming up with your own word for the blank, look for the clue to help you out. In fact, often you can repeat the clue itself in the blank. For example, in the last question, you might have said, "ETS . . . is a *tricky* company." *Tricky* is the word you came up with based on the clue.

Keep in mind that clues can show up anywhere in the sentence: at the beginning, in the middle, or at the end. If you're having trouble finding the clue, look for the most descriptive part of the sentence. That's usually where the clue is. Try to identify the clue in the following example:

Hadrian, one of Rome's second-century emperors, focused his efforts primarily on _____ matters, traveling throughout Rome's territory and personally ensuring that the government of each province was operating efficiently.

| foreign |
| dubious |
| municipal |
| inconsequential |
| martial |

Don't worry if you don't know anything about Roman emperors; the sentence gives us all the information we need. What does it tell us about this Hadrian guy? Well, we know that he spent time traveling throughout Rome's territory and personally ensuring that the government of each province was operating efficiently. Let's use that clue to come up with a blank. Since he cared about the government of each province, our word can be something like *government*.

Now let's do some POE. Does (A), *foreign*, mean *government*? Not really. Cross it off. Same with (B), *dubious*. Since *municipal* matches with *government*, put a check mark next to (C). (D), *inconsequential*, doesn't match with our word, nor does (E). Cross both of them off. The answer is (C).

Notice that everything we need to know about the blank is inside the sentence itself. There will always be a clue in every sentence to tell you what you need to know.

TRIGGERS

Besides the clue, there are other parts of the sentence that tell you what should go in the blank. These other parts of the sentence are what we call triggers.

Triggers are, for the most part, small words. They're important, though, because they usually give structure to the sentence: They either keep the sentence going in the same direction, or they change the direction of the sentence.

Let's take a look at two classic triggers: *and* and *but*. Fill in the blank for each of the sentences below.

- I don't want to go to the party, and _____.
- I don't want to go to the party, but _____.

For the first sentence, you might have come up with something like: "I don't want to go to the party, and you can't make me go." For the second sentence, you might have had something along the lines of "I don't want to go to the party, but I'll go anyway."

Notice the function of *and* in the first sentence. It continues the flow of the sentence. In contrast, *but* in the second sentence changes the flow—it takes the sentence in the opposite direction.

Let's take a look at a question you've already seen to get an idea of how triggers work.

> The actress, though portrayed by the media as an arrogant prima donna, was, in fact, both charming and _____.

improvident
gracious
enthusiastic
exceptional
lithesome

First, let's stop and look for the clue. The most descriptive part of the sentence is "portrayed by the media as an arrogant prima donna." Now, let's look for triggers. Do you see any?

There are not one, but two, triggers in this sentence. The first is the word "though" and the second is the word "and." The "though" tells you the sentence is going to change in direction. Therefore, what goes in the blank should be the opposite of "an arrogant prima donna." What about the second trigger? The "and" tells you the sentence is going to continue in the same direction. So what goes in the blank should be similar to "charming."

More Triggers

Not all sentences have triggers, but many do. The chart below shows some of the most common triggers.

Same-Direction Triggers	Changing-Direction Triggers
and	but, yet
since	though, although, even though
because	
so	
not only . . . but also	
thus	
therefore	
consequently	
hence	
:	
;	

Triggers aren't always words. Note that the last two triggers in the same-direction column are punctuation marks. ETS loves to use the colon (:) and semicolon (;), so always be on the watch for them. Take a look at an example:

Born of the blood of Uranus, the mythic Furies are _____ creatures: they punish those who have wronged blood relatives, regardless of the perpetrators' motivations.

| vehement |
| unforgiving |
| gloomy |
| quarrelsome |
| caustic |

The clue is everything that comes after the colon; the trigger is the colon itself. Therefore, you know that whatever goes in the blank should continue the direction of "they punish those who have wronged blood relatives, regardless of the perpetrators' motivations."

Given the clue and the trigger, a good word for the blank is *vengeful*. You can eliminate (A) since *vehement* isn't a good match. (B) looks okay, but let's go through the rest of the answer choices just to make sure. (C) definitely isn't right, and neither is (D). (E) doesn't fit since *caustic* means sarcastic, so you're left with (B). It's the best answer.

QUICK QUIZ #2

In the following questions, underline the (clue) and circle any (triggers) Then, use the clue and triggers to help you determine what word should go in the blank. Remember, the clue is typically the most descriptive part of the sentence. Also, don't forget you can often repeat a part of the clue as the word that goes in the blank. The answers are on page 43.

1. In the Bible, handwriting appeared on the wall at the feast of Belshazzar, a ____ (+) of doom, according to Daniel; that night, Babylon fell to Cypress.

2. By the late nineteenth century, many of the congressmen had become staunch Conservative ; they firmly believed that the United States should avoid all foreign wars and entanglements.

3. (Even though) the evidence produced did not (i) show his guilt, the jury still believed in his (ii) ~~fault~~ culpability

4. Jane's naiveté was often charming, (but) her (i) ~~trust~~ all too easily led her to be deceived and (therefore) (ii) ~~hurt~~ duped

5. The jealousy of the goddess Hera has been (i) recorded in Greek mythology: numerous stories tell of her (ii) (—) Zeus and his philandering.   resentment toward

6. Many park designers are moving away from the concept of (i) creating play for children, (instead) opting for the freedom offered by open space and other (ii) ~~physical~~ activities. (However) this has come at a cost in our (iii) (—) society, in which protective parents are willing to sue anyone felt to be responsible for their child's skinned knee or stubbed toe.   Cons Constrained   unrestricted   Litigious : 爱诉讼 诉讼的

7. It remains a mystery as to how the stable of the early universe evolved into its present-day diversity.   homogeneity 相似关性.   同质

NO WORD OF YOUR OWN?

Together the clue and the triggers help you come up with your own word for the blank. There are times, however, when you won't be able to come up with your own word—even though you've found the clue and the triggers. What do you do then?

You can still use the clue and the triggers to help you. Even though you may not be able to come up with your own word, you can often tell if what goes in that blank is positive or negative. If you know the word is positive, then you can eliminate any answer choice that contains a negative word. If you know the word is negative, then you can eliminate any answer choice that contains a positive word.

A word of caution: Don't use it as a crutch. It's going to be very tempting to use this technique instead of coming up with your own word, but you shouldn't. Your first goal is always to come up with your own word. Only if you can't do that should you move on to Positive/Negative. For those times when you do use Positive/Negative, remember that you still need to find the clue and triggers. Otherwise you won't know what should go in the blank. Let's try applying Positive/Negative to a question.

> Because he did not want to appear _____,
> the junior executive refused to dispute
> the board's decision, in spite of his belief
> that the decision would impair employee
> morale.
>
> A   –
> B   –
> C   +
> D   –
> E   +

Let's say that you can't come up with your own word, which means you need to rely on Positive/Negative. What's the clue in the sentence? The most descriptive part is "refused to dispute." There's also the trigger "Because." Together, the clue and trigger tell you that a negative word belongs in the blank. So what can you eliminate? (C) and (E).

This is a good example why Positive/Negative can be a very powerful technique. You can't figure out exactly what should go in the blank, but you can still manage to eliminate two answer choices. If you were stuck after that, who cares? You now have a one-in-three chance of getting the question right.

Here's what the complete question looks like:

Because he did not want to appear _____, the junior executive refused to dispute the board's decision, in spite of his belief that the decision would impair employee morale.

contentious
indecisive
solicitous
overzealous
steadfast

(C) and (E) are gone because they're positive words. You can't eliminate (A) if you don't know what *contentious* means. (B) doesn't work because the clue is "refused to dispute." That doesn't work with *indecisive*. For the same reason, (D) doesn't work either. So the best answer is (A). Even though you might not know *contentious*, you can still get to the right answer.

QUICK QUIZ #3

Find the clue and triggers in the following questions and determine whether the word in the blank should be positive or negative. The answers are on page 44.

1. It was only after the end of the grueling and seemingly ceaseless campaign that the soldiers were allowed any measure of _____.

2. Even when injured, Jane has always been a (i) _____ opponent; indeed, a problematic back and foot did not (ii) _____ her from winning several championships during the 2002 season.

3. The nouveau riche often strive for the same social standing as the established wealthy, but they usually find themselves left with only the _____ of affluence.

4. Of particular note is her assertion that verbal transmissions of (i) _____ were not necessary to result in (ii) _____ effects in neighboring social groups; the more violent one group was, the likely nearby social groups were similarly bellicose. A similar effect was not viewed with group feelings of (iii) _____, indicating that conflict spreads far more easily than does amicability.

5. Though it is important to stand by one's beliefs, it is also important not to cling _____ to them.

6. Barbados's approach to debt, however, was radically different than those of similar countries in (i) _____ economic times: By forcing management and workers to discuss outcomes beneficial to both parties, Barbados disproved the most dire forecasts and (ii) _____ in a striking fashion.

7. The novelist's primary skill is his (i) _____ prose, which elevates even his most (ii) _____ scene.

TWO OR THREE BLANKS

So far we've talked mostly about Text Completion questions with only one blank. However, some of the Text Completion questions will have two or three blanks. These Text Completion questions will often be a full paragraph. For each blank, you'll have to choose one out of three possible words.

When you're presented with a two-blank or three-blank Text Completion, treat that question as if it were a series of one-blank questions. Write down letters on your scratch paper (A B C, D E F, and possibly G H I). Read the full sentence or paragraph. Ignore the answers, and decide which of the blanks seems easiest for you to come up with your own word or phrase. If you notice one of the blanks has a really obvious clue, then start with that blank. Now look at the set of answers for that blank. Find the word that matches your word or phrase. Put a question mark next to any word you don't know. Then, move on to the next blank, and then the next.

Sometimes with two- or three-blank Text Completion questions, you may not know the answer to every single blank. In that case, click on the answers you know, guess an answer from what you have remaining in the other blank(s), click the Mark button, make sure that you wrote down the question number next to your work on your scratch paper, and then click Next. Later on in the section, when you've done most of the other questions, you can return to this question (and your scratch paper for the question). You may notice something about the question or answers that you missed the first time. If not, then try one of the other questions you've marked. Remember, you're going to hit some tough questions, and you may not be able to answer them all on the first pass. That's why there's a Mark button. Use it!

Let's try a really long three-blank question. Remember, read the question but ignore the answers.

Economic policy is primarily reactionary, designed solely to avoid downturns rather than foster upturns. As a result, economic policies tend to be (i) _____ the previous crisis, rather than focusing on (ii) _____ management of the current boom. As a result, unrestrained financial growth leads to rampant speculation, and soon even seemingly (iii) _____ investments collapse as another recession begins.

Blank (i)	Blank (ii)	Blank (iii)
ignorant of	prudent	solid
responses to	sparing	tenuous
peripheral to	irrational	unstable

Have fun reading that entire economic textbook? Let's take it apart piece by piece. We'll start with the third blank, because there's a nice clue and trigger close by. We know that the *investments collapse*, which means that there was something wrong with the investments. However, before that clue we have the trigger *even seemingly*, which tells us that although the investments were bad, they didn't seem so bad. We could describe our investments-that-seemed-like-they-weren't-bad with the word *safe*. If we wanted to be more specific, we could say *financially secure*, but *safe* is fine for now.

Now look at the answers for Blank (iii). *Solid* matches with *safe*, because a solid invest-ment is definitely a safe investment, so put a checkmark next to (G). For (H), *tenuous* doesn't mean *safe*, so cross it off (or put a question mark next to it if you don't know what *tenuous* means). For (I), *unstable* doesn't match with *safe*, so cross it off. We only have (G) left, so click on the first word for Blank (iii), *solid*.

Let's try Blank (i) next, because it also has a nice clue for the blank. What's the sentence tell us about *economic policies*? That they are *purely reactionary*. Let's steal the clue for the first blank, and use *reactions*. Cross off (A) and (C), leaving (B), *responses to*.

Now it's time for the middle blank. Most of the work is done at this point, and we now have a much better idea of what this paragraph is about. Blank (ii) is a bit tougher, but there is a clue hiding in the paragraph. What does the paragraph tell us about *management of the current boom*? Well, we know the author thinks that financial policy should *foster upturns*, so we want *helpful* management. (D), *prudent*, means careful, which basically matches our word. (E) and (F) don't, so cross them both off. Our answers are *responses to*, *prudent*, and *solid*.

Don't bite off more than you can chew. If you get a two- or three-blank Text Comple-tion, just work on one blank at a time. Don't get confused by trying to do too much at once. Once you figure out what should go in one blank, use POE *right away*. As you solve each blank, you'll notice that a formerly insurmountable wall of text has become a couple simple sentences.

RELATIONSHIP BETWEEN THE BLANKS

There are a few two- and three-blank questions in which you don't know *exactly* what should go in the blanks. These are rare; most of the time, there'll be a clear clue for at least one blank. Sometimes, however, there will be questions without a nice clue for one or more of the blanks. In that case, you have to see how the blanks relate to each other.

For instance, let's look at this Text Completion question:

Dorsey's film criticisms are (i) _____ in that his critiques (ii) _____ the accepted views of most commentators of film.

Blank (i)	Blank (ii)
impartial	distill
unconventional	conform to
celebrated	defy

The problem with this sentence is there is no clue as to what Dorsey's film criticisms are like. Do they match with the accepted views? Do they go against them? There's no way to know for sure. Rather than look at one blank, let's see how the blanks relate. Make up your own word for one of the blank, and see how it affects the other blank. Then make up another word for the same blank, and see how it affects the other.

Starting with Blank (ii), let's say that his critiques *match* the accepted views. In that case, his film criticisms are *normal, average* reviews. He goes along with whatever everyone else says. But what if for Blank (ii) we say his critiques *go against* the accepted views? In that case, his reviews are probably *unusual*. Looking at the words we came up with, *normal* and *match*, *unusual* and *go against*, notice that *normal* is in the same direction as *match*, and *unusual* is similar to *go against*? Our answers, whatever they are, have to match up.

Now check your answers. The first word for Blank (i) is *impartial*. Are there any words that go in the same direction as *impartial*? Not really. Cross it off. How about *unconventional*? Well, we've got *defy*, which means to go against, so those match up. Put a check mark next to (B) and (E). Check (C) just to be on the safe side. There aren't any words that match up with *celebrated*, so cross off (C).

Remember, these types of Text Completions don't show up that often, so you should still focus on trying to find clues and triggers.

IN SUMMARY...

A text completion is hard only when you get distracted by the answer choices and forget about the sentence itself. Focus on the sentence—that's where the clue and triggers are.

1. Ignore the answer choices. Remember, it's the sentence that's important.

2. Come up with your own word for the blank. If you're having trouble coming up with your own word, look for the clue and triggers.

3. If you can't come up with your own word, use the clue and triggers to determine if what goes in the blank is positive or negative.

4. If it's a two- or three-blank text completion, focus on one blank at a time.

5. If the clue for one blank is actually the other blank, determine what the relationship between the blanks is.

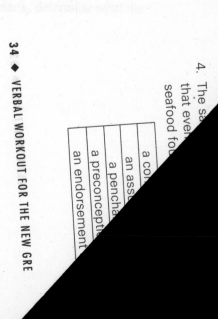

4. The s...
that ever...
seafood fo...

a co...
an ass...
a pencha...
a preconcepti...
an endorsement...

PRACTICE QUESTIONS #1

Directions: Each sentence below has one, two, or three blanks, each blank indicating that something has been omitted. Beneath the sentence are five lettered words or sets of words. Choose the word or set of words for each blank that best fits the meaning of the sentence as a whole. The answers are on page 45.

1. The couple thought that the values represented in traditional services were _____, so they decided to write their own, more modern, wedding vows.

bigoted
archaic
dogmatic
ineloquent
somber

2. An experienced film critic is one who not only calls attention to the (i) _____ of a particular feature, but also puts forth legitimate (ii) _____ that, if employed, would create a more satisfying product.

Blank (i)	Blank (ii)
fascinations	recommendations
origins	statistics
shortcomings	controversies

3. Louis was so painfully shy that his friends had to cajole him not to _____ even the smallest social gathering.

confront
subdue
flout
shun
attend

   almon was prepared with such care
   those who did not have _____
   nd the meal to be delicious.

tention with
urance of
nt for
on of
of

5. The movement in literature known as realism was so named because of its attempt to describe life without idealization or romantic subjectivity; similarly, the realist movement in art had as its intent the (i) _____ of natural forms without (ii) _____.

Blank (i)	Blank (ii)
obfuscation	vulgarity
rendering	embellishment
X adulteration	intrusion

6. Before she applied for the position, Laura thought her qualifications might be considered (i) _____. However, when she learned of the financial (ii) _____ the company was facing, she hoped that her lack of experience might be made up for by her willingness to accept (iii) _____ salary.

Blank (i)	Blank (ii)	Blank (iii)
exemplary	distress	a peremptory
inadequate	approbation	a commensurate
esoteric	abundance	an opulent

7. Known as "The City of Trees," Sacramento has more trees per capita than does Paris, is filled with tree-lined streets and thoroughfares, and even has (i) _____ art installation in City Hall. However, recent budget cuts have (ii) _____ the Urban Forestry workforce, causing some concern about the future of Sacramento's green canopy.

Blank (i)	Blank (ii)
an arboreal	amalgamated
an impressionist	ameliorated
a terrestrial	abridged

PRACTICE QUESTIONS #2

<u>Directions:</u> Each sentence below has one, two, or three blanks, each blank indicating that something has been omitted. Beneath the sentence are five lettered words or sets of words. Choose the word or set of words for each blank that <u>best</u> fits the meaning of the sentence as a whole. The answers are on page 46.

1. In conducting field research, one must observe every detail, no matter how small, for it is often the seemingly unimportant that actually leads to scientific _____.

recessions
obstructions
incapacities
breakthroughs
dissolutions

2. The young researcher's conclusions flew in the face of established scientific knowledge; she therefore stated her findings (i) _____ in her paper. Despite her confidence in her theories, she wanted to avoid accusations of (ii) _____ that might come from more seasoned academics, and determined that she could forgo recognition for the time being. Once her ideas were corroborated by additional experimentation, she would receive her due (iii) _____.

Blank (i)	Blank (ii)	Blank (iii)
eruditely	brazenness	compensation
facetiously	ineptitude	kudos
diffidently	deference	diligence

3. Whereas the flexing of a muscle is viewed as a motion that requires _____ effort, breathing is considered an involuntary act.

careful
conscious
minimal
thoughtful
intensive

4. The count thought his daughter's suitor was naught but a (i) _____; the young man was widely known for his (ii) _____ acts in the taverns and public houses of the village. The nobleman's concerns were therefore (iii) _____ when the wastrel abandoned both the realm and his daughter to seek fortune on the high seas.

Blank (i)	Blank (ii)	Blank (iii)
rake	munificent	broached
maverick	licentious	assuaged
delegate	occult	exacerbated

5. Initially (i) _____ the homeowner's claims of supernatural activity, the Ghost Hunters soon discovered that the house was indeed haunted, but that the ghost was more playful and curious than the traditionally (ii) _____ and solitary spirits they had encountered other places.

Blank (i)	Blank (ii)
credulous of	lugubrious
dubious of	jocund
receptive to	inquisitive

6. The judge was known for his (i) _____ treatment of controversial cases. Hence, it was rare for anyone in the courtroom to request a (ii) _____ for his cases, though he presided over some in which other jurists would feel compelled to (iii) _____ themselves.

Blank (i)	Blank (ii)	Blank (iii)
iniquitous	modification	regale
biased	remonstration	recuse
disinterested	proxy	foment

7. It is easy to assume that the more slow and (i) _____ the study of a disease, the more likely a cure will be found. Historically, however, cures for major diseases have often been found through (ii) _____ breakthroughs and accidental discoveries.

Blank (i)	Blank (ii)
subtle	precipitous
exhaustive	lucid
fortuitous	deliberate

PRACTICE QUESTIONS #3

Directions: Each sentence below has one, two, or three blanks, each blank indicating that something has been omitted. Beneath the sentence are five lettered words or sets of words. Choose the word or set of words for each blank that best fits the meaning of the sentence as a whole. The answers are on page 48.

1. Scientists cannot (i) _____ date when whales evolved to feed using baleen, a filtering structure used to (ii) _____ prey from seawater. Because it is made of keratin, a protein, baleen rarely fossilizes, and the carbon-dating of any fossils found does not conclusively prove age. However, some researchers have attempted to date the modification by (iii) _____ baleen-related skull modifications and formations of the jaw.

Blank (i)	Blank (ii)	Blank (iii)
germanely	sieve	hypothesizing
definitively	consume	assaying
cogently	locate	validating

2. Cleopatra of Egypt and Antony of Rome were allies both militarily and amorously and, together, their armies were (i) _____ at the Battle of Actium. In the chaotic aftermath of the defeat, the two fled and were separated and, tragically, upon hearing a false rumor that his (ii) _____ in battle and (iii) _____ had committed suicide, Antony fell on his sword and killed himself.

Blank (i)	Blank (ii)	Blank (iii)
routed	collaborator	hostility
consoled	antagonist	romance
invigorated	liaison	invasion

3. While there isn't yet enough evidence to prove that any one food can (i) _____ the risk of lung cancer, a "heart-healthy" diet can (ii) _____ other risk factors, such as obesity, that can lead to various forms of cancer.

Blank (i)	Blank (ii)
increase	attack
reduce	detach
assert	diminish

4. Despite his _____ job performance, the administrator did not receive credit for his accomplishments.

incompetent
noticeable
effective
lugubrious
aggressive

5. Although she conveyed the message calmly and without distress, Lin's expression betrayed the message's _____ nature.

facetious
impartial
puerile
uncommunicative
dire

6. Shi-yu's art is to be admired not for its realism, but rather for its distortion of reality: he creates _____ of the world, exaggerating not only its beauty but also its meanness and pettiness.

| a mockery |
| a personification |
| a caricature |
| a sublimation |
| an allegory |

7. Though Bernie is warm and easy-going, she is just as (i) _____, combining her generous nature with an admirable (ii) _____.

Blank (i)	Blank (ii)
affable	recalcitrance
unyielding	benevolence
cantankerous	tenacity

PRACTICE QUESTIONS #4

Directions: Each sentence below has one, two, or three blanks, each blank indicating that something has been omitted. Beneath the sentence are five lettered words or sets of words. Choose the word or set of words for each blank that best fits the meaning of the sentence as a whole. The answers are on page 50.

1. The new film was practically a (i) _____ to Canada, with its shots of Toronto landmarks such as Honest Ed's, Sonic Boom record store, and Parliament Street. Even t-shirts, such as a Canadian coffee shop t-shirt and a Canadian indie-rock band shirt, stress to viewers that the film is (ii) _____ Canadian.

Blank (i)	Blank (ii)
breach	unreservedly
dearth	obscurely
paean	cinematically

2. Some scientists believe that certain human beings may be more _____ than others because the former possess a gene that predisposes them toward aggressive behavior.

reserved
timorous
self-possessed
uncouth
quarrelsome

3. The debate over teacher tenure has recently gained enormous (i) _____; while some believe that tenure is necessary to prohibit arbitrary exercise of (ii) _____ power and to preserve academic freedom, others see tenure as a profligate waste of resources and an obstacle to school improvement. Only through comprehensive comparative studies will we be able to enact a model of teacher recruitment and hiring that will best serve the needs of students, but such studies are difficult to conduct, as districts are often (iii) _____ to experiment with new hiring methods before they have been tested elsewhere.

Blank (i)	Blank (ii)	Blank (iii)
accord	autocratic	eager
ire	whimsical	wanton
prominence	titanic	loathe

4. While some (i) _____, such as Lewis Carroll's lasting creation "chortle" coming from the words "snort" and "chuckle," add meaning and richness to our language, others, such as the recent "reintarnation," can make the speaker simply seem (ii) _____.

Blank (i)	Blank (ii)
chorals	antipodal
neologisms	erudite
canons	benighted

5. While the modern concept of the robot is often (i) _____ to the American science fiction writer Isaac Asimov, the word was actually brought into usage by Karl Čapek, a Czech writer. Čapek wrote about a servant class of creatures who looked almost (ii) _____ to humans, but were actually artificial clones. Čapek noted in his late papers that his brother had contributed the word "robot," deriving it from a Czech word for "slave." Robots, to Čapek, did not symbolize the dream of a future technologically-advanced era, but rather the horror of his current world, filled with the (iii) _____ of fascist dictatorships and mass production.

Blank (i)	Blank (ii)	Blank (iii)
proposed	identical	nuisances
attributed	amenable	actualities
queried	comely	scourges

6. The class was purportedly an exhaustive study of Jane Austen's works, yet since it failed to include either *Emma* or *Pride and Prejudice* in its analysis, it was, by no means, _____.

prudent
acceptable
comprehensive
adequate
authoritative

7. The well-behaved children were (i) _____ and required no (ii) _____ so their parents were always happy to take them on trips.

Blank (i)	Blank (ii)
decorous	supervision
finicky	affluence
exquisite	encumbrance

PRACTICE QUESTIONS #5

1. The two friends, both English teachers, had a tendency to endlessly (i) _____ over small grammatical points; no one else cared whether the word in question was the predicate nominative or predicate adjective of the sentence, but determining who was right was, for them, (ii) _____.

Blank (i)	Blank (ii)
accede	irrelevant
quibble	paramount
kibitz	didactic

2. Although honesty is a trait to be valued, it is not always appropriate because when one is too forthright, one can often be _____.

objective
equitable
deluded
tactless
corrupt

3. Reading D.H. Lawrence's novel *Sons and Lovers* today, it can be easy to forget that its depictions of relationships between men and women were considered (i) _____ for many years after its publication. The types of relationships Lawrence describes, once thought worthy of censure, now seem to appear on film and television on a daily basis and might be considered (ii) _____. Whether one considers it beneficial or harmful, this cultural (iii) _____ marks a profound shift in attitudes toward male/female relationships.

Blank (i)	Blank (ii)	Blank (iii)
prurient	descriptive	transformation
patronizing	pedestrian	assimilation
sacrosanct	vulgar	bias

4. Interpreting data on controversial issues generated from live, as opposed to automated, telephone polls can be complicated by the fact that responders sometimes (i) _____ their views to live pollsters if they believe those views may be considered socially unacceptable. In contrast, automated polling may minimize the (ii) _____ these responders feel, and generate more accurate data.

Blank (i)	Blank (ii)
demonstrate	stagnation
expound	relief
misrepresent	stigma

5. Despite the fact that the (i) _____ writer had no previous publishing experience, she was still able to get a contract for her (ii) _____ novel through hard work and (iii) _____.

Blank (i)	Blank (ii)	Blank (iii)
seasoned	debut	laziness
novice	fiction	persistence
successful	subsequent	expertise

6. Unfortunately, Jeannie's shy demeanor was often misinterpreted by those who did not know her: indeed, strangers typically construed her _____ behavior as coyness.

unresponsive
supercilious
amenable
acquiescent
demure

7. At first, the collector was (i) _____ of the woman's claims that the gold bar was sunken treasure. After he (ii) _____ it, though, he found that coral had grown on the back of the bar, indicating that the bar had been underwater for years. This discovery (iii) _____ the woman's claim.

Blank (i)	Blank (ii)	Blank (iii)
skeptical	briefed	nullified
believing	ignored	validated
tired	examined	contradicted

ANSWERS AND EXPLANATIONS

QUICK QUIZ #1

1. outraged

2. acclaim . . deify

3. mapping . . insight . . shared

4. advent . . defensible

5. moist . . hardy

6. diverse

7. exacerbate

QUICK QUIZ #2

1. In the Bible, handwriting appeared on the wall at the feast of Belshazzar, a _____ of doom according to Daniel; that night, Babylon fell to Cypress.

   portent

2. By the late nineteenth century, many of the congressmen had become staunch _____; they firmly believed that the United States should avoid all foreign wars and entanglements.

   isolationists

3. Even though the evidence produced did not (i) _____ his guilt, the jury still believed in his (ii) _____.

   prove . . culpability

4. Jane's naiveté was often charming, but her (i) _____ all too easily led her to be deceived and therefore (ii) _____.

   credulousness . . duped

5. The jealousy of the goddess Hera has been (i) _____ in Greek mythology: numerous stories tell of her (ii) _____ Zeus and his philandering.

   well documented . . resentment toward

6. Many park designers are moving away from the concept of (i) _____ play for children, instead opting for the freedom offered by open space and other (ii) _____ activities. However, this has come at a cost in our (iii) _____ society, in which protective parents are willing to sue anyone felt to be responsible for their child's skinned knee or stubbed toe.

   constrained . . unrestricted . . litigious

7. It remains a mystery as to how the _____ of the early universe evolved into its present-day diversity.

   homogeneity

QUICK QUIZ #3

1. It was (only after the end) of the grueling and seemingly ceaseless campaign that the soldiers were allowed any measure of _____.

   +

   respite

2. Even when injured, Jane has always been a (i) _____ opponent; indeed, a problematic back and foot did not (ii) _____ her from winning several championships during the 2002 season.

   + . . −

   formidable . . keep

3. The nouveau riche often strive for the same social standing as the established wealthy, (but) they usually find themselves left with only the _____ of affluence.

   −

   trappings

4. Of particular note is her assertion that verbal transmissions of (i) _____ were not necessary to result in (ii) _____ effects in neighboring social groups; the more violent one group was, the likely nearby social groups were similarly bellicose. A similar effect was (not viewed) with group feelings of (iii) _____ , indicating that conflict spreads far more easily than does amicability.

   − . . − . . +

   hostile . . tumultuous . . sociability

5. (Though) it is important to stand by one's beliefs, it is also important not to cling _____ to them.

   −

   dogmatically

6. Barbados's approach to debt, however, was radically different than those of (similar) countries in (i) _____ economic times. By forcing management and workers to discuss outcomes beneficial to both parties, Barbados (disproved) the most dire forecasts and (ii) _____ in a striking fashion.

   − . . +

   dreadful . . rebounded

7. The novelist's primary skill is his (i) _____ prose, which elevates (even) his most (ii) _____ scene.

   + . . −

   rousing . . banal

PRACTICE QUESTIONS #1

1. **B** The couple decided to forgo elements of the *traditional* service in favor of *more modern* vows, so the word in the blank should mean something like too *old-fashioned*. Of the choices, only *archaic* means old-fashioned, so the correct answer is choice (B). Even though traditional vows could be *bigoted*, *dogmatic*, *ineloquent*, or *somber*, none of these words mean old-fashioned.

2. **shortcomings** and **recommendations**

    Start with the second blank. The clues for the second blank are *legitimate* and *would create a more satisfying product*. If a critic offers something legitimate that improve the product, then she puts forth a *helpful suggestion*. Of the three choices, only *recommendations* matches the context you need. The clue to the first blank is *not only calls attention...but also puts forth legitimate*; the first missing word, then, must agree with the fact that there are flaws that need improvement. *Shortcomings* is the only choice that means *problems or flaws*.

3. **D** The clue for this blank is very straightforward: "so painfully shy." If Louis is "painfully shy," is he going to want to attend social gatherings? Probably not. Therefore, what goes in the blank is a negative word—probably something like *avoid*. (A) and (B) are both negative, but they don't mean *avoid*, so eliminate them. Don't cross out (C) if you don't know what *flout* means. (D) looks good, but don't forget to check out (E) just in case. *Attend* in (E) clearly doesn't work, so it's gone. You're left with a word you don't know in (C) and a word that works in (D). Go with what works. The best answer is (D).

4. **C** A good word for the blank is *a liking of* because of the clue "the salmon was prepared with such care that even those . . found the meal to be delicious." Don't cross out (A) if you don't know what *contention* means. (B) doesn't really match *liking*, so cross it out. (C) does mean *liking*, so leave it in. (D) definitely doesn't match *liking*, so cross it out. (E) doesn't match *liking* quite as well as (C). You're left with (A) and (C). Go with what you know. The best answer is (C).

5. **rendering** and **embellishment**

    Start with the second blank. The clue for the second blank is *without idealization or romantic subjectivity*, and the trigger word *similarly* and the semicolon indicate that the two parts of the sentence agree. Recycle the clue and look for a word that means *idealization*. *Embellishment* can mean *an addition to make more interesting*, and comes closest to the meaning you need. The clue for the first blank is *attempt to describe life*, suggesting that the first blank must mean *description*. Of the three choices, only *rendering* matches this meaning.

6.   **inadequate**, **distress**, and **a commensurate**

Based on *her lack of experience*, Laura must have thought her qualifications were insufficient; of the choices, only *inadequate* means insufficient. For the second blank, the trigger *however* suggests a description of the company's financial situation that might make her *inadequate* qualifications acceptable, and only *distress* is sufficiently negative. The third blank needs a word that means Laura will take a salary that matches her *lack of experience*; only *commensurate*, which means proportionate or corresponding, makes sense.

7.   **an arboreal** and **abridged**

The first blank describes the kind of *art installation* that would support the idea that Sacramento is *The City of Trees*, so you need a word that means something like *related to trees*. Of the choices, *arboreal* is the best fit. The second blank refers to an effect of *budget cuts* that would cause *concern about the future of Sacramento's green canopy*, so you something like *reduced* would make sense to describe what happened to the *Urban Forestry workforce*. Of the choices, only *abridged* makes sense.

Practice Questions #2

1.   **D**   Coming up with your own word should be fairly easy for this text completion because the clue is very direct. The clue is "the seemingly unimportant." Well, if the detail only seems unimportant, what is it actually? Very important. Therefore, a good word for the blank might be *wonders*. Does (A) match? No. (B) and (C) definitely don't match. (D) looks good—it's a very positive word— but don't forget about (E). (E) doesn't make any sense, so the best answer is (D).

2.   **diffidently**, **brazenness**, and **kudos**

The second blank has the strongest clue, so start there: The *accusations* the researcher is trying to avoid must be related to *her confidence in her theories*, so you need a word like *overconfidence* for the blank. Of the choices, *brazenness* is the best fit. The first blank should oppose the second blank: The work *flies in the face of established scientific knowledge*, but she's trying to *avoid accusations* and willing to *forgo recognition*. Of the choices, *diffidently* is the best fit. The third blank describes what the researcher hopes to eventually receive: the *recognition* she's currently willing to defer. Of the choices, only *kudos* means recognition.

3. **B** It may be hard to come up with your own word at first, but if you find the clue, it shouldn't be a problem. The clue is "an involuntary act." There's also the changing-direction trigger "whereas." Together, the clue and trigger tell you that what goes in the blank is the opposite of "involuntary." So a good word for the blank is *voluntary*. (A) doesn't give you *voluntary*, so cross it out. (B) could mean *voluntary*, so leave it in. (C) doesn't match, and (D) isn't quite as good as (B)—eliminate both. Finally, (E) is no good. The best answer, then, is (B). This is a great example of why you should never plug and chug. If you go the route of plugging and chugging, guess what? Every answer choice *sounds* as if it could work.

4. **rake**, **licentious**, and **assuaged**

    For the first blank, recycle the clue *wastrel*; of the choices, only *rake* means wastrel. Similarly, the second blank means something like *wastrel-like*, so *licentious* is the best choice there. When the suitor *abandoned both the realm and his daughter*, the count's concerns were *eased*, so *assuaged* is the best fit for the third blank.

5. **dubious of** and **lugubrious**

    The time triggers *initially* and *soon* indicate that the first blank is going contrast with the discovery that *the house was indeed haunted*, so a word that means something like *doubting* would make sense. Of the choices, only *dubious of* fits. The second blank needs to agree with *solitary* while contrasting with *more playful and curious*; of the choices, only *lugubrious* is sufficiently negative.

6. **disinterested**, **proxy**, and **recuse**

    Start with the third blank, where you have the strongest clue. The blank describes what *other jurists* might do, and they're contrasted with the judge who *presided over* cases; hence, something like *not preside* would make sense in the blank. Of the answers, only *recuse* means to not preside. The first two blanks have to work together: Either the judge is known to be *fair*, and it would be rare for someone to request a *replacement*, or the opposite is true. Of the answer choices, only *disinterested* and *proxy* have the correct relationship.

7. **exhaustive** and **precipitous**

For the first blank, you are looking for a word that is similar to (but not a synonym of) *slow. Exhaustive* means comprehensive and thorough, and is in the same ballpark as *slow. Subtle* describes something delicate in intent, and *fortuitous* describes a good accident: Neither word is close to the meaning of *slow.* For the second blank, the trigger word *however* tells you that you want a word that is the opposite of *slow. Precipitous* describes an event that is fast and sudden, and works well in this blank. *Lucid* means easy to understand, and *deliberate* means careful or studied, which is the opposite of what you need in the second blank.

PRACTICE QUESTIONS #3

1. **definitively**, **sieve**, and **assaying**

For the first blank, you need to figure out what *[s]cientists cannot* do when it comes to dating baleen; in the second sentence you're told *any fossils found* don't *conclusively prove age,* so you know scientists can't date the evolution *conclusively. Definitively* is a synonym for *conclusively,* so it's the best choice for the first blank. Both *germanely,* which means relevantly, and *cogently,* which means clearly and convincingly reasoned, may describe the normal actions of scientists, but they don't fit the story. For the second blank, you're told that baleen is a *filtering structure;* therefore it's used to filter, or *sieve. Consume* and *locate* are both common things done to prey, but not by whales and baleen— at least not according to the sentence. For the third blank, you have to again determine what the *researchers* are doing *to date the modification,* so recycle your clue and look for *research.* The best choice is *assaying,* which means examining or analyzing.

2. **routed**, **collaborator**, and **romance**

The first blank describes what happened to their armies at the battle; the second sentence tells you they were defeated, so *routed* is the best choice. The second blank describes the relationship between Cleopatra and Antony; you're told they were *allies* in the first sentence, so *collaborator* is the best choice. An *antagonist* is the opposite of what you're looking for, and a *liaison* is someone who maintains contact between two parties or an illicit affair, so neither definition fits the story. The last blank, when paired with *battle,* mirrors the pair *militarily and amorously* in the first sentence, so *romance* is the best choice.

3. **reduce** and **diminish**

Start with the second blank, which describes a relationship to *other risk factors*: The diet is *"heart-healthy,"* so something like *decrease* would make sense. Of the choices, *reduce* is the best fit. The trigger *while* tells you that the *"heart-healthy" diet* can do what *any one food* seemingly can't—decrease risk—so something like *decrease* would again make sense in the first blank. Of the choices, only *diminish* means decrease.

4. C *Despite* is a trigger word that indicates that the two parts of the sentence go in different directions. The second part of the sentence tells us the administrator did *not receive credit for his accomplishments*. Therefore, the administrator must actually be "accomplished." The answer choice that best fits with "accomplished" is choice (C), *effective*. *Lugubrious* is a more difficult but unrelated vocabulary word meant to distract. *Incompetent* goes in the wrong direction. *Aggressive* would form a coherent thought, but is not directly supported by the rest of the sentence. *Noticeable*, likewise, could conceivably fit into the sentence. However, as *effective* is most directly supported by the rest of the sentence, it is the credited answer.

5. E The clue for the blank is "conveyed the message calmly and without to-do." There is also the changing-direction trigger "although." Together the clue and trigger tell you that what goes in the blank is the opposite of calmness. A good word for the blank might be *serious*. (A) doesn't match, nor does (B). You can't cross out (C) if you don't know what *puerile* means. (D) doesn't work, but (E) does.

You're down to (C) and (E). When one answer choice has a word you don't know and the other works, go with what works. Pick (E). The best answer is, indeed, (E).

6. C The clue for this blank is really everything before the colon—which, don't forget, is a same-direction trigger. That means what goes in the blank should agree with "not for its realism, but rather for its distortion of reality." A good word for the blank, then, is *distortion*. Does (A) match *distortion*? No. What about (B)? No. (C) works, but (D) and (E) don't. The best answer is (C).

This question is a great example of why *not* to rush. If you don't stop to find the clue, then (A) becomes an attractive answer choice.

7.   **unyielding** and **tenacity**

Use the trigger *though* to complete the first blank. The word for blank (i) must mean something different from warm and easy-going, which eliminates *affable*. Since the second part of the sentence indicates that Bernie's qualities are positive, she cannot be *cantankerous*, so *unyielding* is the best choice for blank (i). Blank (ii) must be a positive quality, so *recalcitrance* is out. *Benevolence* is a near synonym for the phrase generous nature, so they would not be used in combination. *Tenacity* is a quality that an *unyielding* person would have, and is thus the best choice for blank (ii).

PRACTICE QUESTIONS #4

1.   **paean** and **unreservedly**

The film contains many references to Canada, including *Toronto landmarks* and t-shirts for *a Canadian coffee shop* and *a Canadian indie-rock band*. From those clues, you know the second blank is a word like *unapologetically* or *clearly*. Eliminate *obscurely*. *Cinematically* is a trap answer because it refers to *a film*, but the film is not *cinematically Canadian*. The items mentioned are all things that are truly in favor of Canadians, and therefore *unreservedly* is the best answer. You now know the first blank is a positive word such as *tribute* or *ode*. *Paean* is *a song of praise* and is the closest match and the correct choice. The other two choices do not pertain to *tribute*.

2.   **E** The clue for the blank is "predisposes them toward aggressive behavior." Since some people have a gene that makes them aggressive, a good word for the blank is *aggressive*. (A) doesn't match *aggressive*, so cross it out. If you don't know what *timorous* means, you have to leave (B) in. (C) isn't a good match, nor is (D). (E), however, works.

You're down to (B) and (E). When you're left with one answer choice that contains a word you don't know and one that works, go with what works. (E) is the best answer.

3.   **prominence, autocratic, and loathe**

The passage begins by describing both sides of a debate, indicating that there is significant disagreement on the issue. Since the two sides disagree, they cannot be in *accord*. Disagreement doesn't necessarily involve anger, so *ire* doesn't work here either. The debate does seem to be gaining in importance, or *prominence*. Blank (ii) must describe a negative type of power, and *autocratic* is the only negative choice in this column. Blank (iii) must mean something that would make it difficult to conduct studies. If the school districts are reluctant or *loathe* to experiment, that would make it difficult to conduct studies.

4.   **neologisms** and **benighted**

Since the word *chortle* was a *creation* that came *from the words "snort" and "chuckle,"* the first blank must be something like *new words*. Of the choices, only *neologisms* means new words. The second blank also describes a creator of a *neologism*, but the trigger *while* indicates a contrast between this second speaker and Lewis Carroll's *meaning and richness*. Of the choices, only *benighted* is sufficiently negative to make sense in the context.

5.   **attributed, identical**, and **scourges**

Use the trigger at the beginning of the first sentence to determine the meaning of the first blank. The word that fits in this blank must make the first part of the sentence disagree with the idea that the word was brought into usage by Čapek; if the concept is often *attributed* to Asimov, then it isn't widely accredited to Čapek. Likewise, the trigger *but* can help us figure out the second blank. The creatures must not look *artificial*, so they may look nearly *identical* to humans. Use the clue in the last sentence to determine that the third blank must mean something like *horror*; *scourges* are sources of affliction or calamity, so that's the answer choice most like *horror*.

6.   **C**   This text completion is actually very easy as long as you take the time to find the clue. The clue for the blank is "purportedly an exhaustive study." The class was supposedly "exhaustive" but if it didn't talk about two of her major books, then what was it? Not exhaustive. Therefore, a good word for the blank is *exhaustive*. (Take note of the two triggers: "yet" and "since.")

Does (A) mean *exhaustive*? No. What about (B)? Not quite. (C)? It could. (D)? No—be careful. The clue doesn't mention anything about the class being bad— just not complete. And finally, what about (E)? It's not a good match. The best answer, then, is (C).

7.   **decorous** and **supervision**

Look for the clue. The children are *well-behaved* and their parents are happy to take them places. *Finicky* is negative word, so it doesn't fit here. *Exquisite* is a nice word, but not a quality that makes children *well-behaved*. *Decorous* means *well-behaved*, so it's a good fit for the blank. *Children* who are *well-behaved* do not require a great deal of *supervision*. *Affluence* means wealth, and *encumbrance* means burden, so those words aren't what you're looking for.

PRACTICE QUESTIONS #5

1.   **quibble** and **paramount**

Start with the second blank: The trigger *but* tells you the word must contrast with the clue *no one else cared*, so something like *important* would make sense. Of the choices, only *paramount* fits. Now you have the whole clue for the first blank: If *determining who was right was, for them, paramount*, then your word for the blank needs to mean something like *argue*. Of the choices, only *quibble* means argue.

2. **D** The clue for this blank is "too forthright." One is "too forthright" when one takes honesty too far. Therefore, what goes in the blank has to be a negative word. (A) is either slightly positive or neither positive nor negative. In either case, throw it out. (B) is positive, so it can't be right. (C) is negative but it doesn't have anything to do with being honest or forthright. (D) is negative and certainly could explain what happens when one is "too forthright." (E) is negative, but it goes too far. (D) is the best answer.

3.   **prurient**, **pedestrian**, and **transformation**

For the first blank, recycle the phrase *worthy of censure* from the following sentence. Of the choices, only *prurient* makes sense. The word in the second blank describes something that can seemingly be seen *on film and television on a daily basis*, so you need a word that means something like *ordinary* or *everyday*; of the choices, only *pedestrian* does. For the third blank, recycle the clue *shift*. Of the choices, only *transformation* means shift.

4. **misrepresent** and **stigma**

The second half of the sentence states that automated polling may *generate more accurate data,* and the trigger word *in contrast* indicates that the two sentences go in different directions. Therefore, the live telephone polls must generate less accurate data, suggesting that the first blank should mean *hide. Misrepresent* is the closest match and is best supported by the rest of the sentence. The first sentence suggests that some responders *misrepresent* when they believe *those views may be considered socially unacceptable.* So, the second sentence suggests the automated polls must minimize this feeling of *socially unacceptability,* and *stigma* is the best match and is correct.

5. **novice, debut, persistence**

The idea for this passage is that a writer with *no previous publishing experience* is able to *get a contract* through *hard work.* Based on those clues in the text, the first blank, which describes the writer, must mean something about having no experience. That rules out *seasoned* and *successful.* The second blank describes the book of the writer, and the only context provided is that the writer has *no previous publishing experience.* Therefore, the only word that makes sense in the blank is *debut.* Finally, the third blank describes how she got her contract. The sentence tells you *hard work* was part of it. The *and* is a same direction trigger, which would allow you to eliminate *laziness. Expertise* can be eliminated, because you know she is not an expert. That leaves *persistence* as the best choice.

6. **E** The clue for this blank is "shy demeanor was often misinterpreted." So what goes in the blank has to be something like *shyness.* (A) doesn't match, nor does (B), so cross them out. (C) doesn't work, so get rid of it, too. (D) isn't quite right, so eliminate it. (E) does work, so it has to be right. (E) is the best answer.

7. **skeptical, examined, validated**

The triggers *at first* and *though* indicate that the first and third blanks are contrasting words. Because the collector finds evidence that supports the *sunken treasure* claim, the third blank needs to be something about substantiating the claim. This lets you eliminate *nullified* and *contradicted,* leaving *validated* as the best answer. That makes *skeptical* the best answer for blank one, because that one most directly contrasts with *validated. Examined* is the best answer for the second blank because the collector made an additional discovery about the bar of gold when he found that *coral had grown on the back of the bar.*

3

Reading
Comprehension

THE TERRAIN OF THE MUNDANE

Practically every test taker in the world hates reading comprehension, and for a very good reason: It's incredibly boring. Well, take heart. Though we can't make the passages any less dull, we can try to make the time spent here a little less painful.

How can we do that? Well, let's talk about how the typical person approaches reading comprehension. First, he reads the passage. That means he reads the *entire* passage—each and every word. He tries to digest this information as much as possible as he reads, and then he moves on to the questions. For each question, he reads the question, goes back to the passage to find the answer, rereads the part of the passage that contains the answer, and only then goes on to the answer choices. Finally, after reading all of the answer choices, he picks the one he thinks is best.

What's wrong with this approach? There's too much reading going on. Basically, the typical person reads the passage at least twice—a big waste of time. Why is reading and rereading passages a bad idea? In order to do well on reading comprehension, you don't need to read that much. It's not *how much* you read that's important; it's *what* you read.

TYPES OF PASSAGES

Subject matter for reading comprehension is going to vary from test to test, but you can expect to see three major categories represented:

- Science
- Humanities
- Social studies

In the end, it doesn't really matter what the subject matter of a passage is. The important thing is not to let a particular category scare you. For example, if you hate science and haven't taken a science class since high school, don't think that a science passage is necessarily going to be a killer. Often, a science passage is relatively easy. Though the jargon may be hard to get past, all the information contained in the passage is factual. Therefore, there's no need for you to do any interpreting or analyzing. The passages ETS selects are pretty cut-and-dried.

POLITICALLY CORRECT

That said, there is one type of passage in which subject matter may count—and that's when ETS uses what we call a PC (or politically correct) passage. Most of the time a PC passage falls into either the humanities or social studies category. We call it a PC passage because it deals with a topic such as women, African Americans, Native Americans, or even the environment.

What can you expect about a PC passage? Everything in the passage is going to be either neutral or positive (sometimes even inspirational) in tone. In no way can a correct answer for a question be un-PC. For example: "Women should not work in the public sphere because they are not as rational as men." That sentence is *very* un-PC, and therefore could never be the right answer. So anytime you have a passage that has a subject matter such as women or minorities, you already know a little something. You know that every right answer must be PC and that any answer choice that is not PC must be wrong.

Keep in mind that ETS, for the most part, is always PC—obviously so on a PC passage, but also on other passages that aren't explicitly PC. Think of it this way: Does ETS want to say anything controversial? No. Why not? Lawsuit, lawsuit, lawsuit. ETS's whole goal is to make money. Lawsuits mean losing money. If anyone was in any way offended by anything, ETS could be subject to a lawsuit. Think of what the National Organization for Women might say if it read the sentence, "Women should not work in the public sphere..." on the GRE. ETS ain't stupid—so it's not going to do anything stupid.

WHAT'S THE BIG IDEA?

Okay, we've established that the typical person wastes time because she reads too much. Quite simply, there's no need to read so much. In fact, reading comprehension only becomes hard when you do read too much. Remember, it's not *how much* you read that counts. It's *what* you read.

So what should you do? Well, what's the primary goal the first time you see a passage? All you really want is a general idea of what the passage is about, right? You want the gist of the passage—that is, the main idea. You don't really care about the specifics, at least not yet. In order to get the main idea of a passage, do you really need to read the entire thing? Well, that depends on a number of factors. If it's a short passage, only 10 lines long, you may want to go ahead and read it. If it's a longer passage, anywhere from 2 to 5 paragraphs, or you find yourself running out of time, then you may need a better approach. We call that approach **2-1-1-F**.

- The first **2** sentences of the first paragraph.
- The first **1** sentence of each middle paragraph.
- The first **1** sentence of the concluding paragraph.
- The **F**inal sentence of the concluding paragraph.

Why can these sentences alone tell you the main idea? You need to consider what good writing is—or rather, how good writing is organized. Good writing is well structured. That means for every paragraph there has to be a *topic sentence*. A topic sentence is a sentence that tells you what's going to happen in a particular paragraph. Technically, a topic sentence can be located anywhere in a paragraph, but usually, it's the first (sometimes the second) sentence of a paragraph.

So if a topic sentence tells you what's going to take place in a paragraph, then guess what? To get the main idea, all you really need to do is read the topic sentence of each paragraph in a passage. We make you read a little more at the beginning because it's the introductory paragraph, and a little at the very end because it often provides some sort of conclusion.

REALLY?

At this point, you're probably thinking, "There's no way that I can read so few sentences and actually get the main idea." You can. But you have to practice using this technique because you're not going to be comfortable with it at first—and therefore, you're not going to like it. But trust us, it works. After reading the first sentence in a paragraph, ask yourself: "Does what I've read give me enough information to *anticipate* what's going to be discussed?" If not, then it's okay to read one or two more sentences. But don't go hog-wild. The whole point is to save valuable time by not reading so much the first time around. Remember, the very first time you see a passage, you don't need to know specifics. All you want to do is find out what is the main idea.

COGITATE AND MASTICATE

In other words, think and chew. Once you've read the topic sentences, stop for a second. Don't leap ahead and start tackling the questions. Ask yourself: "What did I just read?" And then, in your own words, *state the main idea of the passage*. You don't have to articulate a beautiful sentence for the main idea. You just need to say what the main idea is in a short, simple sentence or phrase. It could be: "Macroeconomists good, microeconomists bad."

It is incredibly important that you state the main idea before you go on to the questions. By stating the main idea, you ensure that you understand the sentences that you read. If you aren't able to state the main idea, then you know something isn't right.

2-1-1-F IN ACTION

Now it's time to try out 2-1-1-F, and see how we can apply it to a long, boring passage. We're going to give you a passage in which we've replaced everything but the 2-1-1-F sentences with gibberish. See if you can still get an idea of what the main idea of this passage is.

> The Earth's magnetic field leaves an indelible magnetic "fingerprint" on volcanic rock, a slight magnetization oriented with the Earth's
> Line magnetic field. Since the 1920s, however,
> (5) geologists have known that some rocks are magnetized in the wrong direction, which lead to the theory of geomagnetic reversal. It is a blah blah blah science, blah blah blah. Blah blah blah, blah blah blah blah. Blah blah blah
> (10) blah random fact blah blah blah. Blah blah blah, blah blah blah blah blah blah.
> Computer models, however, have helped give credence to the internal theory of magnetic field reversal. Blah blah blah blah,
> (15) blah blah. Blah blah? Blah. Blah blah blah, blah blah statistic blah blah blah blah. Blah blah blah; blah ferromagnetic something-or-others blah blah blah blah blah.
> This accords well with what scientists know
> (20) of the sun's magnetic field reversals, which occur every decade or so. Blah blah blah blah. Blah blah blah, blah gibberish blah blah blah. Blah blah blah more gibberish blah blah blah blah.

(25)　There remains the problem of the
　　　　simplifications necessary to make the
　　　　computer models work. Blah blah blah: Blah
　　　　blah. Blah blah blah blah. Blah blah blah, blah
　　　　blah blah blah. Blah blah blah blah blah blah
(30)　blah. Consequently, the various theories will
　　　　likely remain in a state of flux until scientists
　　　　have access to simulations of sufficient
　　　　complexity, or we are unfortunate enough to
　　　　watch a magnetic reversal in action.

What's the main idea of that passage? Probably something along the lines of *The internal theory of magnetic field reversal: good stuff and bad stuff about it.* Later on, when we have to answer questions about specifics, we can focus more on the insides of the passage.

WHEN TO READ

Although 2-1-1-F is great, it's not the perfect technique for every passage. You'll have to determine what to do based on several criteria: The length of the passage, the number of questions for a passage, the time you have remaining, and your strength as a reader.

All　　　　　　　　　　　　2-1-1-F　　　　　　　　　　　　None

Short passage　　　　　　　Longer passage　　　　　　Very little time left
Several questions　　　　　　　　　　　　　　　　　　　1 Question
Time left
Good skimmer

For shorter passages, it may be worth it to read the whole passage. If you're running out of time, or know that you frequently run out of time on the Verbal section, then you should 2-1-1-F every long passage, and skip the passage entirely for shorter passages with just 1 question. You'll still end up reading parts of the passage when you answer questions, but it may mean only reading the few sentences asked about, rather than the entire passage.

No matter what part of the reading spectrum you fall on, remember that you aren't getting points for reading the passage. Therefore, don't get stuck in the passage. If you read a sentence and it doesn't make sense, don't keep rereading that same sentence over and over again. Move on to the next sentence, paragraph, or go to the questions themselves.

Read the passage briefly and quickly. Read the questions and answers slowly. Speaking of which…

The Questions

After you've got the main idea in your head, you can move on to the questions. For the purpose of simplicity, we break down all questions into three types:

- General
- Specific
- Weird

Each of these question types will require a slightly different approach, which we'll go into a little later. Because we didn't spend much time reading the passage, we'll have to read each question carefully and try to answer a couple questions: Where in the passage is the answer to this question? What and how much will I need to read to answer this question? What do I think, in my own words, the answer is?

Make sure you read each question carefully. Compare these two questions:

1. Which of the following would most likely refute the author's assertion in line 12?
2. Which of the following would most likely support the author's assertion in line 12?

The answer to question 1 is going to be very different than the answer to question 2. Just that one little word change can completely change the question, and if you're not paying attention and assume that the question is asking something it's not, you could get burned. Here's one more:

3. All of the following would most likely refute the author's assertion in line 12 EXCEPT

Although the word *EXCEPT* is in capital letters, it's still easy to miss if you're reading the question quickly. So take your time. It's not worth it to save 5 seconds speed-reading the question if you end up getting that question wrong.

The Answers

You don't get points based on how well you read the passage or the questions, of course. You get points if you pick the correct answer. Thus, the answers are incredibly important. As with the questions, you'll have to read each answer carefully.

How do we find a right answer? Good question. We don't. Instead, we're going to use our old friend Process of Elimination to find 4 wrong answers. Whichever answer is left must be correct, no matter how awkward it is. POE is the most important part of Reading Comprehension, so we're going to spend a lot of time talking about what makes a wrong answer.

Why focus so much on the wrong answers? Because ETS doesn't write 4 good answers and then 1 best answer. If they did that, everyone would try to argue his or her particular answer as the best one. For instance, what is *Hamlet* about? Revenge, madness, obligation, power, religion, or something else? Everyone has a different opinion, each one valid and supported by different facts. That's great for studying the Danish prince, but not great for a standardized test. ETS needs clear right and wrong answers. So rather than write good answers and then a best answer, ETS writes one answer that actually answers the question and is supported by the passage, and four answers which do not answer the question, or are not supported by the passage.

For each question, you'll have to use your scratch paper and POE to eliminate those 4 wrong answers. We're going to do this in two passes. On the first pass, your job is simply to eliminate the bad, awful, horrible, clearly-not-supported-by-the-passage answers. Cross off any answer that you read that makes you think "the passage didn't say that!" If you're not sure about an answer, skip it. Once you've read over all 5 answers, look at what you have left.

People often end up with two or three answers left on a Reading Comprehension and think "I must be doing something wrong." In fact, the opposite is true. ETS is excellent at writing answers that *almost* match what is said in the passage, but don't. It's going to take some time looking at the remaining answers to realize which ones are wrong. You've eliminated the big, bad, obvious answers, so now you're going to have to look at what's different (even if it's something small) between your remaining answers.

POE

Although each question type will have slightly different criteria for eliminating answers, there are certain categories of wrong answers that will show up over and over again. The better you get at recognizing these wrong answers, the easier Reading Comprehension questions will be.

Even if you find an answer you love, don't stop reading the answers. Put a checkmark next to that answer on your scratch paper, and look at the other answers. You may find that an answer you loved on the first read has problems that become apparent after a second look.

DID THE PASSAGE SAY THAT?

The most important POE criteria is to ask yourself if that answer is actually supported by the passage. Is that *really* what the passage said? Let's look at a sample passage.

> Because dendrites, the portions of a neuron
> which conduct the electrical impulses from
> other neural cells, do not actually process
> *Line* electrical signals, it was long believed that they
> (5) acted essentially as does an electrical cable.
> This theory, the passive cable theory, used
> the same basic equations for the transference
> of electricity by dendrites as are used for
> small lengths of cable. To a large extent, this
> (10) simplification still holds true; surprisingly
> complicated yet accurate models of
> neurological processes have been built using
> the passive cable theory as a mathematical
> basis. Recently, however, work has been done
> (15) analyzing the many different proteins within
> any given dendrite membrane. These proteins,
> rather than simply assisting in the transference
> of electrical signals, may selectively amplify
> certain signals. Because these effects are
> (20) still relatively mysterious at the microscale,
> it is still unknown how they may affect
> neurotransmission on the macroscale.

Ugh. Dense, neurological science stuff. Luckily, we don't have to understand everything about dendrites and what they do, we just need to know what isn't said in the passage. Let's look at the answers to a question. Even without the question itself, we can still eliminate some answers.

○ The passive cable theory gives incongruous results at the macroscale.

○ Dendrites may assist in processing electrical signals.

○ The proteins within the dendrite membrane are too miniscule to study.

○ Previously accurate models of neurological processes may now contain inaccuracies.

○ Certain aspects of dendrites may affect the usefulness of the passive cable theory in certain situations.

Go ahead and write down A B C D E vertically on some scratch paper. Let's go through each answer piece by piece. Choice (A) mentions that *passive cable theory gives incongruous results at the macroscale*. Where does the passage talk about the macroscale? At the very end, it says that *it is still unknown how they may affect neurotransmission on the macroscale*. The passage says we don't know the effect at the macroscale. Does that mean we'll have *incongruous results*, as the answer states? Not necessarily. The passage says we don't know what will happen at the macroscale. Choice (A) makes a guess about what will happen. The passage doesn't support (or undermine) that guess, so (A) isn't the answer. Cross it off.

Choice (B) is flatly contradicted by the passage. Look at the very first sentence of the passage: *Because dendrites…do not actually process electrical signals*. The passage never says they may help *process* signals, it says they may help *amplify* certain signals. The GRE will commonly change words like this to make a wrong answer seem correct. Sure, *dendrites* and the *processing of electrical signals* are both mentioned in the passage, but not in the way that the answer states. Many people gravitate towards answers which contain words they remember from the passage. Be careful, and read the answer choice and the relevant portion of the passage carefully.

Does the passage say why we don't know that much about *the proteins within the dendrite membrane*? Nope, it just says that scientists have been studying them recently. Cross off Choice (C).

From Choice (D), we know that scientists have built *surprisingly complicated yet accurate models of neurological processes*. We also know that recent research on proteins within the dendrite membrane may somehow change that. Do we know how that will be changed? Nope. We don't even know if those changes will affect the previous models. If those models are accurate now, there's nothing in the passage to indicate they won't be accurate later. Answer Choice (D) is gone.

All we've got left is Choice (E). Let's look it over and make sure that it matches the passage. The problem with this answer is that it is heavily paraphrased from the passage, so let's try to un-paraphrase it. What does the answer mean when it says *certain aspects of dendrites*? Well, we know it mentions the *proteins within any given dendrite membrane*. What do we know about those proteins? They actually amplify certain signals, rather than passively pass them on. That *may affect the usefulness of the passive cable theory in certain situations*. The passage states that we don't know yet if it will affect the passive cable theory, and if it does when, so the answer is deliberately left a little vague.

Notice that with every single answer we went back to the passage to check to see if the answer was supported by the text. Although our initial read through (or 2-1-1-F) of the passage was done quickly, when we go back through we'll have to read the question, the answers, and any specific information from the passage carefully.

EXTREME WORDING

Typically, extreme wording in an answer choice will make that answer choice wrong. Take a look at the following sentence:

Everyone loves chocolate ice cream.

ETS would never have this sentence as part of the correct answer. Why? Because it's too easy to prove wrong. All you have to say is, "I hate chocolate ice cream."

The following provides a list of words that usually go "too far" in the land of ETS.

everyone

no one

only

never

always

must

impossible

Keep in mind that, at first glance, some words may not look as if they are extreme. For example, the word *is*. Consider the following sentence:

It is the answer.

Does ETS know for sure that it is? How can ETS prove it without a doubt? Or think about the word *will*:

The United States will buy more imports in the next ten years.

Is ETS capable of predicting the future? This isn't to say that, if an answer choice contains *is* or *will*, it's wrong. Just remember that, in certain contexts, words can take on extreme meanings. Here's a list of words that ETS uses on the Reading Comprehension section that can often be extreme:

resolve

reconcile

prove

define

trace

Well, if extreme wording is bad, then guess what? Wishy-washy wording is good—words like *can, may, most, some, sometimes, possible, seldom, few*.

So, the general rule of thumb: Answer choices that contain extreme wording are usually wrong. Answer choices that contain wishy-washy wording or are moderate in tone are usually right.

Common Sense

The second POE tool to use on reading comprehension is common sense. Use it! Just because something's in print doesn't mean it's plausible. Indeed, ETS often includes ridiculous answer choices on reading comprehension. For example:

> According to the passage, the author believes the purpose of children's literature to be which of the following?
>
> ◯ Expose children to the cruelties of life
> ◯ Instruct children on the difference between right and wrong

Which is the better answer? Clearly (B). You don't have to read anything to know that (A) is wrong. All you have to do is exercise a little common sense.

Paraphrase, Paraphrase, Paraphrase

Finally, the most important POE tool on reading comprehension is to paraphrase. The right answer to a question is never going to be a direct quote from the passage. Rather, the right answer is going to be a paraphrase; that is, a restatement of what's in the passage. Which is why there's one thing you should always do for every question, no matter what type it falls into: Always state the answer to a question in your own words *before* you look at the answer choices. It's the same kind of thinking as coming up with your own word on text completions.

When you state the answer to a question in your own words, what you're doing is paraphrasing. And once you know what you're looking for, it's much easier to be discerning and figure out what's a bad answer choice. Rushing to the answer choices without taking the time to paraphrase is one of the worst mistakes people make on reading comprehension.

GENERAL QUESTIONS

Okay—let's go back and talk about the question types. Let's start off with general questions. These are questions that ask you to provide "big picture" information about the passage. Below are some examples of how general questions can be worded:

- Main Idea

    The primary purpose of the passage is to

    The main idea of the passage is

    The passage focuses primarily on which of the following?

    The passage is primarily concerned with

    Which of the following best states the central idea of the passage?

- Organization/Structure

    Which of the following best describes the organization of the passage as a whole?

    Which of the following is the most accurate description of the organization of the passage?

- Other

    Which of the following titles best describes the content of the passage?

    Which of the following is the best title for the passage?

    The passage would most likely be found in

    The passage would be most likely to appear as part of

- Tone

    The author's attitude toward . . . can best be described as

    The author's attitude toward . . . is best described as which of the following?

To answer any general question, focus on the main idea. Typically, an answer to a general question contains some sort of paraphrased version of the main idea. Also, don't forget about your tools for POE. As mentioned earlier, be wary of answer choices that:

1. Contain extreme wording

2. Don't make common sense

3. Don't match your paraphrase (i.e., the main idea you came up with)

Also, watch out for answer choices that:

1. *Mention something you haven't read about.* If it isn't mentioned at all in the topic sentences, there's no way it can be right.

2. *Are too detailed or specific.* People often miss general questions because they read the entire passage and get caught up in the specifics. That is, in reading the entire passage, they lose sight of the main idea. Therefore, they end up picking an answer choice that contains information from the passage, but that isn't the main idea.

3. *Are too general or beyond the scope of the passage.* Sometimes ETS is too vague. For example, if the main idea was about eighteenth-century *female poets*, an overly general answer choice would say something about eighteenth-century *writers*.

SPECIAL NOTE ON TONE QUESTIONS

Tone questions are a gift. Occasionally, they can be specific questions—that is, they ask about how the author feels about a particular paragraph rather than how he or she feels about the entire passage. But the approach to tone questions, whether general or specific, is basically the same. Take a look at the following answer choices:

    ◯ overwhelming support
    ◯ unabashed admiration
    ◯ qualified appreciation
    ◯ profound ambivalence
    ◯ deep-rooted hostility

What's the right answer? Without reading the passage, you know it has to be (C). Why? Think of extremes. ETS doesn't like extremes, right? Therefore, the right answer to a tone question is never going to be extremely positive or extremely negative. It's going to be somewhere in between. An author can be neutral or objective. He or she can be appreciative or slightly critical. But the author is never going to love something to death or hate something completely. Again, extreme is bad; moderation is good.

(Note that *apathetic* or *indifferent* are always wrong answers on tone questions. If the author didn't care about something, why would he or she write about it?)

QUICK QUIZ #1

For the following passage, find the main idea. The answers are on page 95.

If my colleagues and I are right, we may soon be saying good-bye to the idea that our universe was a single fireball created in
Line the big bang. We are exploring a new theory
(5) based on a 15-year-old notion that the universe went through a stage of inflation. During that time, the theory holds, the cosmos became exponentially large within an infinitesimal fraction of a second. At the end of this period,
(10) the universe continued its evolution according to the big bang model. As workers refined this inflationary scenario, they uncovered some surprising consequences. One of them constitutes a fundamental change in
(15) how the cosmos is seen. Recent versions of inflationary theory assert that instead of being an expanding ball of fire the universe is a huge, growing fractal. It consists of many inflating balls that produce more balls, which in turn
(20) produce more balls, ad infinitum.
Cosmologists did not arbitrarily invent this rather peculiar vision of the universe. Several workers, first in Russia and later in the U.S., proposed the inflationary hypothesis that is
(25) the basis of its foundation. We did so to solve some of the complications left by the old big bang theory. In its standard form, the big bang theory maintains that the universe was born about 15 billion years ago from a cosmological
(30) singularity—a state in which the temperature and density are infinitely high. Of course, one cannot really speak in physical terms about these quantities as being infinite. One usually assumes that the current law of physics did not apply
(35) then. They took hold only after the density of the universe dropped below the so-called Planck density, which equals about 10^{94} grams per cubic centimeter.
As the universe expanded, it gradually
(40) cooled. Remnants of the primordial cosmic fire still surrounds us in the form of the microwave background radiation. This radiation indicates that the temperature of the universe has dropped to 2.7 kelvins. The 1965 discovery
(45) of this background radiation proved to be the crucial evidence in establishing the big bang theory as the preeminent theory of cosmology.

The big bang theory also explained the abundances of hydrogen, helium, and other
(50) elements in the universe.
As investigators developed the theory, they uncovered complications. For example, the standard big bang theory, coupled with the modern theory of elementary particles,
(55) predicts the existence of many super-heavy particles carrying magnetic charge—that is, objects that have only one magnetic pole. These magnetic monopoles would have a typical mass 10^{16} times that of the proton, or
(60) about 0.00001 milligram. According to the standard big bang theory, monopoles should have emerged very early in the evolution of the universe and should now be as abundant as protons. In that case, the mean density
(65) of matter in the universe would be about 15 orders of magnitude greater than its present value, which is about 10^{-29} grams per cubic centimeter.

1. Which of the following best expresses the main idea of the passage?

○ Scientists have proven the big bang theory to be inaccurate and replaced it with the concept that the universe inflated over time.

○ Because the big bang theory cannot account for the actual state of the universe, it is possible that the universe actually evolved through inflation.

○ The big bang theory cannot be discounted completely, but the inflationary theory is also plagued by inconsistencies.

○ The big bang theory is incorrect because of the absence of magnetic monopoles in the universe.

○ Cosmologists have combined the big bang theory with the inflationary theory to produce a new picture of the universe's evolution.

2. The tone of the passage can best be described as

- ⬭ largely nostalgic but also critical
- ⬭ largely concerned but also amused
- ⬭ largely indifferent but also cautious
- ⬭ largely informative but also hopeful
- ⬭ largely appreciative but also modest

3. Which one of the following best describes the organization of the passage as a whole?

- ⬭ A new theory is introduced, a reason for the proposal of that theory is generally described, and certain shortcomings of an older theory are discussed.
- ⬭ A new theory is introduced, a reason for the proposal of that theory is generally described, and an older theory is discarded.
- ⬭ A new theory is introduced, and the reasons for the discarding of an old theory are described.
- ⬭ A new theory is introduced, the evidence supporting that theory is described.
- ⬭ A new theory is introduced, criticism of that theory is considered, and the new theory is further refined.

SPECIFIC QUESTIONS

These are questions that ask about particular details in the passage. Like general questions, specific questions can be phrased in several ways. For example:

The author suggests that . . .

According to the passage, . . .

The author mentions . . .

According to the author, . . .

Since specific questions ask you about details from the passage, there's one thing you must do for every specific question:

> Refer back to the passage.

No ifs, ands, or buts. You must do this. Never, never, never rely on your memory. Your memory is your worst enemy. That being said, let's talk about the two major groups of specific questions: line reference and lead word.

LINE REFERENCE

Line reference questions are easy to identify because they always contain a line reference or a highlighted portion of the passage. For example:

The author mentions T. H. White (line 40) in order to . . .

Which of the following situations is most analogous to the situation described by the author as . . . (lines 15–19)?

You get the idea. Line reference questions are great because they tell you where you should go in the passage to find the information. But they're also a little tricky because the information you're looking for typically isn't contained exactly in the line reference. Rather, it's usually a little bit before the line reference or a little bit after. Therefore, here's your approach to any line reference question:

1. Use the line reference to guide you to the right area of the passage.

2. Read roughly five lines above the line reference and roughly five lines below.

3. Answer the question, based on what you've read, in your own words (i.e., paraphrase) before moving on to the answer choices.

LEAD WORD

Lead word questions are basically line reference questions without the line reference. Well, if you don't have the line reference, how do you know where in the passage to look for the information? The answer is: the lead word.

The lead word is a word or phrase that's easy to skim for. Usually, the lead word stands out in the question because it's the most important or the most specific. What's the lead word in the following question?

> It can be inferred that, during the 1840s, the abolitionist movement did which of the following?

The lead word is *1840s. Abolitionist movement* could be a lead word(s), but only if the entire passage were not about the abolitionist movement. If the main idea were the abolitionist movement, would *abolitionist movement* be easy to skim for? Nope. *1840s* is a good lead word because it's specific and it's very easy to skim for. Numbers, words that have capital letters at the beginning, and italicized words are all good lead words because they're easy to skim for.

Once you've identified the lead word in a question, here's your approach:

1. Skim (not read) the passage for the lead word.

2. Once you find the line that contains the lead word, read roughly five lines before and five lines after.

3. Based on what you've read, answer the question in your own words (i.e., paraphrase). Do this before moving on to the answer choices.

Keep in mind that the lead word may appear more than once in the passage. So if you read the lines surrounding the lead word and don't find the answer to the question, skim the rest of the passage for another appearance of the lead word.

Also keep in mind that the lead word in the question won't necessarily be perfectly represented in the passage. For example, if the lead word in the question is "governmental intrusion," you may find the passage talking about "intrusive actions by the government."

POE FOR SPECIFIC QUESTIONS

Paraphrasing is the key to specific questions. However, you also have some POE tools to help you out as well. As always, watch out for answer choices that:

1. Contain extreme wording

2. Don't make common sense

3. Don't match your paraphrase

Also, watch out for answer choices that:

1. Contain information that's true according to the passage but that doesn't answer the question

2. Misrepresent information found in the same area of the passage as the correct answer

QUICK QUIZ #2

For each of the following questions, locate the answer in the passage by using either a line reference or a lead word. Make sure you paraphrase the answer to the question before looking at the answer choices. The answers are on page 96.

The feminists of revolutionary France were not the only persons hoping that the current paroxysm of social change would bring about
Line improvement of their state. A most singular
(5) category of men, the public executioners, had thought that the advent of a new regime would transform that peculiar disdain in which society held them. For hundreds of years, the post of Master of the High Works in France's
(10) major cities was held by men from ten or so dynastic families, members of an abominable elite that had developed as a consequence of social prejudice: Anyone who had ever been a *bourreau* could never hope to find another job,
(15) nor could he aspire to marry any woman not herself the daughter of a colleague. In this way the dreadful dynasties developed. The best known recipients of this peculiar distinction were the Sanson family, who
(20) operated in Paris and Versailles from 1688 to 1847; the diary kept by Charles Henri Sanson, executioner of Paris during the Terror, provides details of the deaths of many illustrious victims.
(25) Several passages in the Sanson diary suggest that professional executioners did not particularly like having to kill women. This chivalrous repugnance later spread through the Court d'Assizes; while women were
(30) regularly condemned to death in the late nineteenth and early twentieth centuries, in fact they were almost always reprieved. A roughly contemporaneous reluctance to execute women in the United States has been
(35) explained by recent American feminists as evidence of women's almost nonexistent social status at that time; to compensate for legal inegality the men who were women's judges, prosecutors, and jurors adopted a "protective"
(40) stance, frequently acquitting women who, in modern retrospect, seem guilty. In France the egalitarian practices of earlier centuries were ultimately reinstated, which guillotined five women.

(45) This temporary preservation of execution as an exclusively male domain—a thing too necessary and revolting to be inflicted on or endured by half the population—apparently did not strike legislators as being intolerably
(50) illogical, or as being rather a back-handed sort of compliment to men. Proper equality would have involved either equal rights and equal punishment for men and women, or else abolition. However, arguments against
(55) the death penalty tend rather to develop from general humanitarian principles, and less from the putative equality of women.
Chivalry, indeed, would seem to have been the nineteenth century's solution to the
(60) problems posed to the authorities by "female" executions. But more importantly, chivalry enabled society to observe a version of that logic set forth in 1791 by Olympe de Gouges, a logic echoed later in the United States by
(65) Wendell Phillips, who bluntly declared, "You have granted that women may be hung; therefore you must grant that woman may vote." In not executing women, the judiciary body was able to sidestep these irritating
(70) formulations: If women did not receive equal punishment under law, perhaps they need not be assured of equal rights.

1. Which of the following best describes the author's attitude toward the formation of public executioner dynasties?

   ○ Qualified appreciation
   ○ Studied neutrality
   ○ Tempered disapproval
   ○ Vehement condemnation
   ○ Resigned acceptance

2. According to the passage, the unwillingness of men to condemn women to death in the United States during the late nineteenth century was

   ○ a reflection of the influence of the Court d'Assizes on the judicial system in the United States

   ○ in accordance with women's low standing in society and their lack of legal rights

   ○ a result of a popular movement promoting the chivalrous idea that women should be protected from harm

   ○ a misinterpretation on the part of modern historians, who believed many of the women to be guilty

   ○ a reaction to the excesses of the French Revolution and the large number of women who were guillotined

3. The passage suggests that, during the French Revolution, popular arguments against the death penalty did which of the following?

   ○ Emphasized the failure of the death penalty to suppress dissent

   ○ Asserted that the defense of the death penalty was based upon faulty logic

   ○ Supported indirectly the notion that men were equal to women

   ○ Addressed only the needs of men, at the expense of those of women

   ○ Failed to employ the reasoning that men and women should have equal rights

WEIRD QUESTIONS

Finally . . . weird questions. We call these questions weird because they have special formats. They're also weird because they tend to be more time-consuming than usual. The types of weird questions are:

- All That Apply

    For the following question, consider each of the answer choices separately and select all that apply.

    Which of the following can be inferred from the passage about the earliest observations of Mars?

    ◯ Though Aristotle correctly placed Mars farther from the Earth than the Moon, he drew this conclusion from a faulty assumption.

    ◯ Ptolemaeus's writings were based in large part on the work done by Hipparchus, though the two disagreed on the relationship of the Earth to the universe.

    ◯ The recognition of Mars as a planet and not simply a star could not be confirmed until the development of the telescope.

- Except/Least/Not

    All of the following are stated by the author as the advantages of hydroponics EXCEPT

    According to the passage, neutrinos are NOT

    It can be inferred from the passage that which of the following is LEAST compatible with Graham's approach to dance?

- Select-in-Passage

    Select the sentence that offers evidence to support the author's claim about superposition.

- Vocab in Context

    In the context in which it appears, "startling" (line 7) most nearly means

- Argument

    Which of the following, if true, most seriously weakens the argument?

ALL THAT APPLY

All That Apply questions will give you three possible answer choices and ask you to select all of the answers which apply. Other than that, approach these questions exactly like you would a normal, five-answer Reading Comprehension question. Read the question carefully, write down A B C on your scratch paper, and POE. Focus on one answer at a time. If you're not sure whether that answer is correct or not, move on to the next answer choice and come back to it later.

A couple important notes about these questions: There can be 1, 2, or 3 correct answers to these questions. There will always be AT LEAST one answer that is correct. So never leave these blank, but don't be surprised if you eliminate 2 of the 3 answers.

EXCEPT/LEAST/NOT

Often these questions are not that difficult, but they tend to consume a lot of time. Also, they can be a little tricky. What makes these questions easy to miss is the fact that you're trying to find information that's *incorrect* according to the passage—and usually, it's your job to find out the correct information. To sidestep this pitfall, here's how to approach EXCEPT/LEAST/NOT questions.

1. For each answer choice, ask yourself if it is true according to the passage or false.

2. If the answer choice is true, put a Y next to it; if the answer choice is false, put an N next to it.

3. After going through all the answer choices, you should have four Ys and one N. The answer is the one that doesn't belong—the N.

As long as you follow these steps, you should be okay. Just remember, you're looking for information that's *not* true.

SELECT-IN-PASSAGE

Select-in-Passage questions will ask you to click on a sentence from the passage which answers the question. These questions often involve finding the support for an argument, or a specific detail from the passage.

The trick with these questions is to use your scratch paper. Start by figuring out what the question is asking. Where do they talk about that in the passage? Use lead words and what you know from your 2-1-1-F to narrow down which sentences could work. Look through the passage find 2 to 5 sentences that could work, and write down the line number of the first part of each sentence. Pretend each sentence is an answer choice to the question. Does it answer the question? Use POE until you only have one sentence that could be the answer.

VOCAB IN CONTEXT

Vocab in Context questions will ask you for the definition of a word. It may be a simple word, it may be a harder word. The key here, however, is that ETS is not necessarily asking for the standard definition of the word. Instead, they want to know what the word means in the context of the passage.

Consider this sentence: I decided to approach the task more cautiously than usual. The word *approach* in this case doesn't mean to physically walk up to the task. Instead, it's being used metaphorically to imply "getting ready to begin."

Because these questions want to know how a word is used in context, treat them as you would a Text Completion question. Ignore the actual word at first, and focus instead what the passage tells you about that word. What clues are there in the sentence, or in the sentence previous, or in the sentence following, that suggests how the word is being used? Are there any triggers? Come up with your own simple word or phrase to replace the word. Then, POE. Check each answer choice and see if it kind of matches your word.

Remember that although sometimes these questions will ask for the primary definition of a word, they will also often ask for a secondary (or tertiary, et cetera) definition. So if the question asks about the word "table," the passage may be using one of the definitions of table as a verb, such as "to put aside consideration."

ARGUMENT

Argument questions typically appear by themselves, as the only question for a short passage. These questions will often contain the word "argument" in them. The passages for these questions are very similar to the passages supplied for the Argument prompt of the Analytical Writing section.

Start by reading through the passage and identifying the conclusions, premises, and assumptions. (For more help with identifying the parts of an argument, check Chapter 5, which explains what to look for in an argument prompt.)

Say the argument reads as follows:

> Music publishing companies have pointed
> to their decreased revenues as evidence
> that illegal music downloads have hurt
> their business at a time when it should be
> thriving. Although people listen to music
> more frequently now than ever before,
> music publishing company revenues
> continue to decline. Furthermore, more
> people downloaded music illegally in the
> past year than in any years previous.

Argument questions come in several varieties. For each type, we've given a typical correct answer to that style of question, were it to be asked about the argument above.

- **Strengthen** questions ask how best to support or strengthen the argument. With these, the correct answer will show that the argument's assumptions are valid. Eliminate any answers that weaken the argument, or don't support the conclusion.

  ○ Those who downloaded music illegally have
    reported downloading albums which they
    would have purchased if the illegal down-
    loads were unavailable.

- **Weaken** questions ask how to undermine or weaken the argument. Because your goal is to show that the argument sucks, the correct answer will make it clear that the argument's assumptions are invalid, and therefore the conclusion does not follow from the premises. Eliminate any answers that support the argument, or don't weaken the conclusion.

  ○ Those who downloaded music illegally would not have purchased the same music if the option to illegally download it were not available.

- **Assumption** questions ask what the authors assumption(s) are in the argument. If you've already written down the conclusion and the premises, then you just need to look for something that links the conclusion and the premises. Eliminate any answers that, if true, would weaken the argument.

  ○ The decreases in revenue are entirely due to fewer music purchases by illegal music downloaders.

- **Structure** questions are similar to main idea questions in other Reading Comprehension questions. These questions ask about the purpose of certain portions of the argument. Treat these as you would a main idea question: Eliminate any answers that are too specific, too broad, or only half right yet half wrong.

  ○ The first part states a conclusion, while the second part offers support for the conclusion.

- **Explain** questions require you to select an answer which resolves some apparent contradiction or paradox in the original passage. Wrong answers for this type of question won't address the argument's apparent contradiction, or will make the contradiction worse.

  ○ Most people primarily listen to a few albums which they had previously purchased, rather than constantly buy new music.

IN SUMMARY . . .

For reading comprehension, it's the approach that counts. Break bad habits. Don't rely on your memory. Always paraphrase. The bottom line is that reading comprehension is an open-book test. All of the answers are in the passage. It's your job to hunt them down, and you can do that most effectively through POE—that is, getting rid of bad answer choices first.

Finally, don't forget that reading a lot isn't necessarily a good thing. It's not how much you read, it's what you read. We hope that with our approach you're not reading as much as you were before. However, just because you're reading less doesn't mean you can afford to read quickly. You're not reading a lot anymore, so take the time to make sure you understand what you do read.

1. Before you answer any questions, always find the main idea. You can find the main idea by reading the first two sentences of the first paragraph, the first sentence of each succeeding paragraph, and the last sentence of the entire passage. Be sure to state the main idea in your own words.

2. Don't forget that POE is the best way to get the right answer on reading comprehension. Be wary of any answer choice that

   a) contains extreme wording,

   b) doesn't make common sense, or

   c) doesn't match your paraphrase.

3. General questions: These questions ask about "big picture" information such as "what's the main idea" or "how is the passage organized" or "what's the author's tone." To answer general questions, focus on the main idea. Watch out for answer choices that

   a) mention something you haven't read,

   b) are too detailed or specific, or

   c) are too general or go beyond the scope of the passage.

4. Specific questions: These questions ask about particular details in the passage. Use either line references or lead words to guide you to the part of the passage that contains the answer. Always remember to read five lines before and five lines after. Watch out for answer choices that

   a) contain information that's true according to the passage but that doesn't answer the question, or

   b) misrepresent information found in the same area of the passage as the correct answer.

5. Weird questions: These questions are the most time-consuming.

   a) All That Apply: Focus on one answer choice at a time, and use POE.

   b) EXCEPT/LEASE/NOT: Play the Y/N (or T/F) game.

   c) Select-in-Passage: Use lead words to come up with some possible sentences that will answer the question. Treat each sentence as if it were an answer choice, and POE.

   d) Vocab in Context: Answer these questions as you would a Text Completion question. Use the passage to find clues and triggers to come up with your own word for the blank, and then POE.

   e) Arguments: Identify the conclusion and premises. POE.

6. Above all . . . never rely on your memory. Always refer back to the passage. And always, always paraphrase. Paraphrasing helps you see which answer choices are bad because it makes sure you understood what you just read.

PRACTICE QUESTIONS #1

Political parties today are consciously non-ideological, but in the 1840s and 1850s ideology made its way into the heart of the
Line political system. Political sociologists have
(5) pointed out that the stable functioning of a political democracy requires a setting in which parties represent broad coalitions of varying interests, and that the peaceful resolution of social conflict takes place most easily
(10) when the major parties share fundamental values. Such a view implies that the peaceful operation of the political system is the highest social value, an implication which, under certain circumstances, may be justly
(15) questioned. But it does contain important insights about the normal functioning of the American polity. Government by majority rule, Carl Becker observed many years ago, works best when political issues involve superficial
(20) problems, rather than deep social divisions. The minority can accept the victory of the majority at the polls, because both share many basic values, and electoral defeat does not imply "a fatal surrender of . . . vital interests."
(25) Before the 1850s, the second American party system conformed to this pattern—largely because sectional ideologies and issues were consciously kept out of politics. In this sense, the party system had a certain artificial
(30) quality. Its divisions rarely corresponded to the basic sectional divisions which were daily becoming more and more pronounced. The two decades before the Civil War witnessed the development of conflicting sectional
(35) ideologies, each viewing its own society as fundamentally well-ordered, and the other as both a negation of its most cherished values and a threat to its existence.
The development of the two ideologies
(40) was in many ways interrelated; each grew in part as a response to the growth of the other. Thus, as southerners were coming more and more consciously to insist on slavery as the very basis of civilized life, and to reject the
(45) materialism and lack of cohesion in northern

society, northerners came to view slavery as the antithesis of the good society, as well as a threat to their own fundamental values and interests. The existing political system
(50) could not contain these two irreconcilable ideologies, and in the 1850s each national party—Whigs, Know-Nothings, and finally Democrats—disintegrated. And in the end the South seceded from the Union rather than
(55) accept the victory of a political party whose ideology threatened everything Southerners most valued.
At the center of the Republican ideology was the notion of "free labor." This concept
(60) involved not merely an attitude toward work, but a justification of antebellum northern society, and it led northern Republicans to an extensive critique of southern society, which appeared both different from and inferior to
(65) their own. Republicans also believed in the existence of a conspiratorial "slave power" which had seized control of the federal government. Two profoundly different and antagonistic civilizations, Republicans thus
(70) believed, had developed within the nation, and were competing for control of the political system.

1. The primary purpose of the passage is to

○ discuss the requirements for a stable political system, in particular, a democracy

○ present a cause for the breakdown in relations between North and South that led, ultimately, to the Civil War

○ explain the reason why political parties seek to avoid introducing ideology into their platforms

○ analyze the effect of the Civil War on the political party system in the United States

○ propose the theory that the Republican party was responsible for the South's secession from the Union

2. It can be inferred from the passage that political parties today

   ○ do not differ from each other markedly in terms of interests
   ○ consider freedom from conflict the most important social concern
   ○ keep their distance from ideology because of its potential to divide
   ○ look to the Civil War as a lesson on how to maintain national unity
   ○ address only problems of little weight and rarely dispute one another

3. The author mentions Carl Becker in order to

   ○ challenge the position popularly held by political sociologists regarding the power of ideology
   ○ argue that a democracy is characterized by the peaceful transition of power from one party to another
   ○ promote the notion that it is better for a democracy to address only issues that are not divisive
   ○ suggest that, in order for a democracy to flourish, the political system must represent diverse interests
   ○ lend credence to the assertion that political stability is founded upon the absence of ideological confrontation

4. Consider all of the choices separately and select all that apply.

   The author implies that Republicans in the 1850s would be likely to believe that:

   ☐ slaves were going to win many federal elections.
   ☐ their ideas were incompatible with those of their political rivals.
   ☐ northern society was superior to southern society.

5. Select the sentence that provides a practical illustration of why a non-ideological political party system may function well in America.

6. The passage suggests which of the following about politics in America prior to the Civil War?

   ○ Growing divisions between the political parties became increasingly ideological, resulting in the eventual end of the existing political parties.
   ○ While Southern Americans knew slavery was wrong, they were too economically dependent on slave labor to give up slavery.
   ○ Republicans supported Southern Americans in their belief that slaves should not be paid for their labor.

7. The author's attitude toward the Republican party of the mid-nineteenth century can best be described as

   ○ admiring
   ○ appreciative
   ○ sympathetic
   ○ objective
   ○ vehement

PRACTICE QUESTIONS #2

Directions: The passage below is followed by questions based on its content. After reading the passage, choose the best answer to each question. Answer all questions on the basis of what is <u>stated</u> or <u>implied</u> in that passage. The answers are on page 99.

In Anglo-American formalism, surrealism was considered a deviant art movement: improperly visual and impertinently literary,
Line relatively inattentive to the imperatives of
(5) form, and mostly indifferent to the laws of genre, a paradoxical avant-garde concerned with infantile states and outmoded forms, not properly modernist at all. For neo–avant-garde artists who challenged this hegemonic three
(10) decades ago, its very deviance might have made surrealism an attractive object. But such was not the case. Since this formalist model of modernism was staked on the autonomy of modern art as separate from
(15) social practice and grounded in visual experience, its antagonist, the neo–avant-garde account of modernism, stressed the two movements, dada and constructivism, that appeared most opposed to this visualist
(20) autonomy—that sought to destroy the separate institution of art in an anarchic attack on its formal conventions, as did dada, or to transform it according to the materialist practices of a revolutionary society, as did
(25) constructivism. Again surrealism was lost in the shuffle. To the neo–avant-gardists who challenged the formalist account in the 1950s and 1960s, it too appeared corrupt: technically kitschy, philosophically subjective, hypocritically
(30) elitist. Hence when artists involved in pop and minimalism turned away from the likes of Picasso and Matisse, they turned to such figures as Duchamp and Rodchenko, not to precedents like Ernst and Giacometti.

1. Select the sentence that suggests a point of view that, while reasonable to anticipate, was not embraced.

2. The passage suggests which of the following about surrealism as an art movement?

   ⭕ Through its lack of attention to form and indifference to genre, surrealism is understood as an impertinent, but sometimes infantile, form of modernism.

   ⭕ Although surrealism did not always follow the very rules of form opposed by some critics of formal conventions, surrealism was rejected by those critics as dishonest.

   ⭕ Those in the neo-avant-garde movement believed that artists such as Duchamp succeeded in a way that surrealist artists had not.

3. The passage suggests that those sharing a neo-avant-garde point of view objected to which of the following about the formalist model of modernism?

   ⭕ its overly cautious approach to modern art
   ⭕ its use of deviant states and forms
   ⭕ its view of art as a distinct institution
   ⭕ its embrace of materialist practices
   ⭕ its representation of antiquated ideals

Directions: The passage below is followed by questions based on its content. After reading the passage, choose the best answer to each question. Answer all questions on the basis of what is stated or implied in that passage. The answers are on page 100.

E. M. Forster is an Edwardian in point of time, and he is equally so in spirit. His outlook on the world and his literary manner
Line were already thoroughly developed in
(5) that epoch and have passed through the subsequent years of turbulence and cataclysm with remarkably little modification. The various modern revolutions in physics, in psychology, in politics, even in literary style, have not
(10) escaped his intelligent notice, but they can scarcely be said to have influenced him deeply. His response to the explosion of the Victorian dream of benevolent progress has been a modest and orderly retreat to safer ground—
(15) to a tolerant individualism now unmixed with Utopian dreams, but nevertheless closer to Victorian ideals than to any of the popular creeds of today. Rather than conform to bad times, Forster prefers to remind us cheerfully
(20) that his views are atavistic.

The strength of Forster's resistance to the twentieth century is especially apparent when we place him beside some of his fellow writers. If Joyce, Lawrence, Pound, and the
(25) early Eliot represent the main current of the modern literary movement in English, we must admit that Forster's private stream runs in an older channel. These others were radical iconoclasts whose rejection of bourgeois-
(30) democratic life was violent and shattering. Equally shattering was their fragmentation of the polite cadences of Victorian literature. In seeing the falseness of the old psychology, they conceived a scorn for the *hypocrite*
(35) *lecteur*; their role as apocalyptic prophets, as naysayers to the boredom and specious rationality of modern life, demanded that they be obscure and idiosyncratic. Forster, in contrast, unashamedly calls himself a
(40) bourgeois and remains faithful to the tradition of calm intelligibility. He is anti-apocalyptic in both his politics and his literary sense. To some degree his novels return us to the congenial Victorian relationship between writer
(45) and reader, with its unspoken agreement over the usefulness of the sociable virtues and

its apotheosis of the happy family. Though Forster's heroes struggle against "society" as a body of inhibitions, their revolt is never truly
(50) radical. And Forster's ironical style, though it is unsparing in its probing at shams and half-truths, presupposes a confidence in the reader's sympathy and good judgment—a confidence that seemed quite archaic to the
(55) other writers named.

Forster's resistance to modernity may account for the fact that his novels, though they are almost universally esteemed, have never won him a cult of fanatical disciples.
(60) With a few exceptions, critics have tended to explicate and admire his works without becoming heated over the possible merit of his ideas. Yet Forster decidedly *is* a novelist of ideas, and didactic moral content is hardly less
(65) conspicuous in his work than in Lawrence's. Forster's persistent "moral" is that the life of affectionate personal relations, disengaged from political and religious zeal by means of a tolerant eclecticism, is supremely valuable.
(70) This is not a stirring creed; in fact, it is a warning against allowing oneself to be stirred by any creed.

1. The author's primary purpose in this passage is to

◯ discuss E. M. Forster and his writing, particularly in the context of his reaction to modernity

◯ compare E. M. Forster to other writers of the twentieth century such as Joyce and Lawrence

◯ affirm that E. M. Forster is as much a novelist of ideas as other modern writers

◯ suggest that E. M. Forster's writing is a reflection of not only Victorian ideals but also Edwardian

◯ analyze E. M. Forster's response to the revolutions in science and art and how it affected his work

2. According to the passage, Forster's relationship to Victorianism is which of the following?

  ○ He believed Victorian ideals were preferable to those of modernity.
  ○ He did not believe in Victorian ideals but nevertheless clung to them.
  ○ He considered Victorian ideals to be not only oppressive but also false.
  ○ He rejected Victorian ideals, but not so completely as other modern writers.
  ○ He incorporated Victorian ideals into his own personal ideals.

3. The author most likely refers to Forster's "views as atavistic" (line 20) in order to

  ○ make a case for the importance of individualism to Forster and his work
  ○ isolate Forster as a writer unconnected to the revolutions of the modern world
  ○ emphasize that Forster was an atypical modern writer
  ○ suggest that Forster was an ardent supporter of the popular beliefs of his time
  ○ point out Forster's inherent belief in Victorianism

4. Select the sentence that proposes an explanation for the lack of passion among some readers for the ideas often put forth by Forster.

5. The passage suggests which of the following about other writers who produced works in the same period as did Forster?

  ○ These writers, like Forster, rejected bourgeois values and directed their writing away from a style of polite veneer towards peculiar and individualized voices.
  ○ These writers showed a greater willingness to embrace modernity than did Forster, who did not give up his belief in the importance of certain societal virtues.
  ○ These writers, much like Forster, used their writing to instruct readers about their moral viewpoint, even if their styles differed from that of Forster.

6. The author's reaction to Forster's novels can best be described as one of

  ○ disparagement
  ○ skepticism
  ○ neutrality
  ○ appreciation
  ○ enthusiasm

7. It can be inferred from the passage that Joyce, Lawrence, Pound, and Eliot in his early period were all writers who

  ○ wrote in a style ahead of the spirit of their time.
  ○ were often rude and offensive.
  ○ lacked confidence in their audiences' sympathy.

PRACTICE QUESTIONS #4

Directions: The passage below is followed by questions based on its content. After reading the passage, choose the best answer to each question. Answer all questions on the basis of what is <u>stated</u> or <u>implied</u> in that passage. The answers are on page 102.

Natural selection is an immensely powerful yet beautifully simple theory that has held up remarkably well, under intense and unrelenting
Line scrutiny and testing, for 135 years. In essence,
(5) natural selection locates the mechanism of evolutionary change in a "struggle" among organisms for reproductive success, leading to improved fit of populations to changing environments . . .

(10) Yet powerful though the principle may be . . . natural selection is not fully sufficient to explain evolutionary change. First, many other causes are powerful, particularly at levels of biological organization both above and below
(15) the traditional Darwinian focus on organisms and their struggle for reproductive success. At the lowest level of substitution in individual base pairs of DNA, change is often effectively neutral and therefore random. At higher levels,
(20) involving entire species or faunas, punctuated equilibrium can produce evolutionary trends by selection of species based on their rates of origin and extirpation, whereas mass extinctions wipe out substantial parts of biotas
(25) for reasons unrelated to adaptive struggles of constituent species in "normal" times between such events.

Second . . . no matter how adequate our general theory of evolutionary change, we also
(30) yearn to document and understand the actual pathway of life's history. Theory, of course, is relevant to explaining the pathway . . . But the actual pathway is strongly *underdetermined* by our general theory of life's evolution. This
(35) point needs some belaboring . . . Webs and chains of historical events are so intricate, so imbued with random and chaotic elements, so unrepeatable in encompassing such a multitude of unique (and uniquely interacting)
(40) objects, that standard models of simple prediction and replication do not apply.

History can be explained—with satisfying rigor if evidence be adequate—after a sequence of events unfolds, but it
(45) cannot be predicted with any precision beforehand . . . History includes too much chaos, or extremely sensitive dependence on minute and unmeasurable differences in initial conditions, leading to massively divergent

(50) outcomes based on tiny and unknowable disparities in starting points. And history includes too much contingency, or shaping of present results by long chains of unpredictable antecedent states, rather than immediate
(55) determination by timeless laws of nature.

Homo sapiens did not appear on the earth, just a geologic second ago, because evolutionary theory predicts such an outcome based on themes of progress and increasing
(60) neural complexity. Humans arose, rather, as a fortuitous and contingent outcome of thousands of linked events, any one of which could have occurred differently and sent history on an alternative pathway that would
(65) not have led to consciousness . . .

Therefore, to understand the events and generalities of life's pathway, we must go beyond principles of evolutionary theory to a paleontological examination of the contingent
(70) pattern of life's history on our planet—the single actualized version among millions of plausible alternatives that happened not to occur. Such a view of life's history is highly contrary both to conventional deterministic
(75) models of Western science and to the deepest social traditions and psychological hopes of Western culture for a history culminating in humans as life's highest expression and intended planetary steward.

1. The primary purpose of the passage is to

   ○ suggest that the natural selection theory is no longer applicable to today's world

   ○ point out the limitations of natural selection at the lower and higher levels

   ○ propose changes to the natural selection theory to improve its accuracy

   ○ discuss the reasons why natural selection is not a complete evolutionary theory

   ○ expose problems with the natural selection theory in light of recent historical studies

2. Consider each of the choices separately and select all that apply.

   In the first two paragraphs, the author implies that

   ☐ there is strong reason to believe in the accuracy of Darwin's theory of evolutionary change

   ☐ some biological changes are more complex than Darwin's theory allows for

   ☐ biological changes are not necessarily the result of adverse conditions

3. Consider each of the choices separately and select all that apply.

   The passage suggests that the author views the existence of human beings as

   ☐ inevitable, although it may have come about in a different manner

   ☐ a circumstance that began a brief time ago when compared to the existence of the earth itself

   ☐ the result of a linear sequence of related events

4. The author mentions *Homo sapiens* primarily in order to

   ◯ highlight the short period during which humans have lived on the earth

   ◯ suggest the notion that the pathway to consciousness was a long-term process

   ◯ support the idea that the pathway of life is determined, in large part, by random events

   ◯ explain evolution through natural selection by employing a specific species as an example

   ◯ emphasize the intricacy of events that leads to the evolution of an organism or species

5. Select the sentence that explains that the intermingling of highly detailed occurrences makes the prediction of evolution problematic.

6. Which of the following statements is supported by information given in the passage?

   ◯ The study of history will never be completely satisfactory.

   ◯ The theory of natural selection addresses the possibility of random events.

   ◯ The evolution of life does not follow a fixed or determined path.

   ◯ It is possible to determine with a fair degree of accuracy historical events.

   ◯ Theories will always be inadequate because they are at best predictions.

7. Which of the following best describes the organization of the passage?

   ◯ A theory is rejected, and new theories are suggested to replace it.

   ◯ A theory is considered, and conditions are stated under which the theory can apply.

   ◯ A theory is explained, and observations are made that both support and contradict it.

   ◯ A theory is described, and its limitations are noted and then further explored.

   ◯ A theory is outlined, and its relevance questioned by employing it in a different field of study.

PRACTICE QUESTIONS #5

Directions: The passage below is followed by questions based on its content. After reading the passage, choose the best answer to each question. Answer all questions on the basis of what is <u>stated</u> or <u>implied</u> in that passage. The answers are on page 105.

Occupations foster gender differences among workers in a variety of ways, one of the most pervasive being "internal stratification."
Line That is, men and women in the same
(5) occupation often perform different tasks and functions. Even in those occupations that appear sexually integrated, the aggregate statistics often mask extreme internal segregation. Although the proportion of female
(10) bakers increased from 25 percent in 1970 to 41 percent in 1980, for example, the majority of female bakers are found in highly automated baking industries, while their male counterparts are located in less automated bakeries.
(15) The same phenomenon has been detected among pharmacists, financial managers, and bus drivers—all groups where the influx of women workers suggests a diminution of sex segregation.
(20) Another strategy used to maintain gender differences in supposedly integrated occupations is the use of sumptuary and etiquette rules. When women enter male-dominated occupations, certain rules are
(25) often introduced to govern their dress and demeanor. In office settings, for instance, dress codes—either formal or implicit—are not unusual; female employees may be required to wear dresses, nylons, and high-heeled shoes
(30) to enhance their femininity. So it is for female marines and male nurses, both of whom are required to dress differently from their male and female counterparts. Male nurses never wear the traditional nursing cap; female
(35) marines never sport the standard Marine Corps garrison cap.
Informal practices also play a role in constituting femininity in female marines and masculinity in male nurses. As members
(40) of visible minority groups, they stand out at work and receive far more than their fair share of attention. This phenomenon was first documented by Rosabeth Moss Kanter, who found that women in corporations,
(45) simply by virtue of their numerical rarity, were noticed and scrutinized more than their male

counterparts. This added pressure may actually result in different job performances from men and women in nontraditional occupations
(50) and exacerbate gender differences. Kanter's corporate women, for example, became more secretive, less independent, and less oppositional in response to their greater visibility—all traits that have traditionally been
(55) associated with femininity.
Another informal technique that enhances gender differences is practiced by supervisors who evaluate men and women differently. The very qualities that are highly praised in one sex
(60) are sometimes denigrated in the other. Thus, a man is "ambitious," a woman, "pushy"; a woman is "sensitive," a man, "wimpy."
But it would be a mistake to claim that all gender differences are forced on people. In
(65) addition to the external pressures I have just described, male nurses and female marines actively construct their own gender by redefining their activities in terms of traditional masculine and feminine traits. For example,
(70) women in the Marine Corps insist that their femininity is intact even as they march cadence in camouflage units. Likewise, male nurses contend that their masculinity is not at all threatened while they care for and nurture
(75) their patients.

1. The author is primarily concerned with

   ○ explaining how femininity and masculinity can be reconstructed for specific careers

   ○ examining jobs that, at first glance, seem to be nontraditional for men and women

   ○ proving that discrimination based on gender is pervasive in all workplaces

   ○ exploring the reasons why gender differences cannot be ignored in any occupation

   ○ discussing practices that serve to perpetuate gender differences in the workplace

2. Select the sentence that best strengthens the author's claim that informal workplace codes regarding aesthetics can preserve gender disparities.

3. The author suggests which of the following about internal stratification?

- ○ Although women now work in industries once dominated by men, they find it difficult, if not impossible, to be promoted to managerial positions.
- ○ As women enter the work force in greater numbers, men feel their jobs are threatened and their hostility results in increased tension on the job.
- ○ Because men and women rarely engage in the same activities on the job, certain specialties can be feminine-identified and others masculine-identified.
- ○ Since men and women are segregated in the workplace, men tend not to value the work carried out by women.
- ○ Even when men and women are given the same tasks to perform, women continue to receive less pay than do their male counterparts.

4. The primary purpose of the last paragraph is to

- ○ emphasize the importance of outside forces in establishing gender differences
- ○ point out that men and women act to enforce gender differences themselves
- ○ provide an example of men and women who defy the typical perceptions of masculinity and femininity
- ○ demonstrate that, even in a nontraditional context, conventional definitions of "masculine" and "feminine" are preserved
- ○ describe the tension that men and women feel when their sexuality is questioned

5. Consider each of the choices separately and select all that apply.

Which of the following statements about men in the labor force cannot logically be inferred from the passage?

- ☐ In many previously male-dominated industries, men have been displaced by a new generation of female employees.
- ☐ Men are more adept than women at performing tasks that require a high degree of manual effort.
- ☐ In certain industries, men have been forced to disregard convention, thereby encouraging gender disparities.

6. The author specifically mentions all of the following as methods to maintain gender differences in the workplace EXCEPT

○ a manager's use of particular words for men and particular words for women although describing the same quality

○ the designation of dress codes so that the physical differences between men and women are highlighted

○ the internal pressure men and women feel to be traditionally masculine or feminine

○ pressure from coworkers to behave in a conventionally masculine or a feminine way

○ the assignation of different duties for men and women in the same occupation

7. Select the sentence which theorizes that unofficial habits regarding gender in the workplace can influence employee behavior.

PRACTICE QUESTIONS #6

Although meningitis clone III-1 has caused hundreds of thousands of meningitis cases, it does not appear to be uniquely virulent. Now
Line that it is possible to perform clonal analysis
(5) of meningococcal strains, it is clear that other clones have caused similar epidemics in Africa and Asia. These findings do suggest, however, that the introduction of a potentially epidemic clone under the right circumstances can be
(10) devastating. Two explanations have been given for this process: Epidemic clones randomly expand as they progress through a population, or they survive by escaping herd immunity. As an analogy to influenza outbreaks, it has been
(15) proposed that epidemics might result from what are called antigenic shifts. Although all serogroup A meningococci share the same polysaccharide, individual clones differ in the other antigens exposed on the cell surface.
(20) Once immunity to the shared antigens wanes, a new clone with sufficiently different surface antigens might escape immune surveillance and start an epidemic. Epidemiologists following disease patterns will then see an
(25) "antigenic shift" as new clones supersede older clones.

1. Select the sentence that best expresses the author's conclusion regarding the limitations of the usefulness of identifying a similar antigen through clonal analysis.

2. Consider each of the choices separately and select all that apply.

   The passage supplies information for answering which of the following questions?

   ☐ How can we be certain that different epidemics originated in the same cell?

   ☐ Is it possible to develop a method of identifying all clones?

   ☐ Is the mutation of meningitis strains a previously unstudied phenomenon?

3. According to the passage, an antigenic shift takes place when

   ◯ an epidemic causes specific clones to alter their surface antigens so that they are undetectable

   ◯ shared antigens begin to be outnumbered by different antigens, thus allowing certain clones to pass through a population

   ◯ certain clones are able to sidestep a weakened herd immunity and advance through a population

   ◯ clones no longer randomly progress through a population but rather direct themselves toward the weakest elements

   ◯ certain clones build resistance to herd immunity and share this ability with other clones through their antigens

PRACTICE QUESTIONS #7

New York stood at the center of the momentous processes that recast American society in the nineteenth century. Once
Line a modest seaport, the city early took the
(5) lead in developing new forms of commerce and mass production; by 1860 it was both the nation's premier port and its largest manufacturing city. The appearance of new social classes was both cause and result
(10) of industrial development and commercial expansion. Wealth from investments in trade and manufacturing ventures supported the emergence of an urban bourgeoisie; the expansion of capitalist labor arrangements
(15) brought into being a class of largely impoverished wageworkers. The resulting divisions fostered, on each side, new and antagonistic political ideas and social practices.
We know most about the male participants
(20) in these conflicts, workingmen and employers. Politically, bourgeois men upheld their right to protect, improve upon, and increase the private property on which rested, they believed, their country's welfare. In return, many workingmen
(25) affirmed a belief in the superior abilities of those who worked with their hands—as opposed to the idle, acquisitive, parasitical owners of property—to direct American society in accordance with republican values of social
(30) equality, civil virtue, and yeomanry that they inherited from the Revolution.
Class transformation was related to, but not synonymous with, the thorough-going transformation of the gender system in the
(35) first half of the nineteenth century: that is, the changes in all those arrangements of work, sexuality, parental responsibilities, psychological life, assigned social traits, and internalized emotions through which the sexes
(40) defined themselves respectively as men and women. Women of the emerging bourgeoisie articulated new ideas about many of these aspects of their lives. Designating themselves moral guardians of their husbands and
(45) children, women became the standard-bearers of piety, decorum, and virtue in northern society. They claimed the home as the sphere of society where they could most effectively exercise their power. In their consignment to
(50) the household as the sole domain of proper female activity, women suffered a constriction of their social engagements; at the same time, they gained power within their families that also vested them with greater moral authority
(55) in their own communities.
While the cult of domesticity spoke to female interests and emerged from altered relations between men and women, it also contained within it conflicts of class. As
(60) urban ladies increased their contacts with the working poor through Protestant missions and charity work, they developed domestic ideology as part of a vision of a reformed city, purged of the supposed perfidies of working-
(65) class life. Domesticity quickly became an element of bourgeois self-consciousness. In confronting the working poor, reformers created and refined their own sense of themselves as social and spiritual superiors
(70) capable of remolding the city in their own image. From the ideas and practices of domesticity they drew many of the materials for their ideal of a society that had put to rest the disturbing conflicts of class.

1. The author of the passage is primarily concerned with discussing

○ the authority possessed by middle-class women in New York both in public and in private

○ the transformation of New York into an industrial and commercial center of activity

○ social conflict in New York, in terms of class and gender, as a result of economic expansion

○ the social values of the middle class in New York, particularly the cult of domesticity

○ the attempt of the middle class in New York to reform the working class

2. The author states, "We know most about the male participants in these conflicts" (lines 19–20) primarily in order to

- ◯ challenge past studies because they have largely ignored the female participants
- ◯ preface a debate over the motivating factors for class conflict
- ◯ propose possible reasons as to why only men's roles have been examined
- ◯ emphasize the impact that class conflict had on industrial development
- ◯ allude to a later discussion of the women who were active in such conflicts

3. According to the passage, middle-class men were similar to working-class men in that each group

- ◯ perceived the other to be an obstruction to industrial and commercial expansion
- ◯ placed a great deal of weight on private ownership and the entrepreneurial spirit
- ◯ responded to the changing economy with both excitement and aversion
- ◯ felt threatened by the activity of women who sought to lay claim to the home
- ◯ considered itself responsible for the well-being and prosperity of the country

4. According to the passage, bourgeois women did which of the following by taking charge of the home?

- ◯ Both enlarged the scope of their authority and circumscribed their power
- ◯ Portrayed their challenge to male authority as an act necessary to preserve morality
- ◯ Reconstructed the duties of parents as well as the role of children
- ◯ Increased their missionary activity intended to assist the working class
- ◯ Set out to reform the city, in particular the working class

5. Consider each of the choices separately and select all that apply.

According to the passage

- ☐ certain Americans felt that property ownership was in the best interest of the whole country
- ☐ some men who engaged in manual labor believed that those in wealthier classes did not contribute to society
- ☐ the Republican party, which was formed after the American Revolution, believed strongly in social equality

6. Select the sentence that gives a specific arena where the two major social changes discussed in the passage became integrated.

7. Consider each of the choices separately and select all that apply.

Based on the facts about social change described in the passage, which of the following could be an accurate characterization of someone living in New York City in the nineteenth century?

- ☐ A wealthy woman who believes in service to the poor as an important element in leading a truly virtuous life
- ☐ A factory worker who is able to find friends who respect his belief in old-fashioned values
- ☐ A woman, married to a successful investor, who is validated after questioning unethical choices her husband makes

PRACTICE QUESTIONS #8

Directions: The passage below is followed by questions based on its content. After reading the passage, choose the best answer to each question. Answer all questions on the basis of what is <u>stated</u> or <u>implied</u> in that passage. The answers are on page 111.

The societies in which shamanism has flourished have been small, relatively self-sufficient social systems which see themselves
Line as coping directly with their natural worlds.
(5) Like all human beings, the members of such groups lived in a world of uncertainty. The presence of a person who could maintain contact with the cosmic forces of the universe directly, who could make sense of both the
(10) measured order of ordinary times and the catastrophes of drought, earthquake, or flood, was of incalculable value.

More complex social systems tend to have "institutionalized" specialists who transmit
(15) information without explicit recourse to the supernatural. Such societies have priests and prophets, not shamans, at the overt level. But the line between shaman and prophet is tenuous. The prophet usually does not
(20) enjoy the legitimacy within his society that is granted the shaman. His is a voice crying in the wilderness, not that of the legitimate curer and philosopher. Despite these differences, the prophet can be seen as a kind of shaman, and
(25) thus the study of shamanism illuminates some of the obscurities in religious traditions.

1. The primary purpose of the passage is to

   ○ explain the differences between shamans in small and large societies

   ○ describe the reasons why shamans are esteemed in certain societies

   ○ discuss the roles of shamans as well as prophets in social systems

   ○ compare religious leaders in small social systems to those in complex social systems

   ○ argue that the power of the shaman is derived from the supernatural

2. Consider each of the choices separately and select all that apply.

   The author puts the word *institutionalized* in quotation marks in order to

   ☐ support his later statement that such specialists are often not trusted in their societies

   ☐ emphasize that such specialists can only be a part of more advanced societies

   ☐ indicate his lack of belief in the legitimacy of such specialists

3. The passage suggests that shamans and prophets differ because

   ○ shamans are more powerful because they have a mandate from their deity

   ○ shamans possess a higher social status, due to their ability to call upon the supernatural

   ○ shamans are revered as demigods while prophets are considered mortal

   ○ shamans are less likely to be challenged by members of their society

   ○ shamans maintain greater authority because they live in isolated social systems

4. Consider each of the choices separately and select all that apply.

   The passage provides evidence for which of the following statements about shamans?

   ☐ A shaman is unlikely to be well-received in a socially sophisticated community.
   ☐ There are certain aspects of a shaman that are similar to those of an institutionalized specialist.
   ☐ The benefits of a shaman extend beyond assistance in times of need.

5. Select the sentence in the passage in which the author's word choice reveals a degree of irony in the roles of some spiritual specialists.

PRACTICE QUESTIONS #9

Directions: Each passage below is followed by a question based on its content. After reading the passage, choose the best answer to each question. Answer all questions on the basis of what is stated or implied in that passage. The answers are on page 112.

The importance of a well-balanced diet high in fiber and low in saturated fat is understood by most shoppers in Arcadia County. Moreover, *Line* food nutrition labels clearly display important (5) nutritional information. As a result, sales of high-fiber foods in Arcadia County have risen dramatically during the last decade, while sales of foods high in saturated fat have dropped by a similar magnitude. Even so, during the last (10) decade the number of shoppers in Arcadia County who are overweight has increased substantially.

1. Which of the following, if true, most helps explain why during the last decade more shoppers in Arcadia are overweight?

   ◯ Many people who buy food in Arcadia County do not actually live in Arcadia County.

   ◯ Shoppers in Arcadia County who maintain a healthy weight do not all read nutritional labels when purchasing food.

   ◯ People who reduce their intake of saturated fat often increase the number of calories they consume.

   ◯ The obesity rate in Arcadia County has decreased steadily over the past decade.

   ◯ During the past decade, most of the fruits and vegetables grown in Arcadia County were shipped out of the state.

The more the residents of a city exercise, the lower the average number of heart attacks in that city. Likewise, the less the residents of *Line* a city exercise, the greater the average number (5) of heart attacks in that city. Therefore, people who wish to reduce the chance of suffering a heart attack should exercise more.

2. Which of the following, if true, most seriously undermines the argument?

   ◯ Heart attacks are a common cause of death in cities with high exercise rates.

   ◯ The cities with low exercise rates are often those with the highest standards of living.

   ◯ A particular resident of a city whose population has a high exercise rate may not exercise at all.

   ◯ The cities with high exercise rates are also the cities with the lowest number of cigarette smokers.

   ◯ The differences in exercise rates among cities often result from the availability of conveniently located gyms.

In a study, scientists dissected the brains of 10,000 recently deceased people who were all of similar ages and backgrounds.
Line To minimize the risk of contamination and
(5) ensure optimal visual analysis of the brain tissue, the scientists washed the tissue before staining it for analysis. The scientists found that the brain tissue of deceased patients with Alzheimer's disease contained unusually high
(10) concentrations of aluminum. The aluminum was found in tissues that had lesions containing amyloid protein, a protein that damages nerve cells and has previously been shown to cause Alzheimer's. The scientists
(15) hypothesized that Alzheimer's disease results when amyloid protein grows in lesions caused by excess aluminum in the brain.

3. Which of the following, if true, would strengthen the scientists' hypothesis?

○ The brains of some of the deceased people who did not have Alzheimer's disease had unusually low concentrations of aluminum.

○ Some frequently prescribed medications used to control the symptoms of Alzheimer's disease cause stomach irritation, for which patients often take antacids containing high concentrations of aluminum.

○ Amyloid protein has also been shown to play a role in Huntington's disease and Type 2 Diabetes.

○ When the scientists washed the brain tissue, they used water that came from the Stefl Reservoir, a source known to contain water with high concentrations of aluminum.

○ Patients undergoing kidney dialysis sometimes experience disorientation similar to that of Alzheimer's patients due to a decrease in their ability to excrete aluminum.

Some economists have argued that market regulation is antithetical to the ideal functioning of a democratic society because
Line it interferes with the individual's right to make
(5) decisions in his own financial interest. In a regulated market, the citizen is not always at liberty to choose where or how to build his house or whom to hire for his business. If all individuals do not have complete freedom to
(10) make economic decisions purely with respect to their own self-interest, then a society is not a true democracy. Yet this perspective overlooks the fact that the democratic ideal encompasses two separate, but not mutually
(15) exclusive goals: 1) to ensure individual liberty and 2) to promote the overall health and well-being of the population. Some degree of market regulation may be necessary to fulfill the latter goal, for an individual's exercise of
(20) his own liberty can in some instances interfere with the liberty of others.

4. Which one of the following most accurately expresses the main conclusion of the argument?

○ Market regulation ensures individual liberty and promotes the overall health and well-being of the population.

○ Market regulation is not automatically at odds with the ideals of a democratic society.

○ Market regulation does not allow individuals to make choices.

○ Market regulation is a necessary precondition for democracy.

○ Market regulation is antithetical to the ideals of a democratic society.

ANSWERS AND EXPLANATIONS

QUICK QUIZ #1

1. To find the main idea, here's all you need to read:

- "If my colleagues and I are right, we may soon be saying good-bye to the idea that our universe was a single fireball created in the big bang. We are exploring a new theory based on a 15-year-old notion that the universe went through a stage of inflation."

- "Cosmologists did not arbitrarily invent this rather peculiar vision of the universe."

- "As the universe expanded, it gradually cooled."

- "As investigators developed the theory, they uncovered complications."

- "In that case, the mean density of matter in the universe would be about 15 orders of magnitude greater than its present value, which is about 10^{-29} grams per cubic centimeter."

Given these sentences, how might you paraphrase the main idea? That the big bang theory may be wrong and that the inflationary theory may be right? Now you can go to the answer choices.

Eliminate (A) because it's too extreme. Scientists haven't *proven* the big bang theory wrong. Leave (B) in because it's a good match for your paraphrase. Also, note how moderate (B) is. Eliminate (C) because it says the inflationary theory is bad. Remember, it's the big bang theory that's problematic, not the inflationary theory. Eliminate (D) because it mentions stuff (magnetic monopoles) you didn't read about. Eliminate (E) because it suggests the big bang theory is okay. The best answer, then, is (B).

2. **D** Most of the passage provides information about the Big Bang and complications that arise from the theory. However, in the beginning of the first two paragraphs, the authors express hope that their new theory will resolve these complications. Thus, choice (D) is correct. Choices (A) and (C) are wrong because the authors and not nostalgic or indifferent. While the authors may be concerned about the problems associated with the Big Bang, the overall tone of the passage is not one of concern. In any event, the authors are not amused, eliminating choice (B). While the authors do appear to appreciate their new theory of inflation, choice (E) is too strong: The passage as a whole is not largely appreciative, but, rather, mostly informative.

3. **A** Rather than dealing with one answer at a time, start by looking at the first statement of each answer. They are all the same, and they are accurate: The first paragraph introduces the recent theory of inflation. Next, look at the second statement of each answer. Choices (A) and (B) work best: The beginning of the

second paragraph explains that the inflation theory was developed to address complications arising from the big bang theory. Choice (C) is wrong because the authors did not say that the big bang theory was discarded; choice (D) is wrong because no supporting evidence is provided; and choice (E) is wrong because the authors do not discuss criticism of the inflation theory. Finally, look at the last statement in choices (A) and (B). Choice (A) is correct because the remainder of the passage describes the big bang theory and shortcomings of that theory. Choice (B) is too strong; the authors seek to supplement, not discard, the big bang theory.

QUICK QUIZ #2

1. **C** This tone question is specific, not general. Regardless, for any tone question, extreme answer choices are bad. What answer choices are too extreme here? Definitely (D), so cross it out. The other answer choices are fairly moderate, so leave them in for now. What now? Use "dynasties" as your lead word. That takes you to the first paragraph. How does the author feel about the formation of the dynasties? Not too good: She calls them an "abominable elite that had developed as a consequence of social prejudice." So what's the best answer? Something that's slightly negative. Eliminate (A) because it's positive. Eliminate (B) because it's not negative at all. Keep (C) for now because it's slightly negative. Finally, leave in (E) because it's slightly negative.

    The remaining answer choices are (C) and (E). Which one is better? Well, does the author dislike the formation of the dynasties or is she resigned to it? She dislikes it, right? So the best answer is (C).

2. **B** This is a specific question. Use "United States" as your lead words. Once you find the lead words, remember to read about five lines above and five lines below. So where is "United States"? In the second paragraph. What does the passage say about men in the United States? That they took a "'protective' stance" toward women to compensate them for their "nonexistent social status." Always make a paraphrase of the answer before moving on to the answer choices.

    Eliminate (A) because who cares about the Court d'Assizes. Keep (B) because it looks like a pretty good match for your paraphrase. Eliminate (C) because you didn't read anything about a popular movement. Eliminate (D) because who cares about the modern historians. Eliminate (E) because you didn't read anything about lots of French women being guillotined. The best answer is (B).

3. **E** This is a specific question. Use "death penalty" as your lead words. Once you find the lead word, don't forget to read about five lines above and five lines below. So where is "death penalty"? In the third paragraph. What does the passage say about popular arguments against the death penalty? That they focus on humanitarian principles and that they don't focus on equal rights. In other words, men and women are equal, so if women aren't subject to capital punishment, then men shouldn't be either. It's important that you paraphrase the answer to the question before moving on to the answer choices.

Eliminate (A) because it doesn't talk about humanitarian principles or equal rights. Eliminate (B) for the same reason. Eliminate (C) because it misinterprets information in the passage. Popular arguments *failed* to incorporate equal rights. Eliminate (D) because it also misrepresents information in the passage. It's the men that are getting killed, not the women. Keep (E) because it's a good match for your paraphrase. (E) is the best answer.

PRACTICE QUESTIONS #1

1. **B** To find the main idea, all you have to do is read the topic sentence for each paragraph and then the final sentence of the entire passage. Remember, always state the main idea in your own words (i.e., paraphrase) before moving on to the answer choices. So what's the main idea for this passage? You should have come up with something like the following: The Civil War was a result of conflicting political ideologies in the North and South.

(A) is too general. From the second paragraph, you know that the main idea has to have something to do with the Civil War. (B) is a possibility since it talks about the war. (C), like (A), is too broad because it doesn't mention the war. (D) does talk about the war, which is good, but it doesn't really talk about how the war affected the party system, which is bad. (E) is too specific. Though it does talk about the war, it doesn't take into account the topic sentence for the first paragraph. The best answer is (B).

2. **C** Use "political parties" as your lead word. It takes you to the very beginning of the passage. Remember, paraphrase what you read before you move on to the answer choices. What does the passage say about political parties today? That they purposefully avoid ideology.

(A) goes a little too far. The passage does say that parties should try to represent "broad coalitions of varying interests," but that doesn't mean that all parties are the same. (B) misrepresents information in the passage. Lines 11–13 ("Such a view implies . . . ") suggest that "the peaceful operation of the political system is the highest social value" in certain circumstances, but you don't know that to be true for political parties today. (C) is a good match for your paraphrase. (D) isn't mentioned at all in the passage. (E) goes a little too far. It's implied that political parties only address problems of little import because they don't want conflict, but you don't know that parties rarely have disputes. The best answer is (C).

3.　**E**　"Carl Becker," clearly, should be the lead word you use, and you can find the lead word in the first paragraph. Well, why does the author mention Carl Becker? Paraphrase the answer before you look at the answer choices. The author mentions Carl Becker because he wants to cite someone who supports his main idea: Ideology can be very divisive—after all, it caused the Civil War.

(A) misrepresents information in the passage. The passage does talk about political sociologists, but it doesn't say they disagree with Becker. (B) may be true, but it's not the reason *why* the author mentions Becker. (C) goes too far. Becker thinks ideology is divisive, but he's not saying we should therefore avoid it. (D) is really the point the political sociologists are making, not Becker. (E) is the only answer left, and guess what? It matches your paraphrase. (E) is the best answer.

4.　　**B** and **C**

The beliefs of Republicans during the 1850s are most clearly stated in the final paragraph. Choice (A) is incorrect and too literal an interpretation of the text: The *"slave power"* referred to in the passage is the power of the politicians who support slavery, not the political power of the slaves themselves. The last sentence says Republicans thought that *Two profoundly different and antagonistic civilizations...and were competing for control.* Since the Republicans themselves are one of these civilizations, it is reasonable to conclude they believe their ideas are incompatible with those of their political rivals. Choice (B) is correct. The passage says that *southern society...appeared...inferior to their own.* Since Republicans in the passage are northerners, it must be true that they think northern society was superior, which validates choice (C).

5.　　**"The minority can accept the victory of the majority at the polls, because both share many basic values, and electoral defeat does not imply 'a fatal surrender . . . of vital interests.'"**

While most of the passage discusses the increasing ideological divisions between the North and the South before the Civil War, the first paragraph describes the existing political parties' reluctance to embrace ideology. The author explains that such reluctance is part of a stable political system in which the parties largely share the same values. The question asks for a practical illustration of this concept. The final sentence of the first paragraph provides that illustration: If the minority and majority share values, the minority can better accept defeat at the polls. If you selected the sentence before the credited response, make sure you were answering the right question—you were looking for an illustration, not an explanation, of the topic at hand.

6. **A** Choice (A) is supported: The second paragraph describes the growing ideological divide between the North and the South, ending in the disintegration of the existing political parties. Choice (B) is not supported; rather, Southerners are said to have believed that slavery was an important part of civilized life. Choice (C) is not supported, as Republicans opposed slavery. Be careful: In the passage, *free labor* does not relate to slave labor, but a philosophy about work.

7. **D** For a tone question, anything too extreme must be wrong. (E) is out, as a result, as is (A). So you're left with (B), (C), and (D)—each of which is pretty moderate. So use "Republican" as your lead word to find out how the author feels about the party.

    The fourth paragraph talks about the Republicans, and clearly, the author is pretty neutral in tone. So the best answer is (D).

Practice Questions #2

1. **"For neo-avant-garde artists who challenge this hegemonic three decades ago, its very deviancy might have made surrealism an attractive object."**

    The passage, after characterizing surrealism as a deviant art movement, discusses the neo-avant-garde rejection of surrealism. Before explaining this rejection, the author indicates that neo-avant-gardist might have found surrealism's deviancy to be attractive, given the concerns of those embracing the neo-avant-garde viewpoint. However, the author then states "But such was not the case." Thus, the author believes that it would be reasonable to anticipate that the neo-avant-garde would have a positive point of view of surrealism—yet, that anticipation would be incorrect.

2. **B** and **C**

Choice (B) is supported: The author explains that, while neo-avant-gardists might have found surrealism attractive because of its deviancy, they rejected it as *corrupt*, *subjective*, and *elitist*—in short, dishonest. Choice (C) is also supported: The author cites Duchamp as an artist, unlike surrealist artists, that neo-advant-gardists "turned to." Choice (A) may be appealing because it quotes much of the first sentence, properly conveying much of the author's description of surrealism. However, the author states that surrealism "is not properly modernist at all." Thus, Choice (A)'s reference to surrealism as a form of modernism is incorrect. Remember, it takes only one unsupported statement to make an entire answer choice incorrect.

3. **C** This question asks about the neo-avant-gardist view of the formalistic model of modernism, not specifically of surrealism. The neo-avant-gardists are described as antagonists to the formalistic model, which views modern art "as separate from social practice and grounded in visual experience." The neo-avant-gardists "sought to destroy the separate institution of art." Thus, Choice (C) best expresses the neo-avant-gardists' objection to formal modernism. Choices (A) and (E) were not stated in the passage. Choice (B) refers to a characteristic of surrealism, not of the formalist model of modernism. Choice (D) refers to text out of context: The constructivist branch of neo-avant-gardists sought to transform modernist art "according to the materialistic practices of a revolutionary society." They did not criticize formalist art as materialistic.

Practice Questions #3

1. **A** This is a main idea question. To find the main idea, all you have to do is read the first two sentences of the first paragraph, the topic sentence for each remaining paragraph, and then the last sentence of the entire passage. Remember to state the main idea in your own words before looking at the answer choices. So what's the main idea? To talk about Forster and how he really wasn't a very "modern" writer.

(A) talks about Forster and modernity, so it looks okay. (B) is too specific. The passage does compare Forster to these writers, but it's not the main point. (C) is too specific as well. It's a summary of the last paragraph. (D) is off the mark entirely. Finally, (E) is too specific. Revolutions in science and art are mentioned in the first paragraph, but that's about it. The best answer is (A).

2. **D** This is a specific question. Use "Victorianism" as your lead word. Remember, once you find the lead word, read about five lines above and five lines below. So where can you find "Victorianism"? At the end of the first paragraph. What does the passage say about Forster and Victorianism? That Forster stepped away from Victorianism, but not entirely. Don't forget to paraphrase before you go to the answer choices.

    (A) goes too far. Forster did step away from Victorianism, just not completely. (B) goes too far as well. Forster didn't cling to Victorianism's ideals. (C) is too extreme. Forster moved away from Victorianism, but not that completely. (D) looks like a good match for your paraphrase. (E) goes off target. Again, Forster did reject Victorianism, at least to a certain extent. The best answer is (D).

3. **C** This specific question tells you exactly where in the passage to go because of the line reference. Remember, though, you need to read a little bit before the line reference as well as a little bit after. Well, why does the author say Forster is atavistic? To paraphrase: Even though he was a modern writer, and not a Victorian one, he was closer to Victorianism in some ways than he was to modernity. Don't forget to paraphrase before looking at the answer choices.

    Eliminate (A) because it discusses individualism, not Forster's tension with modernity. Eliminate (B) because it's a little off. The author doesn't say Forster was completely unconnected. (C) is okay for now; it suggests that Forster and modernity were somewhat in conflict. (D) is the opposite of what you're looking for. (E) goes too far. Forster didn't belief in Victorianism completely. So the best answer is (C).

4. **"Forster's resistance to modernity may account for the fact that his novels, though they are almost universally esteemed, have never won him a cult of fanatical disciples."**

    Most of the passage concerns Forster's ideas and how they differed in some respects to those of other writers of Forster's generation. Only in the final paragraph is the reaction of others discussed, so the answer must come from that paragraph. After emphasizing in prior paragraphs that Forster's approach and views seem almost archaic compared to other writers, the author proposes in the first sentence of the last paragraph that this very "resistance to modernity" may explain why Forster does not have a cult following.

5.   **B and C**

   Choice (B) is supported: The author tells us that Forster's *resistance to the twentieth century* is best viewed as a contrast to the *radical iconoclasts* who wrote at the same time; they rejected bourgeois life while Forster continued to embrace *the usefulness of the sociable virtues* and *apotheosis of the happy family*. Choice (C) is also supported: After describing the differences in viewpoint and style between Forster and other writers of his day, the author states in the final paragraph that Forster *is a novelist of ideas, and didactic moral content is hardly less conspicuous in his work than in Lawrence's*. Choice (A) correctly describes aspects of the other writers' work, but incorrectly states that Forster shared the values and styles attributed to those authors.

6.   **D** This tone question is general, and it's definitely a "gimme." How do you think the author feels? From the main idea alone, you can tell he likes Forster. That means (A), (B), and (C) aren't right. Between (D) and (E), which is better? The less extreme. So (D) is the best answer.

7.   **A and C**

   Forster is described as *Edwardian in point of time, and…equally so in spirit*. The other writers were Forster's *fellow writers*, and they wrote in the *current of the modern literary movement*, in a way much different from how Forster wrote. Therefore, they must have been *ahead of the spirit of their time*, and choice (A) is correct. Though the passage says that they participated in the *fragmentation of the polite cadences of Victorian literature*, choice (B) is too broad and extreme in that it suggests that they were rude and offensive overall and not just in their literary style. The end of the second paragraph states that Forster did have *confidence in the reader's sympathy*. Since this confidence *seemed quite archaic to the other writers named*, it can be inferred that they *lacked confidence in their audiences' sympathy*. Choice (C) is correct.

Practice Questions #4

1.   **D** This is a general question. For any general question, focus on the main idea. The main idea of the passage can be found by reading the first two sentences of the first paragraph, the topic sentence of each remaining paragraph, and the last sentence of the entire passage. So what's the main idea? To paraphrase: that the natural selection theory doesn't explain all of evolution. Always state the main idea in your own words before looking at the answer choices.

(A) goes too far. Natural selection isn't perfect at explaining all of evolution, but it's still very powerful according to the passage. (B) is true, but it's not the main point of the passage. (C) is a little off. The passage doesn't say anything about making changes to the theory—just that the theory doesn't cover everything. (D) looks like a good match for your paraphrase. (E) is way off target. The best answer is (D).

2. **A, B**, and **C**

The first sentence of the first paragraph explains that natural selection has been thoroughly tested and still holds true. Although in the second paragraph the author reveals that the theory is not comprehensive, this does not invalidate the accuracy of the theory and choice (A) is supported. Choice (B) is also correct because of the discussion in the second paragraph about changes at organizational levels that are above the reproductive focus of Darwin's theory, which was earlier described as *simple*. Finally, choice (C) is correctly inferred from the last sentence of the second paragraph, which discusses changes that are *unrelated to adaptive struggles*.

3. **B** Choice (A) is contradictory to the last sentence of the fifth paragraph, which states that a different manner might "not have led to consciousness." Choice (B) is supported by the author's use of the phrase "just a geological second ago." While the use of the word *not* preceding that phrase may be confusing, *not* refers to the reason that humans appeared on the earth, rather than the time frame. Choice (C) is very close to what the author states; however, the passage does not provide evidence to support the idea that the events occurred in a linear fashion. The passage states that the events were *contingent* and *linked* but these words do not preclude simultaneous events.

4. **C** This specific question has a very easy lead word to find: "*Homo sapiens.*" Still, don't forget that you need to read about five lines before the lead word and five lines after. So why does the passage talk about *Homo sapiens*? Look at the fifth paragraph: to give weight to the idea that life comes about through a random coinciding of events. Always paraphrase the answer before looking at the answer choices.

(A) is mentioned in the paragraph, but it's not the reason why *Homo sapiens* are discussed. (B) focuses on length instead of randomness. (C) talks about randomness, so it should be kept. (D) discusses natural selection, which isn't the point. (E) is a little off. It's not the intricacy of events that matters—it's the randomness. The best answer is (C).

5.	**"Webs and chains of historical events are so intricate, so imbued with random and chaotic elements, so unrepeatable in encompassing such a multitude of unique (and uniquely interacting) objects, that standard models of simple prediction do not apply."**

Look for a sentence that talks about *intermingling, highly detailed occurrences,* and *problematic* prediction. Sentence (12) states that precision is certainly difficult but does not offer reasons. Sentence (13) mentions *minute and unmeasurable differences* and sentence (14) mentions *contingency* and *antecedent states* but each of these are only partial answers to the question. So although the fourth paragraph appears to focus on the problems of prediction, it is actually sentence (11) "Webs and chains of historical events are so intricate…" that fully responds to the question. This sentence discusses *webs* that are *intricate* and prevent the use of *standard models of simple prediction.*

6.	**C**	This is really a general question. What do we need to do for any general question? Think about the main idea. The main idea of this passage is the following: The natural selection theory is not a complete explanation of evolution. The best answer choice has to go with the flow of the main idea.

(A) misinterprets information from the passage. If you use "history" as a lead word, that takes you to the third and fourth paragraphs. Those paragraphs say that the study of history can be satisfactory, at least "if evidence be adequate." (B) isn't true. Natural selection is about the struggle for reproductive success— which doesn't take into account random events. The second paragraph says as much when it discusses lower levels of organisms. (C) goes with the flow of the main idea, especially since it conveys the idea of randomness. (D) goes back to history again. We found out from (A) that history can be satisfactory, but what else? That it's hard to predict, not easy. (E) is too extreme. Theories aren't *always* inadequate. So the best answer is (C).

7.	**D**	This is a general question. So focus on the main idea—in other words, the first two sentences of the first paragraph, the topic sentence of each remaining paragraph, and the final sentence of the entire passage. How is the passage organized? Well, natural selection is explained, and then problems with it are noted in a lot of detail. Always paraphrase the answer to a question before looking at the answer choices.

(A) is a bad answer choice because it says natural selection is rejected. The theory isn't rejected, just noted as incomplete. (B) is okay for the first half, but bad for the second half. Conditions are never stated. (C) is okay for the first half, but bad for the second half. Observations that support it aren't made. (D) is a good match for your paraphrase. (E) is okay for the first half, but bad for the second half. The passage does question natural selection but not by applying it to a different field of study. (Don't get thrown by the discussion of history.) The best answer is (D).

PRACTICE QUESTIONS #5

1. **E** This is a main-idea question. To find the main idea, all you have to do is read the first two sentences of the first paragraph, the topic sentence of each remaining paragraph, and then the last sentence of the entire passage. Don't forget to state the main idea in your own words before looking at the answer choices. So what's the main idea? How gender differences are preserved or enforced in the workplace.

    (A) talks about the reconstruction of gender. Not what you're looking for. (B) discusses nontraditional jobs, not gender differences. (C) mentions pervasiveness, which isn't the point. (D) is a little off because of the word "why." The passage isn't about why we can't ignore gender differences. (E) is the only answer choice remaining, and it's a good match for your paraphrase. The best answer is (E).

2. **"In office settings, for instance, dress codes—either formal or implicit—are not unusual; female employees may be required to wear dresses, nylons, and high-heeled shoes to enhance their femininity."**

    Focus on the word *aesthetics*. Paragraph 2 is the only one that contains a discussion of codes that govern appearance. While sentence (12) does mention visibility of minority group members, the focus is not on the creation of a particular appearance. Within the second paragraph, sentences (9) and (10) may also seem to address the question. However, the question specifically asks for *informal* codes and those two sentences only deal with requirements. Sentence (8) mentions *implicit* dress codes and also states that the specific purpose is to *enhance femininity*; it is therefore the correct answer.

3. **C** This is a specific question. "Internal stratification" is clearly the lead word, and you can find the lead word at the beginning of the very first paragraph. Don't forget to read about five lines before the lead word as well as five lines after. So what is internal stratification? When men and women have the same job, but in that job, they are given different tasks to perform. Remember, it's always important to paraphrase before looking at the answer choices.

    (A) isn't an inference you can make. Women and men have the same jobs is the point. (B) isn't an inference you can make. It might be true, but nothing about internal stratification suggests it. (C) looks good—especially because it agrees with the main idea about gender differences. (D) isn't quite as good as (C). It could be true, but nothing about internal stratification suggests it. (E), finally, is like (B) and (D). It could be true, but nothing about internal stratification suggests it. The best answer is (C).

4. **B** This is a specific question, and the question tells you exactly where to go in the passage: the last paragraph. What's the point of the last paragraph? That gender differences aren't always "forced on people." In other words, people sometimes enforce gender differences themselves. It's always important to paraphrase the answer to a question before looking at the answer choices.

    (A) is the opposite of what you're looking for. It's the internal that's important, not the external. (B) looks like a good match for the paraphrase. (C) is a little off. Male nurses and female marines are nontraditional, but they actually enforce gender differences, too. (D) isn't quite right. The statement is true, but it's not the point of the last paragraph. (E) is way off target. The best answer is (B).

5.   **A** and **B**

    Be careful to choose answers that are *not* supported by the passage. Choice (A) cannot be inferred because the text only indicates an *influx of women workers* in industries such as pharmaceuticals or finance. However, if there are more positions in such industries overall, then the men are not necessarily being displaced. Choice (B) also cannot be inferred. The men work in less automated bakeries, but this is not to say that they are good at their jobs, or that women would be worse at such work if given the chance to try. Choice (C) is the only supported inference, because the second paragraph states that men are *required to dress differently* and *never wear the traditional nursing cap*. Keeping in mind that the question asks which statements *cannot* be inferred, and you should select choices (A) and (B).

6. **D** This is a weird question. What do we know about weird questions? That they're very time-consuming. Okay—what should you do for an EXCEPT question? Play the Yes/No game. Start by finding a lead word for each answer choice. The lead word in (A), "words," takes you to the fourth paragraph. Do managers use language to enforce gender differences? Yes. So put a Y next to (A). The lead word in (B), "dress," takes you to the second paragraph. Do dress codes enforce gender differences? Yes. So put a Y next to (B). The lead word in (C), "pressure," takes you to the last paragraph. Does internal pressure enforce gender differences? Yes. Put a Y next to (C). Use "coworkers" in (D) as a lead word. "Coworkers" doesn't take you anywhere in the passage, so put an

N next to (D). The lead words in (E), "different duties," takes you to the first paragraph. Do different duties for men and women enforce gender differences? Yes. Put a Y next to (E).

Which answer choice is not like the others? (D). It's the only answer choice with an N next to it. So (D) is the best answer.

7.   **"This added pressure may actually result in different job performances from men and women in nontraditional occupations and exacerbate gender differences."**

In sentence (14), the author writes that "added pressure may actually result in different job performance." The *pressure* is referring to the previously mentioned extra attention that some women in corporations receive. The *attention* is the informal habit and the *different job performance* is the behavior, making sentence (14) the correct answer. Sentence (15) is also closely related to the topic but gives evidence for the theory, rather than simply the theory itself. Sentences (16) and (17) also appear to be related to behavior, but focus on the behavior of supervisors, rather than the response of the employees to such behavior.

PRACTICE QUESTIONS #6

1.   **"Once immunity to the shared antigens wanes, a new clone with sufficiently different surface antigens might escape immune surveillance and start an epidemic."**

The question is asking about the author's conclusion, so you can immediately eliminate sentences such as (2), (4), (5), and (7) that are giving factual information. Next, you know that you are looking for a conclusion about the role of antigens in clonal analysis, so you can eliminate sentences (1) and (3) because they appear too early on in the discussion, before the introduction of antigens. That leaves you with only sentences (8) and (9). Sentence (8) tells you that the presence of a sufficient amount of different antigens can cause a clone to escape detection, which is clear drawback. There is no limitation mentioned in sentence (9).

2.   **A and C**

The second sentence of the passage talks about *clonal analysis* as a way to draw *clear* connections between meningococcal strains, so there is an answer for the question in choice (A). Line 14 uses a comparison to influenza outbreaks to explain how clones change, so there is also an answer to the question in choice (C). Choice (B), however, cannot be answered by this passage alone. The passage indicates that currently some clones can *escape immune surveillance and start an epidemic*, but that is not to say that this situation can't be overcome in the future.

3. **C** This is a specific question. Use "antigenic shift" as your lead words. They take you to the middle of the paragraph. Don't forget that you should read about five lines above the lead word as well as five lines after. So what does the passage say about antigenic shifts? That they take place when immunity wanes, which allows some clones to escape surveillance and start an epidemic. Make sure you make this paraphrase before moving on to the answer choices.

    Does (A) match your paraphrase? No. Nowhere in the passage does it talk about clones *changing* their surface antigens. What about (B)? No. There's nothing in the passage about shared antigens outnumbering different antigens. (C)? It's a pretty good match. (D)? No. The passage doesn't say clones direct themselves at the weakest elements of the population. (E)? No. There's nothing about sharing a resistance to immunity. The best answer is (C).

PRACTICE QUESTIONS #7

1. **C** To find the answer to this general question, determine what the main idea is. How do you find the main idea? By reading the first two sentences of the first paragraph, the topic sentence of each remaining paragraph, and then the last sentence of the entire passage. What is the main idea? That the evolving economy in New York produced class conflict and gender conflict. Always paraphrase the main idea before looking at the answer choices.

    (A) is too specific. Middle-class women are discussed, but they're not the main point. (B) is too general. It talks about the economy, but not about class and gender. (C) looks like a good match for your paraphrase. (D) is too specific. The cult of domesticity is mentioned in the passage, but it's not the main point. (E) is too specific. It says nothing about the economy. The best answer is (C).

2. **E** This is a specific question that uses a line reference. Don't forget that you should read not just the line reference, but about five lines above the line reference and five lines below. So why does the author say, "We know most about the male participants"? As a way to discuss class conflict between men *and* as a way to preface class conflict between women. In other words, we don't know a lot about the female participants but here is what we do know. Always paraphrase the answer to a question before looking at the answer choices.

(A) isn't quite right. The author isn't *challenging* the studies about men.
(B) is a little off. Yes, class conflict is at issue, but debate is not. (C) is bad because the passage never talks about why only men have been looked at. (D) contains a true statement—class conflict did have an impact on industrial development—but that's not the point of the author saying, "We know most about the male participants." (E) is the best match for your paraphrase and it is the best answer. This question is a great example of how much of reading comprehension is *not* about finding the best answer. It's about finding the answer that is *least bad*. In other words, get the right answer by eliminating the ones that have to be wrong.

3.   **E**   This is a specific question. Use "middle-class men" and "working-class men" as your lead words. That takes you to the second paragraph. What does the paragraph say about the similarities between the two groups? That they both believed the welfare of the country depended on them. Don't forget that you must paraphrase the answer to a question before looking at the answer choices.

(A) misinterprets the information in the paragraph. It's suggested that the groups didn't particularly like each other, but you don't know whether they saw each other as obstructions. (B) is true of middle-class men, but not working-class men. (C) is not good because the passage does not address feelings that men had about the economic changes. (D) misinterprets information from the passage. You don't know that men felt threatened by the changing roles of women. (E) is a good match for your paraphrase. It's the best answer.

4.   **A**   This is a specific question. Use "home" as your lead word. That should take you to the third paragraph. What does the passage say about women and the home? That "In their consignment to the household as the sole domain of proper female activity, women suffered a constriction of their social engagements; at the same time, they gained power within their families that also vested them with greater moral authority in their own communities" (lines 49–55). In other words, women lost power by being restricted to the home, but also gained power at the same time. Always paraphrase before looking at the answer choices.

(A) is a great match for your paraphrase. (B) misinterprets what you read. You don't know if taking charge of the home was a challenge to male authority. (C) misinterprets information from the passage. You don't know that women were responsible for reconstructing the duties of parents and the role of children. It could have been men. (D) is a little tricky. Women did participate in missionary activity, but you don't know they increased that participation after taking charge of the home. (E) is also tricky because women did try to reform the city, but was this a result of taking charge of the home? You don't know. The best answer is (A).

5.   **A** and **B**

The information relevant to this question can be found in the second paragraph. First, the sentence that begins "Politically, bourgeois men upheld their right..." states that the bourgeois believed the country's welfare rested on private property. This directly supports choice (A). Choice (B) is supported by the description given of the property owners as "idle, acquisitive, parasitical." Choice (C) is incorrect because it confuses Republican, a member of a political party, with republican, an adjective which means supporting a political system that derives its power from the people. In addition, there is no evidence in the passage that the Republican party was formed after the American Revolution.

6.   **"As urban ladies increased their contacts with the working poor through Protestant missions and charity work, they developed domestic ideology as part of a vision of a reformed city, purged of the supposed perfidies of working-class life."**

To answer the question, you must first determine what the two major social changes discussed in the passage are. The organization of the passage should help you realize that those were class struggles, as discussed in the second paragraph, and gender roles, as discussed in the third paragraph. The final paragraph synthesizes these two discussions, and it is where you will find the answer. The next step is to remember that the question requires you to find a *specific arena*. There are four sentences in the final paragraph and all but the correct one give general statements about the incorporation of gender and class struggles. The correct sentence specifically mentions *Protestant missions and charity work*.

7.   **B** and **C**

Choice (A) is not supported, because the passage specifically mentions in the last paragraph that only the bourgeois women participated in reforming the city through charity work. Although the same paragraph also mentions *urban ladies* as charity workers, the first paragraph of the passage equates the urban women with the bourgeois. There is evidence for choice (B) in the second paragraph, which mentions that *many* men believed in manual labor as the propagator of values that were *inherited from the Revolution*. The first paragraph also mentions the manufacturing industry, which supports the mention of the *factory worker* in this answer choice. Proof for choice (C) can also be found through a combination of the first and third paragraphs. The first paragraph mentions that the bourgeois stemmed from investment wealth, and the third paragraph indicates that bourgeois women were empowered in the moral lives of their families.

PRACTICE QUESTIONS #8

1. **C** To find the main idea, just read the first two sentences of the first paragraph, the topic sentence of each remaining paragraph, and then the final sentence of the entire passage. What's the main idea, then? To talk about shamans and prophets.

    (A) is a little too general. It doesn't mention prophets at all. (B) is discussed in the passage, but it's not the main point. (C) looks good because it talks about both shamans and prophets. (D) is too general. Religious leaders is vague—you want an answer choice that mentions shamans and prophets explicitly. (E) is too specific. Shamans and the supernatural are mentioned in the passage, but that's not the main point. The best answer is (C).

2. **A** Later in the passage, the author states that the prophet—that is, the institutionalized specialist—*does not enjoy the legitimacy…that is granted the shaman.* Thus, *institutionalized* is in quotes because the author is using the word in an ironic way: One who is part of an institution in a society should be widely accepted, but the prophet is not. Therefore, choice (A) is correct. Choice (B) is an unsupported and extreme statement: The passage only talks about two types of societies, and only about one vocation within them, that of spiritual conduit. Choice (C) is also not supported: The author is only relaying facts about shamanism and specialists, and there is nothing to indicate his personal feelings toward either.

3. **D** This is a specific question. Use "shamans" and "prophets" as the lead words. That takes you to the second paragraph. What does the passage say about how they differ? "The prophet usually does not enjoy the legitimacy within his society that is granted the shaman. His is a voice crying in the wilderness, not that of the legitimate curer and philosopher." So the prophet doesn't have quite the standing or the power of the shaman. Always paraphrase the answer to a question before going to the answer choices.

    (A) mentions a mandate from a god. You didn't read that, so it can't be right. (B) is half true. Shamans do have more standing, but is that based upon their communication with the supernatural? You don't know. (C) goes too far.

Shamans are respected, clearly, but are they demigods? Who knows. (D) has to be true since shamans have more standing and power than do prophets. (Note the moderate language—"less likely.") Finally, (E) is half true. Shamans do have greater authority—but is it because they live in isolated social systems? You don't know. The best answer is (D).

4.   **B** and **C**

Although the passage says that *more complex social systems tend to have "institutionalized" specialists*, there is no evidence to substantiate the idea that if a shaman were to go to a complex society, he would be rejected by the people. Therefore, choice (A) is not supported. Choice (B) is supported because the author says that *the line between shaman and prophet is tenuous* and that *the prophet can be seen as a kind of shaman*. These phrases imply a similarity between the shaman and the prophet, who is an example of a specialist. Choice (C) is supported by the last sentence of the first paragraph, which describes the shaman as one of *incalculable value* even in *ordinary times*.

5.   **"His is a voice crying in the wilderness, not that of the legitimate curer and philosopher."**

The word *his* in this sentence refers to the prophet; previously, the text describes the prophet as an *"institutionalized"* spiritual specialist, while the shaman helps those who deal *directly with their natural worlds*. For the author to describe the prophet as the one who is really in the *wilderness*, then, while the shaman is *legitimate*, can be said to be ironic.

Practice Questions #9

1.   **C**   Before looking at the answers, try to come up with an explanation for how better food choices can still lead to weight gain. A terrific explanation would be that people eating well-balanced diets eat a greater quantity of food. With your answer in mind, review the answer choices. Choice (C) is a match. Choice (A) might seem appealing, but the passage did not suggest that the people who are gaining weight live in Arcadia County, just that they shop there. Choice (B) might introduce a new paradox (healthy people don't read labels), but it is irrelevant to why more people are now overweight. Choice (D) is similarly irrelevant: That fact that fewer people are obese does not explain why more people are overweight. Choice (E) might seem appealing, but the fact that local fruits and vegetables are shipped away does not mean shoppers in Arcadia are not eating fruits and vegetables, and the passage states that shoppers in

Arcadia are eating more foods high in fiber. Thus, this answer choice does not explain the weight gain.

2. **D** This argument contains one of GRE's favorite flaw patterns. The author notices a correlation (more exercise and lower average heart attack rates) and assumes causation (exercise causes reduced heart attack rates). Anytime you see a causal flaw, the correct answer will involve the possibility of another explanation for the effect (here, for lower heat attack rates). Choice (D) does this: It could be that having fewer smokers explains why there are fewer heart attacks. If you picked choice (A), you may have done so because you thought it undermines the premise that there are fewer heart attacks in cities with high exercise rates. However, a correct answer may not undermine a premise, just an assumption. Moreover, the fact that heart attacks are a common cause of death in cities with high exercise rates is not inconsistent with the premise that those cities nevertheless have lower average heart attack rates than do other cities. Choice (B) is irrelevant without knowing how or why standards of living might be relevant to heart attacks, and Choice (C) is irrelevant because a single atypical individual does not seriously undermine a general conclusion. Choice (E) may explain why some cities have lower exercise rates, but that does not weaken the causal link between more exercise and fewer heart attacks.

3. **E** The scientists' hypothesis effectively suggests that aluminum causes Alzheimer's disease by showing a correlation between the presence of aluminum in brain tissue and the presence of the disease. Correlation, however, does not equal causation, so to strengthen the argument the scientists would need to show evidence that the aluminum has actually *caused* the brain lesions. Choice (A) is about *low concentrations of aluminum*, whereas the study concerns high concentrations, so that choice is out of scope. Choices (B) and (D) suggest other possible explanations for the high concentrations of aluminum in the brains of the Alzheimer's patients, so they would actually weaken the hypothesis. Choice (C) does not directly address aluminum at all, and so cannot form a causal link between aluminum and Alzheimer's disease. Only choice (E) illustrates a situation in which patients' brains are negatively affected by aluminum, suggesting that aluminum can in fact cause brain disease and providing strong support for the possibility that aluminum could cause the particular brain disease that the scientists were studying.

4. **B** The author begins by presenting and explaining an idea with which he does not agree: *Market regulation is antithetical to the ideal functioning of a democratic society*. The word *Yet* indicates the author's disagreement on the basis of a factor that the economists did not consider. The main conclusion then should be something like *market regulation is not antithetical to the ideal functioning of a democratic society*. Choice (E) is the conclusion that the argument is structured to refute, not the conclusion of the argument itself. Choice (C) is an extreme restatement of the economists' position, and is not consistent with the main conclusion. Choice (A) takes part of the premise out of context to form an idea that is not expressed by the author or by the economists. Choices (B) and (D) both look similar to the author's main conclusion stated above. The difference between these two answer choices is in tone. Choice (D) draws a conclusion stronger than is warranted by the argument. Choice (E) is not as extreme, and thus is a closer match to the argument's conclusion.

4

Sentence Equivalence

THE GOAL: FILL IN THE BLANK

Sentence Equivalence questions are very similar to Text Completion questions, and we will approach them similarly to how we did one-blank Text Completion questions. Sentence Equivalence questions will give you a sentence with one blank, and you need to find the two words which fill in the blank. Inserting either word into the blank will result in equivalent sentences. For example:

> Although he had inherited a large fortune, his _____ spending quickly drained his family's coffers, leaving him in poverty.
>
> ☐ timorous
> ☒ extravagant
> ☐ pernicious
> ☐ provident
> ☐ frugal
> ☐ profligate

The steps for solving a Sentence Equivalence question are:

1. Write down A B C D E F vertically on your scratch paper.

2. Read the sentence. For now, do not read the answers.

3. Locate clues and triggers in the sentence. Use these to figure out your own word or phrase to fill in the blank. Write down this word or phrase on your scratch paper.

4. Compare each answer choice to your word or phrase. If they kind of match, put a check mark next to that answer choice on your scratch paper. If they don't, cross off that answer. If you don't know a word, put a question mark next to it and leave it.

VOCABULARY

Sentence Equivalence questions are basically a way to test your vocabulary. Because of this, make sure you're studying GRE vocabulary words every day. As you do POE, remember that you can't eliminate any answer you don't know. If you come across an unknown (or barely remembered) vocabulary word, put a question mark next to that answer on your scratch paper.

Once again: *Never cross off words you don't know.*

CLUES AND TRIGGERS

When you read a Sentence Equivalence question, look for clues and triggers. Remember that clues tell us what could go in the blank. A clue is basically "what does the sentence tell me about this?" There will always be a clue in the sentence. A trigger tells us if the blank goes in the same or opposite direction as the clue. (For more about clues and triggers, see Chapter 2: Text Completions.)

QUICK QUIZ #1

In the following sentences, find any clues or triggers. Then, use the clues and triggers to help you determine what word should go in the blank. Remember the clue is typically the most descriptive part of the sentence. Also, don't forget you can often repeat a part of the clue as the word that goes in the blank. The answers are on page 135.

1. The house had been abandoned in the 1920s, and years of disuse and _____ had left it in severe disrepair.

2. Rather than shift the company's focus immediately, a series of initiatives were implemented to apply the new directive _____.

3. Contemporary critics _____ Keaton's *The General*, although later audiences and critics would eventually hail it as a masterpiece.

4. Smith's friends, dismayed at his avarice, soon abandoned him to his _____ and self-centered pursuit of profit.

5. They were nearly polar opposites: he sociable, she insular, he garrulous, she _____.

6. In contrast to Newton's formulation of light as a series of discrete particles, Goethe viewed light as a _____ unit.

TIME FOR POE

Once you've filled in your own word or phrase in the blank, it's time to find some answers. As always, using your scratch paper is important. Match each answer choice to your word or phrase. If the two kind of match up, put a check mark. If they don't, cross off that answer.

Let's look at some scratch paper possibilities, and talk about what to do for each one. Say that your scratch paper looked like this:

14.	A ✓	15.	A̶	16.	A̶	17.	A ✓
	B̶		B ✓		B̶		B̶
	C ?		C ✓		C ?		C ?
	D ?		D̶		D̶		D ?
	E ✓		E̶		E ?		E̶
	F̶		F ✓		F̶		F ?

Look at the work you did on question 14. Although you didn't know what the words from (C) or (D) meant, they don't matter. Why? You've got two words that you know work. In that case, pick (A) and (E) and move on.

How about question 15? Now we've got 3 checks, which is a problem because we should only have 2 words. No problem. If that happens, it just means your word or phrase was a little too vague. See if you can change your word or phrase to match the clue more closely, and try each remaining answer choice again.

Question 16 is the type of question that freaks most people out, but it shouldn't. Whatever question 16 was, you knew you could cross off (A), (B), (D), and (F). Sure, (C) and (E) were apparently tough vocab words you didn't know, but who cares? They're the only words left, which means that they must be the answers. Choose (C) and (E) and move on.

ONE FOOT IN THE DOOR

Look at the scratch paper for question 17, above. One of the answers is definitely (A), but it looks like you've got three words you didn't know: (C), (D), and (F). What should you do now?

If you don't know any of those three words at all, then guess one of them and move on. Hey, it's not great, but you've got a much better shot at getting that question right than most people do. Flee, and the time you saved by not staring blankly at those hard vocab words can be used on Reading Comprehension questions.

On the other hand, if you sort of recognize the question marked words, then you've got a couple options.

- **Positive/Negative**

  Is your original word a positive or negative word? Put a + or – next to your word and the answer you picked. Look at the words you didn't know. Are they positive are negative words? If your original word was positive, cross off any negative words. If your original word was negative, then cross off any positive words.

- **Word Association**

 Look at the words you didn't know. Do you remember where you've heard any them? Can you think of a phrase that uses them? If so, then ask yourself if that same association applies to the word you did know (or your original word or phrase). If not, then cross off that answer. But if it sort of fits, then pick it and click Next.

SPEECHLESS?

Finally, let's look at the worst case scenario: You have no idea what word goes in the blank. You've read the sentence several times, but you can't find the clue or any triggers. If that happens, then the first thing you should do is click Mark so you can return to that question later, and then click Next. Once you've worked on the other questions in that section, you can come back and possibly see something you missed the first time.

If, when you return to that question you still can't think of a word to go in the blank, then it's time to match up some answers.

Let's say we couldn't figure out what the question was asking for, but the answers were:

☐ manifest
☐ arduous
☐ graceful
☐ elegant
☐ grueling
☐ eloquent

Look through the answers. Are there any words that match up? They don't have to be synonyms, they just have to mean, very roughly, the same thing. Choice (C), *graceful*, matches with choice (D) *elegant*. Draw a line connecting those two answers. Now to check to see if there are more matches (there are often 2 pairs of matching words). Choice (B), *arduous*, matches with choice (E), *grueling*. Draw a line connecting those two. The only words we have left are choice (A), *manifest*, and choice (F), *eloquent*, which do not even come close to meaning the same thing. Cross off choices (A) and (F). Now we've got two choices: Either pick choice (C) and choice (D) or pick choice (B) and choice (E). Choose one of those pairs of words and move on to the next question.

In Summary

Sentence Equivalence questions are, like Text Completion questions, basically a way to test your vocabulary. Use your scratch paper, and keep studying those Hit Parade words!

1. **Write down A B C D E F** vertically on your scratch paper.

2. **Read the sentence**. For now, do not read the answers.

3. Locate clues and triggers in the sentence. Use these to **figure out your own word or phrase to fill in the blank**. Write down this word or phrase on your scratch paper.

   If you can't come up with your own word or phrase for the sentence, then try to match answer choices up. If you can only find one match, choose those two words. If you can find two sets of matching words, choose one of those pairs.

4. **Compare each answer choice to your word or phrase**. If they kind of match, put a check mark next to that answer choice on your scratch paper. If they don't, cross off that answer. If you don't know a word, put a question mark next to it and leave it.

   If you're left with one check and multiple question marks, use Positive/Negative or Word Association to figure out which question marked answer you should pick.

PRACTICE QUESTIONS #1

<u>Directions</u>: For each sentence, select the <u>two</u> answer choices that when used to complete the sentence blank, fit the meaning of the sentence as a whole <u>and</u> produce completed sentences that are alike in meaning. Remember to use your scratch paper and POE. The answers are on page 135.

1. After successfully conning the investors out of millions of dollars, the crook _____ with the money in the middle of the night and managed to avoid arrest.

   - [ ] indicted
   - [x] absconded 潜逃
   - [ ] squandered
   - [ ] converged
   - [x] divested
   - [ ] decamped 逃走

2. Because there is now such a _____ of vampire novels on the market, the excitement they once evoked has been deadened by their sheer number.

   - [ ] lack of
   - [ ] dogma
   - [x] glut
   - [x] inundation
   - [ ] dearth
   - [ ] deviance

3. Although the accusations against the politician were _____, they were believed by enough voters to seriously damage his bid for office.

   - [ ] credible
   - [x] specious 似是而非的
   - [x] ephemeral 轻易的
   - [ ] presumptuous
   - [x] spurious
   - [x] transient 短暂的

4. Even though the curator actually spent several months arranging the exhibit, the paintings seemed as if they had been hung with _____.

   - [ ] guile
   - [x] haste
   - [x] deliberateness
   - [ ] creativity
   - [x] celerity
   - [ ] slowness

5. The critical analysis of the works of Shakespeare is not, as yet, _____; the sheer volume and complexity of his writings ensure that there will always be more to analyze.

   - [ ] abstruse
   - [ ] pedantic
   - [x] comprehensive
   - [x] elaborate
   - [ ] learned
   - [x] exhaustive 详尽·彻底

6. Both Darius and Xerxes continued the Persian tradition of showing leniency to beaten foes who showed themselves to be _____, while punishing ruthlessly those who chose to remain defiant.

   - [ ] bellicose
   - [x] complaisant
   - [x] obeisant
   - [ ] prolix
   - [ ] turbulent
   - [ ] venerated

7. Most historians credit the influence of
   Clovis's deeply religious wife, Clotild, for
   his decision to _____ paganism in favor
   of Christianity.

   ☐ desiccate
   ☒ abjure
   ☒ exacerbate
   ☒ legitimize
   ☒ espouse
   ☒ renounce

   B F

PRACTICE QUESTIONS #2

Directions: For each sentence, select the two answer choices that when used to complete the sentence blank, fit the meaning of the sentence as a whole and produce completed sentences that are alike in meaning. Remember to use your scratch paper and POE. The answers are on page 137.

1. Widely disseminated since its publication during the reign of Caesar Augustus, Virgil's *Aeneid* has served as the _____ of perfect Latin expression for hundreds of generations of students.

   - ☒ paragon
   - ☒ epithet
   - ☐ anomaly
   - ☐ epitome
   - ☐ nadir
   - ☐ epitaph

2. The analyst's report indicated that Gaines Corp. had significantly underreported its capital depreciation; rather than remaining steady, the company's value had actually _____.

   - ☐ grown
   - ☒ declined
   - ☐ underestimated
   - ☒ diminished
   - ☐ augmented
   - ☐ amortized

3. Elements of the author's work are undeniably autobiographical; however, the piece as a whole has been _____ to such an extent that it cannot properly be called a historical record.

   - ☐ narrated
   - ☐ inscribed
   - ☐ documented
   - ☒ fabricated
   - ☐ contrived
   - ☐ catalogued

4. The obligation to perform charitable acts is a central _____ of many world religions.

   - ☐ tenet
   - ☐ paradigm
   - ☐ model
   - ☐ idyll
   - ☐ precept
   - ☐ sanctity

5. Words rely on their contexts as well as their texts to create meaning, but this does not mean that language is inherently incapable of possessing _____ definitions; after all, many words have only one meaning that can be reasonably inferred regardless of the situation in which they are uttered.

   - ☒ concrete
   - ☐ hermetic
   - ☒ definitive
   - ☐ heterogeneous
   - ☐ iconoclastic
   - ☐ diverse

6. Charitable appeals often feature a single individual, whether animal or human, because people tend to react more _____ to individuals than to groups.

   - ☐ magnanimously
   - ☐ quietly
   - ☐ discreetly
   - ☐ perniciously
   - ☐ nefariously
   - ☐ benevolently

7. Dean always seemed to go along with the group and changed his opinion to complement those around him, and this _____ nature often irritated his friends.

- ☐ vociferous
- ☒ indelible
- ☒ malleable
- ☐ tractable
- ☐ strident
- ☐ immutable

PRACTICE QUESTIONS #3

<u>Directions</u>: For each sentence, select the <u>two</u> answer choices that when used to complete the sentence blank, fit the meaning of the sentence as a whole <u>and</u> produce completed sentences that are alike in meaning. Remember to use your scratch paper and POE. The answers are on page 139.

1. The members of the team were already upset that they were losing, but their anger escalated when the _____ members of the opposing team boasted about their considerable lead in points.

   ☐ fortunate
   ☐ vigorous
   ☐ haughty
   ☐ incensed
   ☐ humble
   ☐ arrogant

2. The president of the company was shocked when he arrived at the quiet boardroom the day after the stock market crash; rather than exhibiting outrage, the members of the board were completely

   _____.

   ☐ impassive
   ☐ histrionic
   ☐ stoic
   ☐ impassioned
   ☐ empathetic
   ☐ fetid

3. The law student was bent on augmenting his transcript with challenging classes; as a result he was completely vexed by the involute, _____ tax law textbooks.

   ☐ transparent ✗
   ☐ luculent
   ☐ convocational
   ☐ labyrinthine
   ☒ byzantine
   ☐ perspicuous

4. In the new age of the internet, blogs and chat rooms have become forums for some normally _____ people to say what they might not otherwise have the intrepidity to utter out in the real world.

   ☐ pusillanimous
   ☐ mettlesome
   ☐ ingenious
   ☐ plucky
   ☐ recreant
   ☐ impudent

5. While her neighbors found her new lawn decorations absurdly _____, Josie thought they were tasteful, even sophisticated.

   ☐ cosmopolitan
   ☐ unkempt
   ☐ meretricious
   ☐ tawdry
   ☐ viridian
   ☐ svelte

6. The newly appointed chief financial officer had saved millions for the company in the last year; unfortunately, his _____ attitude was making the employees miserable, as they were forced to give up some of the luxuries afforded to them in previous years.

   ☐ magnanimous
   ☐ penurious
   ☐ prodigal
   ☐ parsimonious
   ☐ dispassionate
   ☐ hedonistic

7. When the town's water supply ran low during the summer drought, the residents received a notice that _____ them to take heed of the dearth of water and avoid any water-related activities that weren't necessary.

- ☐ lambasted
- ☐ beseeched
- ☐ wheedled
- ☑ inundated
- ☐ castigated
- ☑ importuned

PRACTICE QUESTIONS #4

Directions: For each sentence, select the two answer choices that when used to complete the sentence blank, fit the meaning of the sentence as a whole and produce completed sentences that are alike in meaning. Remember to use your scratch paper and POE. The answers are on page 141.

1. Although the President had been accused of reducing defense spending, the new report revealed that during his administration military _____ had actually increased.

   ☐ adventurism
   ☐ outlays
   ☐ successes
   ☐ gaffes
   ☐ expenditures
   ☐ efficiencies

2. The government assistance program provided both subsidized and free meals to children from _____ families.

   ☐ imperious
   ☐ imperturbable
   ☐ impecunious
   ☐ impious
   ☐ impennate
   ☐ impoverished

3. The _____ of available housing units meant that supply surpassed demand and drove down the price that renters were willing to pay.

   ☐ dearth
   ☐ glut
   ☐ paucity
   ☐ decrepitude
   ☐ excess
   ☐ temerity

4. Supported as it was by legislators from across the ideological spectrum, the recently enacted parks bill was rightly labeled a successful _____ of bipartisanship.

   ☐ rostrum
   ☐ exemplar
   ☐ antithesis
   ☐ illustration
   ☐ forum
   ☐ tenet

5. Many Britons were surprised by the results of the ethnographic survey, which revealed that nearly five percent of the population of England and Wales were of South Asian _____.

   ☐ extraction
   ☐ pretense
   ☐ arbitration
   ☐ affectation
   ☐ descent
   ☐ antecedence

6. While the film critic was _____ in her conviction that sequels are generally inferior to their predecessors, she did acknowledge occasional exceptions such as *The Godfather Part II*, a film she considered superior to the original.

   ☐ wavering
   ☐ vacillating
   ☐ adamant
   ☐ perturbed
   ☐ disconsolate
   ☐ resolute

7. After decades of stability, the past 15 years have borne witness to a remarkably _____ period for airlines, during which virtually every airline has been part of a merger, filed for bankruptcy, or both.

- ☐ fallow
- ☐ avionic
- ☐ erratic
- ☐ malignant
- ☐ volatile
- ☐ desolate

PRACTICE QUESTIONS #5

Directions: For each sentence, select the <u>two</u> answer choices that when used to complete the sentence blank, fit the meaning of the sentence as a whole <u>and</u> produce completed sentences that are alike in meaning. Remember to use your scratch paper and POE. The answers are on page 142.

1. Despite its _____ as a plot device in films and television programs, multiple-personality disorder is in reality remarkably rare.

   - ☐ simplicity
   - ☐ coincidence
   - ☐ pervasiveness
   - ☐ correlation
   - ☐ ubiquity
   - ☐ facility

2. Psychologists define "confirmation bias" as a fallacy whereby facts that _____ one's previously held beliefs are emphasized and those that diverge are downplayed.

   - ☐ calibrate
   - ☐ corroborate
   - ☐ facilitate
   - ☐ extrapolate
   - ☐ qualify
   - ☐ substantiate

3. While the ascent of online classified advertising has coincided with the _____ of newspapers, the journalist was reluctant to attribute the diminution of the latter to the former.

   - ☐ appropriation
   - ☐ concatenation
   - ☐ wane
   - ☐ consolidation
   - ☐ aggregation
   - ☐ dwindling

4. Aspirant writers may take _____ in the example of Frank Herbert, whose magnum opus *Dune* was, at the outset, rebuffed by every publishing house in the country.

   - ☐ consolation
   - ☐ insinuation
   - ☐ succor
   - ☐ allusion
   - ☐ solstice
   - ☐ instruction

5. In an era in which mass media is but a thrall of its corporate masters, the amateurish _____ of commercials for local businesses provide a tonic for the slick homogeneity of most advertising.

   - ☐ amalgamations
   - ☐ eccentricities
   - ☐ synergies
   - ☐ conglomerations
   - ☐ syllogisms
   - ☐ idiosyncrasies

6. Though the futurist conceded that Apple's iPhone was a revolutionary device, she was adamant that it would not be immune to the same forces that caused such previous "game changing" products as Ford's Model T and Sony's Walkman to be considered _____.

   - ☐ avant-garde
   - ☐ electronic
   - ☐ circuitous
   - ☐ antediluvian
   - ☐ superannuated
   - ☐ radical

7. Unlike Lacey, who is nearly emaciated due to her eating habits, Marty's other cat, Marco, has _____ appetite.

- [ ] an edacious
- [ ] a meager
- [ ] a spurious
- [ ] a scanty
- [ ] a sporadic
- [ ] a voracious

PRACTICE QUESTIONS #6

Directions: For each sentence, select the two answer choices that when used to complete the sentence blank, fit the meaning of the sentence as a whole and produce completed sentences that are alike in meaning. Remember to use your scratch paper and POE. The answers are on page 144.

1. The economics professor had a plan to discourage her _____ students who thought blandishments would get them higher grades: any wheedling student would have to complete an additional 15-page research paper by the end of the semester.

   ☐ lumbering
   ☐ viable
   ☐ fawning
   ☐ candid
   ☐ obsequious
   ☐ ingenuous

2. Most singers of a style of Portuguese music called "fado" sound and appear appropriately _____ as they sing lyrics about lost love and regret.

   ☐ fatuous
   ☐ morose
   ☐ buoyant
   ☐ melancholy
   ☐ nonplused
   ☐ discordant

3. The horse trainer thought her newest client had a penchant for picking ironic names for their _____ horses; one example was Tractable, a horse that did not live up to his name.

   ☐ auspicious
   ☐ compliant
   ☐ obdurate
   ☐ serendipitous
   ☐ tranquil
   ☐ recalcitrant

4. The guileless politician's responses at the debate disconcerted some of her potential voters, and she was worried that her opponent's _____ statements would encompass a wider range of voters' interests.

   ☐ affable
   ☐ ambiguous
   ☐ conspicuous
   ☐ benevolent
   ☐ equivocal
   ☐ candid

5. When Becca brought home the irascible puppy, her more quiescent dogs were rattled by their new _____ housemate.

   ☐ pugnacious
   ☐ languid
   ☐ bellicose
   ☐ juvenile
   ☐ diminutive
   ☐ phlegmatic

6. When Howard began his career as a professional mediator, he had no idea that some of his clients would be so _____; he thought that having a job that requires one to deal with disputing parties would entail placating their enmity.

   ☐ acquiescent
   ☐ indignant
   ☐ churlish
   ☐ disparate
   ☐ amenable
   ☐ distinct

7. The newspaper's humor columnist, while talented, puts off writing her columns until the last minute; as a result, she submits pieces that are so _____ that her editor emails her after almost every deadline to remind her of the minimum line requirement.

- ☐ fallacious
- ☐ terse
- ☐ jocular
- ☐ waggish
- ☐ laconic
- ☐ erroneous

PRACTICE QUESTIONS #7

Directions: For each sentence, select the two answer choices that when used to complete the sentence blank, fit the meaning of the sentence as a whole and produce completed sentences that are alike in meaning. Remember to use your scratch paper and POE. The answers are on page 146.

1. In the summer of 1911, merchant Nathan Steinberg beamed with pride as he placed his order for 3,000 pairs of high-button shoes; little did he know that they would be _____ come that fall!

   ☐ outmoded
   ☐ passé
   ☐ chic
   ☐ inapplicable
   ☐ repulsive
   ☐ disagreeable

2. The port city of Galveston, Texas, was once a great _____ of economic activity, but though great effort went into its reconstruction after the floods of 1900, it never returned to its former prosperity.

   ☐ bounty
   ☐ maritime
   ☐ abundance
   ☐ hub
   ☐ chronicle
   ☐ center

3. Anthony's general sense of restlessness and rash approach to life have compelled him to rush headlong into decisions that less _____ men would think twice about.

   ☐ lethargic
   ☐ audacious
   ☐ torpid
   ☐ exotic
   ☐ aggrandized
   ☐ intrepid

4. The misapprehension that lemmings commit mass suicide by jumping off cliffs has been fostered by legends, films, and television commercials; one reason people believe the myth may be that lemmings are _____ to Scandinavia, a region with an unusually high suicide rate.

   ☐ inherent
   ☐ organic
   ☐ endemic
   ☐ prodigious
   ☐ indigenous
   ☐ titanic

5. An exceptionally sophisticated predator, the platypus uses the electroreceptors on its bill to locate _____, resulting in a remarkably efficient and effective hunting practice.

   ☐ iniquity
   ☐ provender
   ☐ quintessence
   ☐ pith
   ☐ victuals
   ☐ lassitude

6. Though Salsa takes its roots from various countries in Central and South America, it is fundamentally and essentially Cuban: its development was a _____, but ultimately the music belongs to one country.

   ☐ collaboration
   ☐ mélange
   ☐ feat
   ☐ coup
   ☐ lyric
   ☐ denouement

7. The praise the students received for their flashy presentation and detailed handouts was utterly unwarranted, for their apparent diligence was motivated merely by _____.

- ☐ prepossession
- ☐ cronyism
- ☐ assiduity
- ☐ sycophancy
- ☐ torpidity
- ☐ obsequiousness

ANSWERS AND EXPLANATIONS

QUICK QUIZ #1

1. *neglect*
2. *gradually*
3. *savaged* or *harshly criticized*
4. *greedy*
5. *taciturn*
6. *continuous*

PRACTICE QUESTIONS #1

1.   **B** and **F**

Because the clues in the sentence tell you the crook *successfully conned the investors* and *managed to avoid arrest*, the blank should mean something like *escaped* or *bolted*. Choice (A) could be appealing at first because it deals with criminals, but it has nothing to do with escaping. Choices (C) and (E) both have to do with getting rid of money, so they might also be attractive, but neither of them has anything to do with escaping, either. *Converged* means coming together, so that can be eliminated. Choices (B) and (F) both mean to leave secretly or to sneak out, so those are the best answer choices.

2.   **C** and **D**

The clue in this sentence is *sheer number*. Possible words for the blank might be *abundance* or *flood*. This makes choices (C) and (D) both solid fits for the blank. Choices (A) and (E) are also synonyms, but they have the opposite meaning of what you're looking for in this sentence. Choice (F) is connected to the idea of vampires and deadening, but has nothing to do with *sheer number*. Choice (B) can be eliminated because it doesn't have anything to do with the sentence.

3.   **B** and **E**

The sentence says that the accusations were *believed by enough voters* and did *serious damage to his bid to office*. The *although* trigger lets you know that the blank should contrast with the clues, so the blank should mean something like *false* or *untrue*. Choices (B) and (E) both mean *false*, so those are the best words for the blank. Choice (A) means *believable*, so that could be attractive if you didn't pay attention to the trigger. Choices (C) and (F) both mean short-lived, which could contrast appropriately with the *serious damage to his bid for office* clue. Because the sentence specifically tells you the voters *believed* the accusations, though, those answers can be eliminated. Choice (D) can be eliminated because it doesn't have anything to do with the clue.

4.   **B** and **E**

Even though is a trigger that changes direction, therefore the paintings would have been hung in a way opposite of what the sentence tells you. Since the curator *spent several months*, the paintings would seem as if they were hung in a very short amount of time. Check the answer choices. *Haste* and *celerity* both indicate swiftness of motion, and so choices (B) and (E) work best. *Deliberateness* and *slowness* is a synonym pair, but the trigger *even though* makes the meanings of these words opposite of the meaning of the blank. Neither *creativity* nor *guile* (which means skillful deceit) matches the meaning.

5.   **C** and **F**

Because *there will always be more to analyze*, the critical analysis could not be complete and therefore you are looking for words that mean complete. *Comprehensive* and *exhaustive* both describe a complete analysis. Synonyms *pedantic* and *learned* both refer to scholarly endeavors, but don't fit the meaning of the blank. *Abstruse* describes something that is difficult to understand and *elaborate* describes something intricate or involved. Although both words could describe the analysis of Shakespeare, neither fits the story of the sentence and the meaning of the blank.

6.   **B** and **C**

The trigger *while* indicates that leniency was shown to those who did the opposite of *remain defiant*, so the blank must mean something like *submissive*. Both *bellicose* and *turbulent* are nearly the opposite of what you're looking for, so eliminate answer choices (A) and (E). Neither *prolix*, which means verbose, or *venerated*, which means esteemed, mean submissive, so eliminate choices (D) and (F). Both *complaisant* and *obeisant* mean submissive, so answer choices (B) and (C) give you appropriate, equivalent sentences.

7.   **B and F**

The clue tells you that whatever Clovis did to paganism, he did it *in favor of Christianity*, so something like *give up* would make sense in the blank. Both *legitimize* and *espouse* are nearly the opposite of what you're looking for, so eliminate choices (D) and (E). Neither *desiccate*, which means to dry out, or *exacerbate*, which means to make worse, mean give up, so eliminate choices (A) and (C). Both *abjure* and *renounce* mean give up, so choices (B) and (F) give you appropriate, equivalent sentences.

PRACTICE QUESTIONS #2

1.   **A and D**

The clue tells you that the *Aeneid* has been *widely disseminated since its publication*, so a word like *model* or *example* would fit the blank. Both *anomaly* and *nadir* are nearly the opposite of what you're looking for, so eliminate choices (C) and (E). Choices (B) and (F) are commonly confused words, but neither works here: An *epithet* can be a descriptive word or phrase or an expression of contempt, and an *epitaph* is an inscription on a grave marker. Both *paragon* and *epitome* mean perfect example, so choices (A) and (D) give you appropriate, equivalent sentences.

2.   **B and D**

If the company *underreported its capital depreciation*, then its actual value was lower than reported; instead of remaining steady, its value must have *gotten smaller*. Both *grown* and *augmented* are nearly the opposite of what you're looking for, so eliminate answer choices (A) and (E). Neither *underestimated* nor *amortized*, which means paid off in installments, make sense in the blank, so eliminate choices (C) and (F). Answer choices (B) and (D) give you appropriate, equivalent sentences.

3.   **D and E**

You know that parts of the work are *autobiographical*, but the trigger *however* indicates that the second part of the sentence goes in a different direction; combined with the fact that the work *cannot properly be called a historical record*, you know that it must have been *fictionalized*. Answer choices (D) and (E) are the only ones that fit the context. Choices (C) and (F) are synonyms, and might be attractive because they are words that can be associated with *historical records*, but they don't contrast with *autobiographical*.

4.   **A and E**

The word in the blank must mean something like *idea*. While *idyll* sounds like *idea*, the meaning is completely different (an *idyll* is a lighthearted artistic work). *Sanctity* is the quality of being sacred, which is related to religion, but not what we're looking for. Choices (B) and (C) are synonyms, but neither of them mean *idea*. Choices (A) and (E) both mean *idea*, and are often used in religious contexts, so they fit best in this sentence.

5.   **A and C**

The word that fits the blank must describe a type of definition. To determine what type, look for clues and triggers. If words *rely on their contexts*, that must mean that their definitions sometimes change. The trigger *but* suggests a change in direction; however, the trigger *does not mean* counteracts the *but*, so we're looking for a description of a definition that does not change. Choices (D) and (F) would suggest things that do change. *Hermetic* means *sealed*, and *iconoclastic* means *unusual*, so those words have nothing to do with changing or not changing. Choices (A) and (C) both describe things that do not change.

6.   **A and F**

The blank describes the goal of *charitable appeals*, so *charitably* or *generously* would make sense. Both *perniciously* and *nefariously* are nearly the opposite of what you're looking for, so eliminate choices (D) and (E). Choices (B) and (C) give roughly synonymous meanings, but there's no clear connection between discretion and generosity. Both *magnanimously* and *benevolently* can mean charitably, so choices (A) and (F) give you appropriate, equivalent sentences.

7.   **C and D**

The clue *goes along with the group and changed his opinion to complement those around him* signals he is *flexible* to a fault and it *irritates* his friends. The best answers are choices (C) and (D), which most closely mean *flexible and easily lead* and produce equivalent, appropriate sentences. Incorrect choices (A) and (D) both could mean *loudly crying out*, and incorrect choices (B) and (F) are synonyms that go in the opposite direction of the missing word.

Practice Questions #3

1. **C and F**

   The clue in this sentence is *boasted*, which implies that the opposing team was conceited, which would have been a good guess for the blank. *Haughty* and *arrogant* both mean the same thing. Choice (E) is the opposite definition you were looking for. Choices (A) and (B) are traps if you didn't catch the clue—you might think that because they were winning, the other players were *fortunate* or *vigorous* (strong), but that's not the definition you should have been looking for. Choice (D) describes how the losing players are feeling.

2. **A and C**

   The trigger in this sentence is *rather than*, and the clues are *quiet boardroom* and *exhibiting outrage*. You should fill in your own word based on the meaning you need, such as apathetic. Choices (A) and (D) look quite similar, which means they're either both wrong, or they're opposites. The latter is the case here. *Impassive* means without emotion and *impassioned* means excited. Choice (A) looks good, so you should find an answer that means the same thing. *Stoic* fits the bill. The rest of the answer choices, with the exception of (F), are traps. *Fetid* means stinky, *histrionic* means overly emotional, and *empathetic* contains the root *path*, but doesn't have the meaning you're looking for.

3. **D and E**

   There are three main clues in this sentence: *challenging, vexed*, which means confused, and *involute,* which means complicated. Recycle the clue *involute* for the blank. The first two answers, choices (A) and (B), as well as (F), are direct opposites of what you want. *Convocational* might have looked good if you had been thinking of "convoluted.", but it is incorrect. You might have studied *byzantine*, which can mean intricate and complex, and *labyrinthine*, which has a similar meaning. (D) and (E) are the correct answers.

4. **A and E**

The clue here, *intrepidity*, coupled with the trigger, *might not otherwise*, lets you know that you want a word that means the opposite of *intrepid*. Eliminate choices (B) and (D), as these are synonyms of *intrepid*. *Impudent*, choice (F), doesn't necessarily mean brave, but it's still on the wrong side of the fence for this blank: It means bold and disrespectful. Also eliminate choice (C), as *ingenious* (intelligent), has nothing to do with this question—though you personally might think internet trolls are unintelligent.

5. **C and D**

The clue here, *tasteful, even sophisticated*, and the trigger, *while*, let you know that you want a word that means the opposite of *tasteful*. Choices (A) and (F) are antonyms. Choices (B) and (E) are both trap answers: *[U]nkempt* may describe a neglected front lawn, and *viridian* means green. Answer choices (C) and (D) give you acceptable equivalent answers.

6. **B and D**

The fact that the employees had to *give up some of the luxuries* lets you know that they're dealing with someone stingy; the trigger *unfortunately* also points you in that direction. Answer choices (A) and (C) are opposites of *stingy*. *Hedonistic* describes someone who loves luxury, which is also in the wrong direction. *Dispassionate* describes someone unaffected by emotion, which might describe this CFO, but not necessarily. Choices (B) and (D) appropriately describe his attitude.

7. **B and F**

There aren't clear clues to this sentence, but it's not hard to fill in your own word for the blank: You want something like "asked." *Beseeched* and *importuned* mean just that—but in a stronger sense, which is probably warranted when there's a water shortage. Answer choices (A) and (E) are too negative, and choices (C) and (D) are trap answers. You might have been thinking about watering your lawn when you read this sentence, as that's usually the first water-related activity to go during a shortage. *Wheedled* doesn't have anything to do with weeds, it just sounds like it does, and *inundated* means filled quickly with water.

Practice Questions #4

1.   **B and E**

Since the sentence begins with the Trigger *although*, you know that the first and second parts of the sentence will be different. The first part talks about *reducing defense spending*, so the second part must talk about the *spending* being *increased*. Check the answer choices. Choice (B) outlays and choice (E) expenditures both mean the same thing as *spending*. While choice (C) successes and (F) efficiencies are similar in meaning, they do not mean *spending*. Choice (A) adventurism and choice (D)gaffes are not similar in meaning. Choices (B) and (E) are correct.

2.   **C and F**

The sentence states that the purpose of the program is to provide *assistance* by offering low-cost or no-cost meals. The group most likely to need such assistance would be those from poor or low-income families. Check the answers. Impecunious and impoverished both mean poor. None of the remaining answers are similar in meaning to each other. Choices (C) and (F) are correct.

3.   **B and E**

The sentence states that *supply surpassed demand*, meaning that there were "too many" *available housing units*. Check the answer choices. Both glut and excess mean "too many." While dearth and paucity have similar meanings, they both mean "too few." Decrepitude and temerity are not similar in meaning to each other. Choices (B) and (E) are correct.

4.   **B and D**

The sentence says that the bill had support from across a "range" of political opinions. Since *bipartisanship* means cooperation from both sides, the bill would be an "example" of such cooperation. Check the answer choices. Both exemplar and illustration mean "example." Even though rostrum and forum are similar in meaning (a place for speaking), neither mean "example." Antithesis and tenet are not synonyms. Choices (B) and (D) are correct.

5.   **A and E**

The sentence discusses surprise at the results of an *ethnographic survey*, which would relate to the national or cultural background of peoples. Of the answer choices, only *extraction* and *descent* relate to ancestry. The best answers are choices (A) and (E).

6.   **C and F**

The sentence begins with the trigger *while*, indicating a change or contrast in the sentence; the second part states that the critic *acknowledged the occasional exception*, so you need a word like *firm* to describe her normal conviction. Both *wavering* and *vacillating* are nearly the opposite of what you're looking for, so eliminate choices (A) and (B). Neither *perturbed*, which means disturbed, nor *disconsolate*, which means gloomy, makes sense in the blank, so eliminate choices (D) and (E). Both *adamant* and *resolute* can mean firm, so choices (C) and (F) give you appropriate, equivalent sentences.

7.   **C and E**

The time trigger *after* indicates that something has changed; the first part of the sentence states that the past 15 years were characterized by *stability*, so you need a word like *unstable* for the blank. Both *erratic* and *volatile* can mean unstable, so choices (C) and (E) give you appropriate, equivalent sentences.

PRACTICE QUESTIONS #5

1.   **C and E**

The trigger *despite* indicates that the two parts of the sentence are different; the second part of the sentence describes *multiple-personality disorder* as *rare* in real life, so you need a word like *commonness* to go with *films and television*. Both *pervasiveness* and *ubiquity* can mean commonness, so choices (C) and (E) give you appropriate, equivalent sentences.

2.   **B and F**

The sentence includes the trigger *and*, which means that the two parts of the sentence agree; the second half of the sentence states that facts that *diverge are downplayed*, so you need something like *agree* for the blank to go with *emphasized*. Both *extrapolate* and *qualify* are nearly the opposite of what you're looking for, so eliminate choices (D) and (E). Both *corroborate* and *substantiate* can mean agree, so choices (B) and (F) give you appropriate, equivalent sentences.

3.   **C and F**

The sentence contains the trigger word *While*, which signals that the second part of the sentence is different from the first. The second part states that the journalist was *reluctant* to conclude that *ascent* of the *former*, *online advertising*, caused the *diminution* of the *latter*, *newspapers*. Thus, the first part must convey that there is some relationship between the *ascent* and the *diminution*, so a good word for the blank is "descent." Only *wane* and *dwindling* mean "descent." Choices (C) and (F) are the best answers.

4.   **A and C**

The sentence states that a novel now considered a *magnum opus* was at first *rebuffed*, or rejected. Aspirant, "hopeful" or "beginning," writers would take "comfort" in such an example, as it would encourage them. Check the answers for words similar in meaning to "comfort." Both *consolation* and *succor* mean "comfort." The best answers are choices (A) and (C).

5.   **B and F**

The sentence says that *local* commercials are a *tonic* or "cure" for *homogeneity* or "sameness," so a good word would be "quirks" or "individualities." Check the answers. Both *eccentricities* and *idiosyncrasies* mean "quirks." The best answers are choices (B) and (F).

6.   **D and E**

The sentence contains the trigger word *Though*, indicating a shift in the meaning of the sentence. In the first part, the futurist *conceded* that the iPhone was *revolutionary*, thus the second part must mean that it was "old-fashioned." Check the answers. Only *antediluvian* and *superannuated* mean "old-fashioned." Choices (D) and (E) are the best answers.

7.   **A and F**

The trigger, *unlike*, lets you know you want a word that is the opposite of *emaciated*. *Emaciated* is used to describe someone who has become thin or feeble, so Marco must have a *large* or *healthy* appetite. *Edacious* and *voracious* both mean devouring, so answer choices (A) and (F) are your best options. *Meager*, *scanty*, and *sporadic* are on the wrong side of the fence; so eliminate choices (B), (D), and (F); *spurious* means fake, so eliminate choice (C).

PRACTICE QUESTIONS #6

1. **C and E**

    There are two clues in this sentence to describe the students: *blandishments* and *wheedling*. Both describe people who use flattery to try to persuade people. *Fawning* and *obsequious* both mean flattering, so answer choices (C) and (E) give you appropriate, equivalent sentences. Both *candid* and *ingenuous* are nearly the opposite of what you're looking for, so eliminate answer choices (D) and (F). Neither *lumbering*, which means ponderous or clumsy, nor *viable*, which means feasible or capable of living, make sense in the blank, so eliminate choices (A) and (B).

2. **B and D**

    Lyrics about lost love and regret lets you know you want a word that means something like *sad*. Both *fatuous* and *buoyant* are nearly the opposite of what you're looking for, so eliminate answer choices (A) and (C). Neither *nonplused*, which means baffled, nor *discordant*, which means dissonant, make sense in the blank, so eliminate choices (E) and (F). Both *morose* and *melancholy* can mean sad, so answer choices (B) and (D) give you appropriate, equivalent sentences.

3. **C and F**

    The clue *tractable* means obedient, and this horse was anything but, so you need a word like *disobedient*. Both *compliant* and *tranquil* are nearly the opposite of what you're looking for, so eliminate answer choices (B) and (E). Both *auspicious* and *serendipitous* are positive words, so eliminate choices (A) and (D). Both *obdurate* and *recalcitrant* can mean disobedient, so answer choices (C) and (F) give you appropriate, equivalent sentences.

4. **B and E**

    The first politician is described as *guileless*, which means she was honest and straightforward in her speech; her opponent's statements, then, must have been *dishonest* or *not straightforward*. *Ambiguous* and *equivocal* both mean not straightforward, so answer choices (B) and (E) give you appropriate, equivalent sentences. Choices (C) and (F) would better describe the first politician, not the second, and are therefore opposites of what you want. Neither *affable*, which means friendly, nor *benevolent*, which means well-wishing, mean dishonest, so eliminate choices (A) and (D).

5. **A and C**

You have two clues about the puppy: He is described as *irascible*, and the other dogs are described as *more quiescent*. This tells you that the new puppy must be *aggressive*. Answer choices (A) and (C) mean aggressive, and so give you appropriate, equivalent sentences. Choices (B) and (F) are on the other side of the fence and would better describe her other, quieter, dogs. Choices (D) and (E) are trap answers that address the fact that the new dog is a puppy—and therefore *juvenile*, which means young, and likely *diminutive*, which means small—but not his problematic behavioral issue.

6. **A and E**

The most important trigger in this sentence is a time trigger: *When Howard began* in the beginning of the sentence and *he thought* later both indicate that Howard eventually realized he was wrong. He *thought* that his clients would be argumentative, so you need a word that means something like *not argumentative*. Choices (B) and (C) are the opposite of what you want and can be eliminated. *Disparate* and *distinct* may describe two disputing parties, but don't mean not argumentative. *Acquiescent* and *amenable* mean that the clients were willing to listen to Howard and agree to his suggestions, so answer choices (A) and (E) give you appropriate, equivalent sentences.

7. **B and E**

Since the columnist *puts off writing her columns until the last minute* and needs to be reminded of the *minimum line requirement*, her columns must be too *short*. *Terse* and *laconic* both mean using few words, so answer choices (B) and (E) give you appropriate, equivalent sentences. Choices (A) and (F) both suggest things an editor would be unhappy about, and choices (C) and (D) suggest things that likely describe a humor columnist—but none are supported by the sentence.

1.   **A and B**

Steinberg placed his order with excitement, presumably because he thought that he would be able to sell many shoes, but there was some relevant detail that he did not know. This fact must be something that would happen that fall that would interfere with his ability to sell the shoes. *Chic* means *stylish*, a characteristic that would likely make the shoes easier to sell, not harder. *Inapplicable* means *cannot be applied to a particular situation*, and would not likely be used to refer to shoes. *Repulsive* and *disagreeable* are both negative qualities that would indeed make shoes difficult to sell, but these words are both stronger in meaning than is warranted by the sentence. *Outmoded* and *passé* both mean *out-of-fashion*; if the shoes fell *out-of-fashion*, they would be very difficult to sell.

2.   **D and F**

Galveston once had *prosperity*, so it must have been a place where lots of *economic activity* took place. *Bounty* and *abundance* both refer to a large amount of something (usually positive), and so could refer to great wealth, but these words would not be used to refer to a place. *Maritime* means *having to do with the sea*; while Galveston is a port city, the blank does not refer to that quality. A *chronicle* is a listing of events, which isn't what you're looking for. The word in the blank needs to mean something like *a place where activity happens*: Both *hub* and *center* fit this definition.

3.   **B and F**

Anthony has a *sense of restlessness and rash approach to life*, suggesting that he has a strong sense of adventure, so the blank must need a word describing that type of nature. *Lethargic* and *torpid* both describe people with little energy, so they would mean the opposite of what you're looking for. While Anthony probably likes *exotic* things, he himself is not obviously *rare or unusual*. *Aggrandized* means *made greater in status*, and there is no indication in the sentence that Anthony is of high status. *Audacious* and *intrepid* both mean *fearless*, which is consistent with Anthony's adventurous nature.

4.   **C and E**

According to the sentence, some people believe that lemmings commit suicide because they are in some way related to a region where people often do the same thing; a word that means something like *native* would be a good fit for the blank. Choices (C) and (E) both mean native. *Inherent* means intrinsic, and cannot be used to refer to a living animal, and *organic* means natural, not native, so eliminate choices (A) and (B). *Prodigious* and *titanic* both mean large, which would have nothing to do with the potential for suicidal tendencies, so eliminate choices (D) and (F).

5.   **B and E**

The platypus is a *sophisticated predator* that uses an *effective hunting practice* to locate something, so you need a word like *food* or *prey* for the blank. Choices (B) and (E) both mean food. *Iniquity* means evil, and *lassitude* means listlessness, so eliminate choices (A) and (F). Choices (C) and (D) can both mean important part; while the platypus presumably thinks food is important, it is not looking for just any important thing, but specifically for prey.

6.   **A and B**

Keep track of the triggers in this sentence. The *but* means that the development had a characteristic inconsistent with *belongs to one country*, so you're looking for something like *belongs to more than one country*. Choices (C) and (D) mean *achievement*, and while the development of the music was an achievement, that's not the word you need. A *lyric* is a rhythmic composition, and a *denouement* is an outcome. Neither of these words mean anything like *belongs to more than one country*. *Collaboration* and *mélange* both describe a mixture of different influences. Since salsa *takes its roots from various countries*, these words would describe its development accurately.

7.   **D and F**

If the students' diligence was only *apparent* and the praise they received was *unwarranted*, then their motivation must be negative. *Prepossession* and *cronyism* are both negative words, but they refer to a bias in someone's favor. The students desire to gain such a bias, but they don't have it themselves. *Assiduity* is a near synonym for *diligence*, so that word is the opposite of what you're looking for. *Torpidity* means *sluggishness*, and these students aren't lazy. Choices (D) and (F) both refer to a desire to win favor from an authority figure, a less-than-pure motivation.

5

Analytical Writing

WELCOME TO ANALYTICAL WRITING

So, as you are aware, one of the tasks that ETS has deemed essential for evaluating your grad school potential is writing two short essays. You won't be writing these essays on a topic in your graduate field. In fact, you won't be writing these essays on any academic topic at all. There will be no research involved, no careful consideration of evidence, no peer review, no faculty supervision. In short, it's about as far away from the type of academic writing you'll be doing in grad school as you can imagine. But don't worry. With the right knowledge and some practice, you can learn to score higher on the Analytical Writing section. It's no different from the rest of the GRE in that regard.

How Much Does Analytical Writing Matter?

We asked this question about the GRE as a whole in the Introduction chapter, and the answer here is fundamentally the same: It depends. However, it's probably safe to say that right now the Analytical Writing section will matter the least of the three sections. It doesn't distinguish between candidates as well as the multiple-choice sections do. About 60 percent of test takers score between 4 and 5.5 on the Analytical Writing section, which means most people get a 4, 4.5, 5, or 5.5.

The best way to be certain, however, is to call the schools you're interested in, and ask them directly. Some will tell you that they don't really care about the Analytical Writing section at all, and some will tell you that they want a minimum score of 5. It's important to find out what the situation is at the schools you intend to apply to, so you can determine how much time and effort to devote to this chapter.

Structure

First, let's review the basics of the Analytical Writing section. This section contains two parts. The first part lasts 30 minutes and is officially titled "Present Your Perspective on an Issue." The second part also lasts 30 minutes and is officially titled "Analyze an Argument." For ease of reference, we'll continue to refer to the two tasks as the Issue essay and the Argument essay. The Analytical Writing section will always be the first section on your test, and will never be experimental.

Scoring

Each essay will receive two scores, ranging from 0 to 6. If the scores are within one point of each other, they will be averaged. If the scores are not within one point of each other (this is rare) then an expert reader will be brought in to read and score the essay. The final scores for the two essays are then averaged and rounded to the nearest half point.

For example, your Argument essay may receive a 5 from both readers, so your average for that essay would be a 5. Your Issue essay may receive a 5 from one reader and a 4 from the other, so your average for that essay would be a 4.5. The average of 5 and 4.5 is 4.75, which rounds up to 5. Thus, you would get a 5 as your Analytical Writing score.

The essays are scored "holistically," which means the readers assign a score based on their overall impression of the essay. There's no checklist that they use to sum up the points (e.g., half a point for good grammar, one point for a good conclusion, etc.). It's okay to make minor grammatical or spelling errors as long as the essay as a whole is strong. The readers aren't going to examine your essays carefully enough or long enough to notice all the details. They have a lot of essays to grade and are probably not going to spend more than two or three minutes reading each one. Later, we'll talk about how to make your essay cater to a short attention span.

Think of the scores for Analytical Write section as 0–3: bad, 4–6: good. A score from 4–6 means that you, to a varying degree of success, answered the question asked. It was clear what your position was, and your support clearly connected to your position. A score from 0–3 means that you did not actually answer the question asked. Maybe your position wasn't clear, or your support didn't seem to connect to your position, or maybe you just wrote about something only tangentially related to the question asked.

Consequently, your goal your essay should be to make sure you answer the question. If you have a free minute at the end of your essay, it's always helpful to look over the prompt, then look over your essay. Did you do what they asked you to do? If so, you'll probably get a 4, 5, or 6.

WHAT YOU'LL SEE ON THE SCREEN

Don't expect to get a fancy word processor on the Analytical Writing section. In fact, what you get barely deserves the name "word processor." There's no spell check, no grammar check, no italics, no underlining—basically no formatting features at all. Here's what your screen will look like:

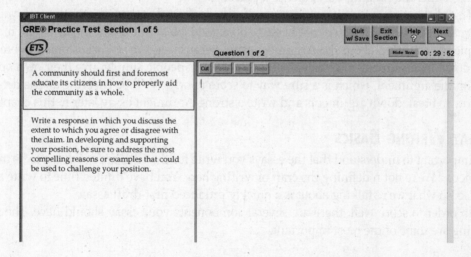

As you can see, it's not much. The essay prompt will stay in front of you the whole time at the left side of your screen. You type your essay into the field at the right. You'll have to scroll eventually to see everything you've written, because the field isn't very big. To navigate in the text field you can use the arrow keys or click with the mouse. There are also four editing buttons on the right side of your screen: Cut, paste, undo, and redo. By highlighting text in your essay, you can move it around with the cut-and-paste feature. You shouldn't need to use these buttons, however. In fact, if you're using the cut-and-paste feature heavily, it's already a bad sign: a pretty clear indicator that your essay isn't well planned. By the way, you have to type your essays—no writing them by hand—so brush up on your typing if it's a little rusty.

Topics

The topics are about issues of general interest and don't require any special knowledge. Make sure to read the directions for each essay prompt. The directions sometimes have subtle differences. Visit the ETS website at **www.ets.org/gre** for a complete list of all the potential essay topics and directions. (Yes, you really get to see this information in advance of the test!) Practice responding to these essay prompts. Practicing with a variety of these essays will prepare you for whatever comes your way on test day.

There are nearly 250 topics listed for each essay, so the point isn't to memorize them to be ready for your actual GRE topic in advance. Rather, by browsing through the lists, you'll get an idea of what kinds of topics you'll be asked to write about.

Understanding the Two Tasks

The two essays that ETS requires you to write have distinct features, and it's important to know exactly how they differ. The simplest way to understand the distinction is that the Issue essay requires you to present your own opinion and support it with examples, while the Argument essay requires you to evaluate someone else's opinion without giving your own. Another way to put it is that the Issue essay requires you to develop your own argument by making claims and providing evidence to support and explain those claims, while the Argument essay requires you to critique another person's argument by analyzing its claims and judging the evidence it presents.

This distinction is important, because if you don't understand clearly the task you're being asked to perform, you're not likely to do a good job on the essay. In particular, many people get confused about the Argument essay because they're not accustomed to breaking down an argument and analyzing its logic. Many people simply give their own opinion on the argument, which is a sure way to score poorly. We'll be covering all the details of how to break down arguments and write a strong Argument essay later in this chapter.

Essay Writing Basics

It's important to understand that the essays you write for the GRE are not going to be masterpieces. We're not redefining the craft of writing here. You have limited time to write and revise, so what we're talking about is a quickly produced first-draft essay.

In order to score well, there are several components your essay should have. The following are some of the most important:

- **Length.** This is a good example of the difference between GRE writing and real writing. In the real world, good, vigorous writing is concise. Unnecessary things are cut out. On the GRE, you want to write as much as you can. That doesn't mean that you're filling the screen with blather or repeating yourself a hundred times, but you do want to expand on your ideas as much as possible and explore as many of their ramifications as you can. Be thorough. However, in your quest for length, know that depth is better than breadth. It's much better to have a few well-chosen examples that you explore in depth than many examples that you discuss only superficially. The bottom line is that high-scoring essays are usually long, and low-scoring essays are usually short. Make it as long as time permits. Aiming for about 500 words is a good guideline.

- **Organization.** Remember, the readers are going to go through your essay very quickly, and they're grading holistically. You need to make a good overall impression. No brilliant example, no amazing turn of phrase will save your essay if it is disorganized. One of the primary things the readers are looking for is a well-structured, well-organized piece of writing. In a sense the structure is much more important than the content. No one *really* cares what you say—they're not reading your essay to decide whether they agree with you. They care how you say it—whether you write a well-planned, logical response to the prompt. The easiest way to organize your essay is to use the old boring four- or five-paragraph essay format that you first learned in sixth grade: introduction, two or three body paragraphs, and a conclusion. Hard to believe something so basic could work on the GRE? Believe it. We're not writing real essays here, we're learning how to tackle a standardized test.

- **Introduction and Conclusion.** This is really part of organization, but it's important enough to discuss separately. Your essay must have an introduction and a conclusion. You can't simply launch into an example in the first sentence of your essay—the reader will be jolted. You have to ease the reader into the essay by spreading out a road map of where the essay is going. A good introduction can do a lot for you, because a reader who comes away with a good impression from the introduction is more likely to keep that good impression throughout the rest of your essay. Think of it as building good will. A conclusion is also crucial, because you don't want your essay to just en—. Wow. See how jarring that was? Now you probably wouldn't end in mid-word, but the point is that you have to bring your reader home with some kind of summation. The essay needs closure. A strong introduction gives the reader a good first impression; a strong conclusion leaves the reader with a good last impression.

- **Clear Point of View.** Unlike the other points mentioned so far, this one is not structural but rather content-based. It should always be clear to someone reading your essay exactly where you stand. Whether you're presenting your opinion in the Issue essay or critiquing the argument in the Argument essay, your own position should always be clear. When a clear point of view isn't present, your essay is weak and abstract, and the reader doesn't know why you wrote it—you clearly had nothing to say. When this situation arises, most of the time it's because you haven't actually figured out what you think. You're hoping to uncover it by writing about it, but that rarely works. Instead you end up with an essay that reads as though you were trying to discover your point of view along the way—which is exactly what you are doing. In order to write a high-scoring essay, you need to know what it is you want to say. And that means that you have to think before you write. Writing is just thinking on paper, but the thinking has to come first. We'll discuss this in more detail shortly.

- **Proper Grammar and Effective Language.** To some degree, of course, your essay score will be affected by how well you write. If your sentences are all the same length and same structure, your writing will be monotonous. If you make numerous or prominent grammatical errors, it will seem careless and unsophisticated. Using language well is part of good essay writing. We can't really teach you in this book to be a better writer (that's an entire book in itself), but we'll try to give you some helpful guidance along the way. In general, try to write as well as you can, but don't think that you need complicated syntax or fancy rhetorical flourishes to be successful on the Analytical Writing section. Use language that you're comfortable with and you should be fine. This is the GRE. You don't need the essay-writing skills of E. B. White to score well.

THE FOUR RULES

There are four basic rules we're going to follow while writing an essay. Poorly written essays tend to be essays which don't have a clear purpose. Although the Issue and Argument essays each have their own peculiarities we'll have to take into account, remembering the following four rules will keep your essay, whichever one it is, focused.

1. Spend time thinking.

2. Make a plan and stick to it.

3. One thought per paragraph.

4. Clearly link each paragraph to your thesis.

SPEND TIME THINKING

Time is ticking. We know. It's scary. There's even a little clock, right there in the corner of the screen, counting down tick by tick. Take a deep breath. Even though time is limited, don't rush into writing before you're ready. If you do, you'll find that you quickly run out of things to say, and you'll have a screen full of random, unconnected sentences in front of you. It's better to spend some time up front thinking about what you'll say.

So relax a bit. Read the prompt. You've got scratch paper, so use it. What's your initial thought after you read the prompt? Write it down. Write down all your thoughts, even the stupid ones. The idea is just to get your thoughts down without any inhibitions. (No one will take away points from your essay because you wrote something stupid down on your scratch paper.) Play devil's advocate. Think about the other side of the issue or argument. What examples can you use?

You will probably spend around 5 minutes without typing a single word. If so, good. Trust us, it will pay off later.

MAKE A PLAN AND STICK TO IT

Now you've got some ideas. Perfect. Lay them out into the rough outlines of an essay. What's your introduction? If it's the Issue essay, you'll need to state your opinion, also known as your thesis, clearly. If it's the Argument, it will probably be some variation of "This argument is potentially flawed, and we will need more information to determine whether or not to use it."

How will you support your thesis? What examples will you use, or what flaws will you point out? As soon as you know, you know exactly what your paragraphs will be. Write down that outline on your scratch paper.

That is your roadmap for the essay. Do not deviate from it. It's a good plan. Many people have the impulse to change their entire essay at the last second. Don't. Stick with your plan. Whenever you get lost in your essay, look back to your scratch paper to see what you should be writing about.

ONE THOUGHT PER PARAGRAPH

The people who grade your essay are not going to take printouts of your essay to a luxurious reading room, sit upon large padded velvet chairs, pour themselves glasses of brandy, light their pipes, and settle in to examine your thoughts. They will read your essay from a computer monitor as quickly as possible while sitting in an office chair with poor back support. They're not going to give you the benefit of the doubt.

Therefore, you need to make each point incredibly easy for them to find. Each paragraph will contain one, and only one, point, and support for that point. Nothing else.

You already know, from your plan, what each paragraph will be about. If you start wandering from that plan, and from the point of the paragraph, you're going to lose the reader. The teddy bear was invented in two places independently of each other: 1902 in the United States, and in 1903 in Germany. If you're confused, you're not alone. Switching from one point to another in the middle of the paragraph makes for jarring, incomprehensible writing.

CLEARLY LINK EACH PARAGRAPH TO YOUR THESIS

Once you have your thesis, every single thing you write in your essay should exist for one purpose, and one purpose only: to prove your thesis. If you are not actively supporting your thesis, then you're not answering the question.

It may not be as obvious to the graders how your paragraphs link to your thesis as it is to you. So once again, make life easy for those poor, harried GRE essay graders. Let them know exactly how that paragraph connects to the thesis, and how it answers the question they asked.

In other words, don't assume that if you show them Points A and C, that they will know that point B connects the two. Explicitly write that Point A leads to Point B, and Point B leads to Point C, and Point C leads back to your thesis.

THE ISSUE ESSAY

The first essay that we're going to look at is the Issue essay. We've already discussed the basic tasks for an essay. Now we're going to look at how you do it.

THE PROMPT

The first thing the GRE will give you is a prompt, a short sentence displayed inside a box. They want to know your opinion about that prompt. The prompt will be what they call a "topic of general interest," which means that ETS thinks almost everyone will have an opinion about it.

Here's a sample Issue Prompt:

> *The best indicator of a glorious nation is the emphasis it places on educating its populace.*

One thing you may have noticed about this prompt is that it not only presents an issue, but it takes a side. The GRE will never simply say "Education: Discuss." Instead they'll take a definite position. It is up to you to agree or disagree with that position, and explain exactly *why* you agree or disagree.

ETS doesn't actually care about your opinion on the Issue Essay. What they are actually looking for is that you *have* a clear opinion, and that you back that opinion up. It's not better to agree than it is to disagree, or vice versa. They don't care. They simply want to see how you support your position.

Directly following the prompt will be an assignment. Although these take a couple different forms, they are always some variation of:

> *Write a response in which you agree or disagree with the above statement and explain your reasoning for the position you take.*

Most of the prompts will be similar to the one above: a claim about some sort of topic of importance to society as a whole (laws, education, ideals, technology, et cetera) which you can agree or disagree with. There are sometimes slight variations such as:

- Given a claim and a reason for that claim, discuss how much you agree or disagree about the claim and the reason given.

- Given two opposing views, discuss the view that you agree with most and explain your reasons. Address both the side you agree with and the opposing side.

Even these, however, are hardly different from the typical prompt and assignment. ETS still wants you to clearly state your opinion and the reasons you hold it. (For a full list of Issue topics that the GRE will use, go to **www.ets.org/gre**)

EXAMPLES

Once you've read the prompt and the assignment, write down "Yes" and "No" on your scratch paper. Now it's time to brainstorm. Think of examples to support each side of the prompt. Don't worry about which side of the prompt you actually agree with for now. Just focus on the support you could use to argue either side.

For our prompt above, for Yes we could list any glorious nation which emphasized education, or any decidedly non-glorious civilizations which did not emphasize education. Note that we can argue the claim by saying "Doing what we say is good, so do what we say," and we can also argue it by saying "Not doing what we say is bad, so do what we say." The examples could be from history, current events, literature, film, or your personal experiences. Write down anything you can think of to support your position under Yes on your scratch paper.

For No, we could list any glorious nation which did not emphasize educating its citizens, or we could list some non-glorious civilizations which did emphasize education. List anything you can think of to show that education ain't so needed under No on your scratch paper.

Now look at your lists of examples. Was there one side, Yes or No, which had more examples? Are there any particular examples you came up with that you think you could write about particularly well? If so, you've found out what you think about the claim. If you've got better examples under Yes, then you are 100% for education, because it is the most important thing to make a society great. If you've got better examples under No, then you are now whole-heartedly devoted to nations focusing on something other than education, because it's not as necessary as those eggheads think it is.

After you've chosen a side, put a star next to your strongest 2 or 3 examples.

To review: Come up with your examples before you come up with an opinion. Go with whichever opinion has the better examples. Again, the GRE doesn't care about your opinion, it cares about your support. So focus on support first.

THESIS

Now that you know your position, it's time to tell the world. A basic thesis can be something along the lines of:

> *Education is the best indicator of a glorious nation.*

Or:

> *Education is not the best indicator of a glorious nation.*

These are fine theses. They state directly what we think with a minimum of fuss. Although they don't use the words "Yes" or "No," it's still clear what we think. You can always use this sort of clear, simple thesis. However, let's see if we can do a bit better. Rather than simply restate the claim, we can look at our examples a bit and ask ourselves "How do those examples support my point?" Use that to write your thesis. For instance:

> *Without education, a great nation will not last beyond the current generation.*

Or:

> *Education is no substitute for food, jobs, or military might, all of which are the true indicators of a major nation.*

Remember that every paragraph you write must link back to your thesis, so feel free to rewrite it a couple times. No matter what, however, make sure it is obvious how your thesis answers the question asked. The most eloquent, profound thesis doesn't do you any good if it doesn't have anything to do with the prompt or the assignment.

OUTLINE

Remember those examples you put stars next to? Each one of those will be a paragraph. Figure out which example will go first, and which next. Keep in mind that you will need to transition from one paragraph to the next, so if you know that mentioning one example will allow you to segue naturally to the next, put them in an order to allow you to use that transition.

Now you've got your outline:

- Thesis (with introduction paragraph)
- Example (tied back to thesis)
- Example (tied back to thesis)
- Conclusion

You won't always stick simply to the above outline, but if you're ever stuck it's a nice simple format to follow. You may only use 1 example, or 3 examples, but no matter how you lay out your essay, figure out a plan beforehand and stick to it.

You can also (and sometimes will be required to) use one of the examples from the *other* side of the argument, and show why it doesn't actually invalidate your side of the argument. "Sure, some may point to the Athenian city-state as evidence that education is important, but their education was in fact limited almost entirely to a select few. It was Athen's navy that had far more to do..."

WRITE

Here is where all that planning pays off. Using your outline, start writing your essay. Anytime you're stuck, look back to your outline and ask yourself "What do I need to say right now to support my thesis?"

Although you may decide to sparge your essay with a miscellany of abstruse words in order to give your essay a veneer of erudition, don't. Using advanced vocabulary is fine, but never let it hinder the reader. If you're not sure if you're using a word correctly, just using a vocabulary word to use it, or if you think that using a word may obscure your point rather than clarify it, then use a simpler word or phrase instead.

Whenever you're stuck, say things as directly as possible. If you have time, you can always go back later and modify your sentences if necessary, but it's better to end up with simple, direct sentences at the end than it is to have a couple great sentences that end abruptly because you ran out of time.

Time is incredibly important in this essay. Keep watching the clock. You'll want to spend 5–7 minutes on each paragraph. When you've got 10 minutes left, move on to the conclusion as soon as possible.

SAMPLE ESSAY

> In order to accomplish anything great, one must seek unpopularity.

Write a response in which you agree or disagree with the above statement and explain your reasoning for the position you take. In developing your position, consider situations in which the statement may or may not hold true and explain how these situations shape your decision.

Many people who have achieved important objectives have done so at the cost of being unpopular. It is sometimes argued that unpopularity is necessary in order to accomplish anything great and that nothing important is achieved by those who worry about being liked. While this may be true in some situations, many great things have been achieved by people who needed to court popularity in order to do them. In other cases, great things have been achieved by people for whom popularity or unpopularity were irrelevant. The key factor is the particular nature of the objective.

When the goal is to accomplish a change in society, unpopularity is probably inevitable. Most people resist large changes, and therefore the people who are pushing for the changes are bound to be unpopular with the section of the population that wants to keep things the way they are. For example, when civil rights leaders such as Malcolm X and Martin Luther King, Jr., were pushing for equal civil rights for black Americans, they were despised by much of the country. The goals they were advancing were controversial and confrontational and this made them deeply unpopular with millions of Americans. Despite this, the cause of civil rights was undoubtedly a great and noble one.

In other situations, however, great things can be accomplished and sometimes can only be accomplished by people with popular support. For example, when Britain was in danger of being defeated by Germany in 1940, Franklin Roosevelt was able to use his popularity and political skill to gather support for programs such as the Lend-Lease Act, which gave badly needed supplies to the British military. Without Roosevelt's skill in rallying the American people, the necessary support might not have been there to defeat the Axis powers and win the war. Victory in World War II is an example of a great thing that could only have been accomplished by a popular leader.

Finally, in some circumstances popularity is irrelevant to the achievement of an important task. Some examples of this would be scientific and medical research. When Jonas Salk developed the polio vaccine, a dangerous disease was eradicated, which is a great thing. Salk's accomplishment, however, did not depend on whether he was popular. Similarly, when Einstein wrote his 1905 paper on the photoelectric effect, his achievement in recognizing that the speed of light is constant for all observers did not depend on whether other scientists liked him. A scientific advance is not judged by the popularity of the scientist who discovers it. It just doesn't really matter either way.

In the end, to know whether unpopularity will be a necessary component of achieving something great, you need to know the type of achievement under discussion. Achievements that require large-scale social change will probably make those who fight for them unpopular, but other types of achievements will only be possible when their supporters are popular. And with still other types of achievements, such as scientific ones, it doesn't matter if their proponents are well liked or not. It's all a question of circumstance.

Now let's discuss a few things about this essay. First, this is not a flawless essay. It's not supposed to be perfect. However, this would get a high score on the GRE. Here are some of its features.

Introduction

The introduction accomplishes a few things, all of which you want to do in your essays. First, it establishes what the issue under discussion is. It does this by paraphrasing the prompt in the second sentence. Paraphrasing is usually better than quoting it verbatim, because it's less boring to the reader, and even seems less lazy. (If the prompt is very short, you may have a hard time paraphrasing it; if this is so, don't worry about it.) There are other ways to make it clear to the reader what issue is under discussion, but paraphrasing is the simplest.

Second, the introduction clearly establishes the point of view of the essay. After reading this introduction, you know quite clearly that the writer believes the prompt is sometimes true, but not always. And it leads you to believe that the following paragraphs will back up those assertions by providing examples of the different types of situations.

Body Paragraphs

The body paragraphs follow the implicit promise of the introduction to back up the writer's position. The first paragraph not only explains *why* the prompt is sometimes true, but presents concrete examples in Malcolm X and Martin Luther King, Jr., to support the point. You always want to make sure that your body paragraphs have concrete detail. Abstractions are not persuasive. Specifics and particulars are needed to back up your thesis.

The third paragraph logically follows by discussing an example of the opposite situation, exactly as the introduction has led you to expect. It gives a concrete example backed up by historical details.

The fourth paragraph continues the logical structure and organization of the essay by giving concrete examples of the last situation described in the introduction. Thus, all the body paragraphs give details and examples that support the basic point of view of the essay.

Conclusion

The most important thing about the conclusion is that it's there. You'll notice that it doesn't really say anything that wasn't already said in the introduction. The purpose of the conclusion is to tie a bow on the essay and give it the feeling of closure. It's a matter of ending the essay on the right note, with the right tone.

TIME GUIDELINES

You have 30 minutes to write the Issue essay. How should you spend your time? Here are some guidelines.

Brainstorm Outline }	5–7 minutes
Write	20–22 minutes
Proof	3 minutes

These are only rough estimates, but they should give you a sense of how to apportion your time. You should develop your own essay-pacing plan by writing some practice essays and adjusting your timing if necessary.

THE ARGUMENT ESSAY

Now it's time to take a look at the Argument essay. You'll find that even though the Argument essay is the more unfamiliar of the two essay types, once you learn how arguments are constructed, it's actually not that difficult to write one. If you read and practice the material in this section, you'll be able to bang out a high-scoring essay on any Argument topic ETS throws at you. Let's begin.

WHAT IS AN ARGUMENT?

On the GRE, an argument isn't about you and your roommate yelling at each other over whose turn it is to buy toilet paper. An argument is a short paragraph that attempts to convince you of something by providing evidence. Your job on the GRE is to analyze that argument and discuss how well-reasoned it is—whether it's logical and persuasive.

THE *REAL* TASK OF THE ARGUMENT ESSAY

The directions on the GRE describe your task as "analyzing" the argument. There's a simpler way to understand what you're really supposed to do, however. Your job is to *criticize* the argument. "Analyzing" sounds like an even-handed evaluation of the argument. That's not what you're doing here. On the Issue essay, there's no right answer; you can take any position you like. On the Argument essay, however, there *is* a right answer. How well-reasoned will you find the argument? The answer will always be, "Not very well. In fact, rather poorly. This argument is terrible."

If the argument were a well-reasoned piece of writing, there wouldn't be much to say about it. "Great argument! Airtight logic! The reasoning is ironclad! The conclusion must certainly be true!" That wouldn't make for much of an essay. So the first thing you need to do is reorient yourself to understand the real situation: ETS provides you with a weak, badly reasoned argument, and your job is to rip it apart and demonstrate why it's so bad. We'll be showing you how to do exactly that in the following pages.

THE PARTS OF AN ARGUMENT

Arguments consist of three basic parts:

- Conclusion

- Premises

- Assumptions

Let's look at each of these components in detail.

Conclusion

The conclusion is the most basic part of an argument. There's no point in writing an argument unless there's some conclusion you're trying to reach. The conclusion is simply the main point of the argument, the primary thing that the author is trying to convince you of.

Let's look at a simple argument.

> *Bobby needs to watch the Red Sox game. His TV is broken. Therefore, he should buy a new TV.*

What is the conclusion of the above argument? Pretty clearly, the ultimate point the author is trying to make is that Bobby should buy a new television. In addition to the general thrust of the argument, the tip-off we have here is the word "therefore." Certain words tend to indicate that the conclusion is about to follow. Among them are *therefore, thus, so, clearly, hence, consequently*, and *in conclusion*.

The first thing you should always do is identify the conclusion of the argument.

Premises

Think of premises as the reasons that the author gives to make you believe the conclusion. An argument can't simply assert something without backing it up. That wouldn't be an argument at all. The author of an argument needs to provide evidence to support the conclusion. Those pieces of evidence are the premises. Let's take another look at our sample argument.

> *Bobby needs to watch the Red Sox game. His TV is broken. Therefore, he should buy a new TV.*

We know that the conclusion is that Bobby should buy a new television. What are the premises of this argument? What evidence did the author provide to support the conclusion? This time it's pretty clear that the premises are the other two sentences in the argument: Bobby needs to watch the Red Sox game; his TV is broken.

After identifying the conclusion, you should always identify the premises of an argument.

The "Why?" Test

There's a simple way to determine if you've correctly identified the conclusion and premises of an argument. It's called the "Why?" test, and this is how it works. After you have identified what you believe to be the conclusion of the argument, ask yourself, "Why should I believe this is true?" The premises should answer that question. For example, ask, "Why should I believe that Bobby should buy a new TV?" The answer here is clearly, "Because he needs to watch the Red Sox, and his TV is busted." That means we've correctly identified the conclusion and premises. What if we'd misidentified them?

Let's say we had thought that the conclusion was the first sentence. When we ask, "Why should I believe that Bobby needs to watch the Red Sox?" there's nothing to point to. Nothing in the argument provides any support for that statement. The argument just says so. We just have to accept it as given.

So the "Why?" test helps us to make sure we've correctly broken down the argument into its basic pieces.

Assumptions

So far, we've seen how to find conclusions and premises. Assumptions are the third part of arguments. Assumptions are similar to premises in that they also provide reasons to support the conclusion. But they have a key difference. While the premises are explicitly stated in the argument, the assumptions are by definition *unstated*.

Assumptions are things that must be true in order for the conclusion to make sense, but that the author left out of the argument. Instead of establishing the truth of those facts, the author simply *assumed* that they were true. Let's go back one more time to our sample argument.

Bobby needs to watch the Red Sox game. His TV is broken. Therefore, he should buy a new TV.

What must the author be assuming in order for the argument to make sense? What else must be true for the conclusion to follow properly from the premises?

Well, for one, we have to assume that Bobby can't get his TV fixed, or can't get it fixed soon enough to watch the game. If he could get it fixed, then he wouldn't have to buy a new one.

Second, we have to assume that there's no other way Bobby can watch the Red Sox game. For example, he can't go over to his friend Johnny's house and watch the game there. Or he can't go to Fenway Park and see the game live. If he could do either of these things he wouldn't have to buy a new TV.

So, let's summarize the breakdown of this argument:

Conclusion: Bobby should buy a new TV.

Premises: He needs to watch the Red Sox Game. His TV is broken.

Assumptions: He can't get his TV fixed. He can't watch the game some other way.

Why Assumptions Are So Important

It's important to understand that assumptions are necessary for an argument to work. If the assumptions aren't true, the argument falls apart. In the argument above, if Bobby can fix his TV, or watch the game another way, then he doesn't have to buy a new TV. The conclusion is effectively destroyed. This is the key because, as we said, your task on the Argument essay is to weaken the argument. You do that by identifying the assumptions of the argument and attacking them.

Here are a few more tips to help you spot assumptions:

- **Focus on the gap in the argument.** There is always a gap between the premises of an argument and the conclusion, some unjustified leap of logic that needs to be filled by the assumptions. If you look for the gap in the reasoning, and think about what information will bridge that gap, it will be easier to find the assumptions.

- **Look for new stuff in the conclusion.** If the conclusion talks about things that weren't mentioned at all in the premises, then the author must have simply assumed there was a connection.

- **Think about weaknesses in the argument.** What are the possible flaws? An argument is always weakest at its unstated parts. Pretend you're a lawyer in a courtroom and your job is to raise doubt in the minds of the members of the jury about the truth of the argument's conclusion. What could you say? What counterexamples and alternative possibilities could you suggest?

QUICK QUIZ #1

Try to break down the following arguments. Write down the conclusion and premises, using the "Why?" test to check yourself. Then write down any assumptions you spot. The answers are on page 174.

1. *All the classrooms in the Dover school district have computers. The children in Dover have higher standardized test scores than the children in Wilmington, where there are no computers in the classrooms. Clearly, Wilmington should put computers in its classrooms to raise students' scores.*

Conclusion: _____

_____

Premises: _____

Assumptions: _____

_____

2. *Tony's Macaroni is the best-selling brand of macaroni and cheese at FreshStar supermarket. Therefore, more people in town must prefer its taste to that of any other brand.*

Conclusion: _____

_____

Premises: _____

_____

Assumptions: _____

_____

3. *This new food additive has been shown to cause cancer in laboratory rats. Consequently, any product that uses it will be dangerous for humans.*

Conclusion: _____

_____

Premises: _____

_____

Assumptions: _____

_____

All of the examples we've looked at so far are much shorter and simpler than the arguments you'll get as prompts for the Argument essay, but you break them down in the exact same way. The arguments you'll actually be writing about have a lot more than two assumptions. There will be more things wrong with them than you'll have time to write about. This is good because it means you don't have to find every assumption in order to write a high-scoring essay. You only have to find a few.

THE PROMPT

Now we're ready to tackle a sample prompt for the Argument essay.

The following is a memo from the circulation manager of National Newsletter, Inc.

"To make the home delivery service of our national newsletter more profitable, we should focus on Holden County rather than Plymouth County. First, the residents of Plymouth County are more geographically spread out, which would require us to spend more money per customer delivering the newsletter to them than to the residents of Holden County. Furthermore, a study by a nearby university indicates that Plymouth County residents prefer local news to national news, since they spend 50 percent more time watching local television news broadcasts than national broadcasts. Lastly, because Holden County has a higher average income per resident than Plymouth County, we can expect to make more money delivering newsletters in Holden County than in Plymouth County."

The assignment itself can take a variety of forms, but is always some variation of one of the four questions:

• What evidence is needed to evaluate the argument?

• What are the assumptions of the argument?

• What questions would we have to ask to determine the argument's feasibility?

• What other plausible explanations could there be other than the proposed explanation?

Each question type will require a slightly different approach to how we use the argument's assumptions. (For a full list of all the Argument Essay topics the GRE will use, see **www.ets.org/gre**. If you find you still have trouble breaking down arguments, it's a great place to find some real GRE arguments to tackle.) We'll talk about each specific question type in detail a bit later, but for the first part of the your essay it doesn't matter what question they ask. First, we'll have to look at the parts of the argument.

FIND THE ASSUMPTIONS

The conclusion is that National Newsletter, Inc.'s home delivery service will be more profitable if they concentrate on Holden County rather than Plymouth County. The premises are: 1) Plymouth residents are spread out so it will cost more to deliver the newsletter to them; 2) A study suggests that Plymouth residents care more about local news because they watch local news programs more than national programs; and 3) Holden residents have more money on average than Plymouth residents.

So far this is not too difficult because the structure of the argument is fairly straightforward. But now comes the important part: spotting assumptions. So let's think about what else must be true for this argument to work, and what implicit facts are being left out. Where is the gap in the reasoning? How might we challenge this argument? What possibilities could we suggest that would cast doubt on the conclusion?

First, we might notice that they're assuming that the higher per-customer cost of delivering to Plymouth County (due to geographical spread) won't be compensated for by higher sales there, or by a slightly higher subscription rate, or by some other factor.

Second, we can point out that the argument assumes that this university study is valid and accurate.

Third, they're assuming that although the residents of Plymouth County may watch more local TV news than national news (according to the study), the residents of Holden County *don't*. (Remember, the argument is making a comparison between two counties, so the claim about Plymouth County's TV news preferences is only helpful to the argument if Holden County's preferences are different.)

Fourth, the argument assumes that because Plymouth County residents aren't interested in national TV news programs (compared with local programs), they won't be interested in a national newsletter. In other words, it assumes that their television preferences are the same as their newsletter preferences.

Fifth, we can point to the assumption that higher income leads to higher home-delivery subscription sales.

We could probably find a few more if we kept looking, but five assumptions are more than enough to write the Argument essay.

It's also important during this step to think about some concrete counterexamples you can use in your essay to attack the assumptions. Being specific and using concrete details is just as important in the Argument essay as in the Issue essay. It's not enough to just say, "The argument assumes [insert assumption], but maybe that's not true." You have to demonstrate why it might not be true, why it's a bad assumption.

Let's come up with some specific criticisms of the assumptions we identified for this argument.

Assumption 1:   Higher cost of delivery to spread-out people means less profit.

Why it's a bad assumption: Because higher costs can be counterbalanced by higher revenue. If they sell more subscriptions, they could make more money. Or maybe they can charge a higher rate because of the extra delivery distance.

Assumption 2:   The university study is valid.

Why it's a bad assumption: We have no idea how it was conducted. We don't know that the sample it used was representative of the Plymouth County population. Maybe it only surveyed people who watch television, rather than people who read to get their news.

Assumption 3:   The preference for local TV news by Plymouth County residents does not apply to residents of Holden County.

Why it's a bad assumption: Because maybe residents of Holden County also watch 50 percent more local TV news than national TV news. In fact, perhaps they watch 150 percent more local news than national news. Perhaps they don't watch any national news at all.

Assumption 4:   The preference of Plymouth County residents for local television news over national television news indicates that they won't want to read a national newsletter.

Why it's a bad assumption: Because people's preferences for written material may be very different from their television preferences. Perhaps people really like seeing local events covered on television, but prefer to read about national events in newspapers and newsletters.

Assumption 5:   Higher average income means more sales and more profits.

Why it's a bad assumption: Because we don't know what the difference in income actually is. It could be $5 a year, which would be insignificant. Furthermore, we have no evidence that the newsletter is expensive and therefore more likely to be bought by wealthier people.

Remember, we're not going to write about all of these assumptions. We only have to pick a few of them.

Outline

Choose two or three of the assumptions you listed out. Note that you may only spot two or three assumptions in an argument; that's fine. You won't always come up with five assumptions. Out of the assumptions you could find, however, choose whichever ones you want to write about. You may also find that some of your assumptions are very similar to each other; it may be better to treat them as variations on the same assumption, and use that mega-assumption and one other assumption.

Each assumption will be a separate paragraph. Look to see if you can think of any transitions between assumptions to help you order your paragraphs, but if not then just pick whichever assumption you want to write about first. Your outline will probably look like this:

- Introduction
- Assumption #1
- Assumption #2
- Conclusion

If you have time, you may have a third assumption paragraph. After writing a couple Argument Essays, you'll know whether not you reliably have time to write 2 or 3 body paragraphs. Writing about 3 assumptions is not necessarily better than writing about two, so don't feel as if you must have 3 separate assumptions to get the highest score. It's far more important to have each assumption you found clearly explained than it is to simply list assumptions. Whatever your specific outline, however, stick to it.

Write

The introduction for every Argument question, no matter which type it is, is always basically the same. The introduction will be a variation of "The argument comes to this conclusion, but that may not necessarily be true. We need more information to know for sure."

The body paragraphs, however can change quite a bit depending on what type of question was asked.

- **State the Assumptions**: As you write your body paragraphs, don't simply state the assumptions and leave it at that. After you state each assumption, describe why that assumption may not be valid. Emphasize as much as possible the difference between the argument's premise and conclusion. If possible, use specific counterexamples to show the problems with each assumption.

- **Necessary Evidence**: The evidence we will need to evaluate the argument will be information to tell us whether or not each assumption is valid. For instance, this argument claims that the higher cost of delivery to spread-out people will result in less profit. To know for sure whether or not that's true we're going to need to evidence of exactly how much money is lost due to extra mileage in Plymouth County, and how much revenue we can expect to accrue from those residents. Until we know that the extra revenue won't make up for the added mileage costs, we don't know if it's a good or bad idea to expand into Plymouth County.

- **Ask Some Questions**: The questions we ask will be focused on the argument's assumptions. With each question, we need to make it clear why we need to ask that question, and the results the answers could have on the argument's recommendation. For the current argument, we may need to ask if the preference of Plymouth County residents for local news applies to the residents of Holden County. If the residents of Holden County similarly prefer local news to national news, then we may need to consider an alternate location for our newsletter, or ignore the study in our recommendation since both locations are similarly biased. If the residents of Holden County do not prefer local news, unlike the residents of Plymouth County, then we would need to know if they would still be interested in the national newsletter. If they watch so much national news, would they need our national newsletter, or do they receive all the national news they require from television broadcasts?

- **Other Explanations**: Here we will use our assumptions to see what other conclusions we could get from the initial premises. The initial argument will give a definitive conclusion or explanation, and we need to show that the conclusion is not necessarily correct. Consider the following argument:

Students from Astoria High School consistently score better on standardized tests than do students from Midtown High School. The school day at Astoria High School is 30 minutes longer than the school day at Midtown High School. Astoria High School's higher test scores can therefore be attributed to its longer school day.

There are several assumptions in this argument. Two major ones are:
1) Astoria High School and Midtown High School are comparable schools
2) That extra 30 minutes is connected to the test scores. Either assumption gives us a possible alternative explanation. If the two schools are not comparable, for instance if Astoria High School is well-funded whereas Midtown High School is not, or Astoria High School has small classes and Midtown High School has large classes, then the difference in test scores could be due to either of those reasons. (In an actual essay, we'd explain how each difference could result in higher scores in one school and lower schools in the other.)

As with the Issue essay, timing is important. When you have 10 minutes left, start to transition to your conclusion. You don't want to have a great essay marred by the fact that you didn't get to finish it.

SAMPLE ESSAY

> Write a response in which you discuss the stated or unstated assumptions of the argument. Be sure to explain how the argument depends on these assumptions and what the implications are if the assumptions are unsupported.

The argument concludes that in order to increase the profitability of the home delivery service for its national newsletter, National Newsletter, Inc., should concentrate on Holden County rather than Plymouth County. This conclusion is based on the premises that Plymouth County is more geographically spread out than Holden County, that people in Plymouth County watch more local TV news than national TV news, and that Holden County residents have a higher average income than residents of Plymouth County. The reasoning in the argument is logically flawed, however, because it relies on numerous assumptions that appear to be wholly unsupported.

First, the argument assumes that because the residents of Plymouth County are spread out geographically, making delivery more costly, there is less potential for profit. However, higher costs could be compensated for with higher revenues. For example, if more home delivery subscriptions were sold in Plymouth County than Holden County, the revenue from higher sales would lead to more profit. People in Plymouth County may even be more likely to order home delivery precisely because they live in far-out places. Furthermore, Plymouth County residents might be willing to pay a higher subscription rate because of the distance, compensating for the extra cost of delivery. The argument fails to address any of these potential situations.

Second, the argument ignores the possibility that residents of Holden County watch the same amount of local television news as do the residents of Plymouth County. The argument mentions a university study that says Plymouth County residents watch 50 percent more local TV news than national TV news. However, no information is provided about television viewing in Holden County at all. For all we know, everyone in Holden County also watches 50 percent more local TV news than national TV news. In fact, Holden County residents might not watch any national TV news at all. If any of this is true, it would severely weaken the argument.

Finally, the argument fails to take into account that the higher average income of Holden County does not necessarily mean more sales and more profit. We don't even know how much higher the average income is, for one thing. It could be higher by an insignificant amount. Moreover, there's no reason to believe that higher income will lead to more newsletter subscriptions. A newsletter isn't a luxury item like a yacht that can only be afforded by the wealthy.

In conclusion, the argument that focusing on Holden County rather than Plymouth County will make home delivery of the newsletter more profitable is rather weak. If the author demonstrated that higher delivery costs couldn't be balanced with higher revenues, that Holden County residents watch more national news than residents of Plymouth County, and that higher incomes lead to higher subscription sales, the argument would be greatly strengthened. Without this additional support, however, there is no reason to accept the conclusion of the argument.

As was true of the sample Issue essay earlier, this is not a perfect essay. It's not a particularly creative essay, but it gets the job done and would rate a high score on the GRE. Let's look a little closer.

Introduction

The introduction accomplishes a few things. It demonstrates understanding of the argument (and of arguments in general), and it establishes the point of view of the essay very clearly. This introduction follows a very easy template that you can use for your essays.

The argument concludes [paraphrase conclusion]. This conclusion is based on the premises [paraphrase premises]. The reasoning in the argument is logically flawed, however, because it relies on assumptions that appear to be wholly unsupported.

The first two sentences of the introduction demonstrate that you understand the argument and that you understand how arguments work. You're using the jargon of arguments such as "conclusion" and "premises" and later "assumptions." You're not giving your own opinion at all. Instead, you're showing the reader that you understand the task of the Argument essay. The final sentence of the introduction establishes your point of view, which will always be the same: This argument is terrible because of its unsupported assumptions.

Body Paragraphs

The body paragraphs logically follow the introduction and proceed to systematically address major assumptions of the argument and show them to be dubious. Each body paragraph does two things. First, it identifies an assumption, and then, it criticizes that assumption with specific, concrete details and counterexamples.

There are many ways to introduce assumptions. Here are a few good ones.

The argument assumes [assumption]. However ...

The argument fails to consider that [assumption may be false]. For example ...

The argument ignores the possibility that [assumption may be false]. For example ...

The argument does not take into account that [assumption may be false]. For example...

Notice that the body paragraphs make heavy use of structure words to indicate the overall organization of the essay and the organization of the paragraphs themselves—words like, *first, second, finally, last, furthermore, in addition, moreover, for example.*

Also notice that the body paragraphs use specific details and counterexamples to attack the assumptions. If the assumption is false, then something else must be true, and you should always suggest what that alternative could be. Otherwise your argument will be too abstract and too vague.

Conclusion

As in the Issue essay, the conclusion is really just restating the basic perspective of the introduction. Here it recaps the three assumptions from the point of view of how the argument could be improved. After all, if you're ripping the argument to shreds, it's only polite to suggest ways that the author could begin to fix it. Ultimately, though, your goal is to wrap up the essay with a final restatement of your position and end the whole thing on a conclusive note.

TIME GUIDELINES

You have 30 minutes to write the Argument essay. Here are some guidelines on how to use your time.

Brainstorm ⎫	
Outline ⎭	5–7 minutes
Write	20–22 minutes
Proof	3 minutes

Again, these are only suggestions. You have to find something that works for you. With practice, you'll become better and faster at producing these essays, so you'll feel less pressed for time.

FINAL THOUGHTS

Now you have the knowledge you need in order to raise your score on the Analytical Writing section. The only thing missing is the experience. Practice writing these essays and you'll find that they become easier and easier. Writing GRE essays is a craft, not an art, and anyone can learn how to do it. Work hard, and when your real test comes you'll finish the first 60 minutes with confidence. Those essays aren't going to hold you back.

ANSWERS AND EXPLANATIONS

Quick Quiz #1

1.   The conclusion is that putting computers into Wilmington classrooms will raise students' test scores. Why should we believe that? Because Dover has higher scores and there are computers in all of its classrooms. Those are the premises. Lastly, what are the assumptions? First, that the computers are the actual explanation for the higher test scores in Dover, rather than something else such as better teachers or access to Princeton Review books. Second, even if the computers are the cause of the higher test scores, you have to assume that the two towns are similar enough so that what works in one town will work in the other. Maybe the students in Wilmington don't know how to use computers and so computers won't help them.

2.   The conclusion is that Tony's Macaroni is the best-tasting brand of mac and cheese in town. The evidence for this conclusion (in other words, the premises) is that it's the best-selling brand at FreshStar supermarket. What are the big assumptions here? One is that the sales at FreshStar are representative of the sales at all other supermarkets in town. Maybe Tony's Macaroni sells very poorly at other stores. (If you were thinking that FreshStar is the only supermarket in town, you were just assuming that. The argument never says it.) The second big assumption is that best sales = best taste. In other words, the argument assumes that Tony's Macaroni sells well because it tastes better than other brands. But that's not necessarily true. Maybe it's just cheaper.

3.   The conclusion is that any product using the food additive will be dangerous for humans. The premise is that it caused cancer in lab rats. The assumptions? Well, for one, they're assuming that humans are like lab rats (kind of like how ETS views you when you're working on the multiple-choice experimental section). More precisely, they're assuming that something that is dangerous to lab rats will also be dangerous to humans—that humans and lab rats are similar in this way. The second assumption is that any product using the additive will use similar quantities to those that were given to the lab rats. After all, if the rats were fed 20 grams of the additive per day, and a typical product for human consumption would only use .05 grams, maybe we shouldn't be as concerned (especially given the difference in body weight between rats and humans).

SAMPLE ESSAYS

The following essays are intended to give you additional exposure to the points that were made in this chapter. They are not models of perfection and are not supposed to be. Despite their flaws, however, they do the important things well enough to receive high scores on the GRE. Remember, reading these essays is not a substitute for practicing writing essays yourself. Ultimately, you're the one who has to sit at the computer and type out two essays—this book can't do it for you. But these essays will help you get a better feel for what the graders are looking for.

ISSUE ESSAYS

Issue Essay #1

> *A good decision is one that takes into account its future consequences more than its present benefits.*

Write a response in which you agree or disagree with the above statement and explain your reasoning for the position you take. In developing your position, consider situations in which the statement may or may not hold true and explain how these situations shape your decision.

When trying to decide a course of action, it is important to consider both its short-term and long-term consequences. Looking at only one of these factors may lead to sound decisions sometimes, but in other cases will bring on disaster. Some argue that the future ramifications of a decision are more important than whatever present advantages it may have, but that will not always be true. Sometimes, the immediate benefits of a choice are important so that steps should be taken to achieve them even at the cost of future problems. Two examples from history demonstrate that neither present benefits nor future consequences are enough to justify a decision by themselves.

First, consider the compromise that British Prime Minister Neville Chamberlain struck with Nazi Germany. The Munich Compromise was supposed to accomplish "peace in our time," but Hitler soon seized more territory and invaded Poland. Seeking to avoid war is a good thing, and Chamberlain's actions kept Britain out of the war longer than it otherwise would have been. However, all it really did was postpone the day when appeasement would no longer be possible and confrontation would become necessary. In the meantime, Hitler became stronger and solidified his hold over more and more of Europe. Britain would likely have lost far fewer men in the war had it been more willing to sacrifice the short-term benefits of appeasing Hitler for the longer-term necessity of defeating him. In this case, the future costs far outweighed the present advantages.

In contrast, however, sometimes the immediate benefits of a decision are so great that they outweigh future problems. For example, when the U.S. Constitution was being drafted, a controversy arose over how representatives would be apportioned. The southern states wanted black slaves to be counted for population purposes, because this would give them more representatives in Congress. The northern states did not want to do this and argued that only free men should be counted. Eventually, the 3/5 compromise was adopted, which determined that a slave would count as three fifths of a free man. Condoning and recognizing slavery in the Constitution led to tremendous problems, culminating 75 years later in the Civil War. However, without that compromise the Constitution would never have been ratified and the states would never have been able to form a unified country. In this situation, the importance of establishing a new country and government was high enough that making such a compromise was necessary. Despite the terrible future consequences that almost destroyed the country, at least there was a country to be preserved.

In conclusion, as the above examples demonstrate, neither the long-term consequences nor the short-term benefits of a decision can determine definitively whether that decision was proper. Rather, it is the relative importance of the benefits and consequences themselves that determine the best course of action. In some situations, the immediate advantages will be great enough to justify future problems. In others, short-sighted decisions will lead to terrible costs down the road. Good decisions must be based on circumstances, not principles alone.

Analysis

The introduction of this essay makes clear that the author believes that the prompt is sometimes true, and sometimes not. The point of view is clear. Furthermore, it gives some general description of why that might be. There are two solid body paragraphs that back up the author's thesis, contrasting the importance of focusing on long-term consequences vs. short-term benefits. The body paragraphs also use concrete, specific examples rather than vague assertions or hypothetical situations. The body paragraphs are well developed, giving the essay depth and length. Finally, the conclusion restates the point of view and ends with a good sentence to give the essay a proper note of closure. This is an example of a well-organized essay that uses only two examples, but uses them well to support its point.

Issue Essay #2

> *The arts (music, dance, visual arts) are much less important to students' futures than academic subjects such as Math, History, English, and Science. The arts should be deemphasized in schools.*

Write a response in which you agree or disagree with the above statement and explain your reasoning for the position you take. In developing your position, consider situations in which the statement may or may not hold true and explain how these situations shape your decision.

The question of how to use limited time and resources in schools is a contentious one. Schools are where kids learn the basic skills and knowledge they will need in life, such as reading and math. Schools traditionally are also where kids are exposed to other important aspects of a well-rounded education, such as sports and the arts. Many people believe that academic subjects like history and science are much more important than music, dance, or the visual arts, and therefore that the arts should not receive much emphasis in schools. However, the arts are an important aspect of what gives life beauty and meaning. Depriving kids of exposure to the arts would leave them less able to understand and enjoy one of the primary things that can give their lives satisfaction and purpose.

For example, music education gives a tremendous number of benefits to students. Nearly all students listen to music, but far fewer know much about how it actually works. Studying music gives one a new appreciation for composers and songwriters that enhances the experience of listening to music. Furthermore, studying music gives students the chance to make music themselves, by singing or learning to play an instrument. The ability to play music even gives some students career opportunities, but more often it gives students the opportunity to find a life-long passion and hobby. The joys of having music in one's life are hard to calculate.

Another reason why the arts should be taught in school is that students will develop skills that are not emphasized in academic subjects. For instance, students that practice drawing and painting develop hand-eye coordination and the ability to translate things from the imagination to the reality of paper. Students that practice dance learn about their own bodies and how to express themselves with body language and gestures. These are all useful skills that are neglected in regular classroom subjects.

Finally, studying the arts taps into students' inborn sense of creativity and stimulates their work in other academic subjects. Someone who studies painting or photography is likely to be able to write in a more visually descriptive way. Someone who has learned about the history of sculpture and tried to make pottery will have a greater appreciation for the history of ancient civilizations and their cultural artifacts. Studying the arts can in fact enhance the study of academic subjects.

In conclusion, it would be a terrible mistake to de-emphasize the arts in schools. While no one can deny that it is important for students to learn math and English and history, ways should be found to teach these subjects better, rather than simply giving them more time at the expense of the arts. Students who get no exposure to the arts in school are likely never to be exposed to them later. Without the arts, their lives will not be as full and fulfilling as they would otherwise have been, and that would be a terrible loss.

Analysis

This essay also shows an author arguing one side of a prompt, but unlike the previous essay, this one disagrees with the prompt. The introduction begins by outlining the problem, pointing out one perspective on the problem, and then clearly rejecting that perspective to argue that the arts are important. We know what the issue is and we know where this author stands. The three body paragraphs use clear transition words (*for example, another reason, finally*) to make the structure and organization obvious. They show three specific ways that the arts are beneficial to students, thus providing solid support to back up the thesis of the essay. The conclusion paragraph reiterates the main point and sums up the author's argument, ending on the right kind of conclusory note.

Issue Essay #3

> Today's world offers many ways to learn; reading books is no longer necessary to become a well-educated person.

Write a response in which you agree or disagree with the above statement and explain your reasoning for the position you take. In developing your position, consider situations in which the statement may or may not hold true and explain how these situations shape your decision.

For centuries, books were the primary means of passing on knowledge. There was no television, no radio, no Internet, no study-at-home videotapes. Now that all these things exist, books no longer have a monopoly on information. This leads some to the conclusion that reading books isn't necessary for becoming educated anymore. There is some truth to this. Today, people learn things in other ways and from other sources. However, much of the world's knowledge is still only available in books, and therefore reading them will continue to be an important part of people's education. How important will depend to some degree on what exactly we mean by education.

For example, if we consider an educated person to be one who knows the basic facts of history, then there are many sources for this information outside of books. Much information about world history can be found online and can help a person learn about the basic facts and dates and people that we believe educated people should know. History is also available on CD-rom encyclopedias. Beyond the computer, there are many historical documentary films that can educate people about the realities of the past. Even some Hollywood movies convey accurate historical information that can properly be called educational.

However, many kinds of information that we feel educated people should know are not available anywhere but in books. Literature is an obvious example. Most people would not consider an education complete if it did not include exposure to some of the world's great literature. Shakespeare and Milton and Dickens and Austen have much to teach us through their stories and characters. And right now, experiencing literature still means reading books. Despite such things as books on tape and e-books, reading books is still the only realistic way for people to become knowledgeable about literature.

Finally, if we believe that being a well-educated person means having some special knowledge about a particular field, then reading books will also be essential. Becoming a lawyer requires reading case books on contracts and evidence in law school. Becoming a doctor requires reading textbooks on anatomy and neurology. Being a scientist requires reading scientific journals to learn about new scientific discoveries. For almost any "major" in college, the information that one would need to study is only available in books, whether you want to study sociology, religion, anthropology, philosophy, or something else.

In conclusion, while there are many sources outside of books for some types of information, many other types of information are still largely restricted to books. Radio, movies, television, the Internet, and other sources of knowledge are certainly places where you can educate yourself, but their scope is limited. Whether the reading of books is truly "necessary" to be a well-educated person will depend on how exactly you define "well-educated," but most people will probably define it in a way that will make the reading of books essential still.

Analysis

This essay is finding truth in both sides of the issue, similar to the way the first essay did, although the introduction shows it to be leaning somewhat toward the claim that reading books will still be necessary. The first body paragraph describes one situation that could support the idea that education can be obtained outside of books, but the second and third suggest two other definitions of education that indicate that books are still necessary. So this essay entertains the thesis of the prompt, but ultimately moves in the direction of rejecting it. Remember, there is no right answer, no correct perspective to take. As long as you support your opinion, your essay will be fine. The conclusion here recaps the points made in the introduction and body paragraphs, which is the main thing it needs to do.

ARGUMENT ESSAYS

Argument Essay #1

The following is from a state report on safety procedures in various towns.

The Peabody health department requires that all mine workers be screened at least once every four months for health problems that may arise from working underground. However, this requirement may be unnecessary and of no benefit to workers. In the town of Orange, the health department has no such requirement, and surveys show that workers are screened on average only once every three years. Not only is the reported number of workers with job-related illnesses lower in Orange, but the number of deaths known to be the result of exposure to harmful agents on the job is half as large. Clearly, increased frequency of health screenings neither prevents illness nor saves lives.

Write a response in which you discuss the stated or unstated assumptions of the argument. Be sure to explain how the argument depends on these assumptions and what the implications are if the assumptions are unsupported.

> The argument concludes that more frequent screenings for job-related health problems don't reduce illness or save lives. The conclusion is based on the premises that although Peabody screens workers every four months and workers in Orange are screened on average every three years, the reported number of sick workers is lower in Orange and the number of deaths is half as much. The argument is not logically persuasive, however, because it relies on numerous shaky assumptions for which no evidence has been given.
>
> First, the argument does not address the possibility that the populations of Peabody and Orange may be very different. The argument claims that half as many people die in Orange from exposure to harmful agents as do in Peabody. But comparisons of absolute numbers are only valid if the populations are similar. For example, say the population of

Peabody was 1,000 and 10 people died, while the population of Orange was 100 and 5 people died. Even though twice as many people died in Peabody as in Orange, Peabody's rate was only 1 percent while Orange's rate was 5 percent. The argument fails to address this issue.

Moreover, the argument assumes that the condition of mine workers is identical in Peabody and Orange except for the difference in frequency of screening. However, there are many other potential explanations for the reported differences. Perhaps the mine workers in Orange have better protective equipment, which means they get sick less often. Or perhaps they work in less toxic mines. There could even be differences in screening procedures that account for the differences. No information has been presented to show that other plausible explanations have been ruled out.

Lastly, the argument fails to consider that workers in Orange may be screened more often than the averages suggest. Averages can be deceptive because they are subject to distortion by extreme values. For example, most workers in Orange could be screened every few months, but if there were a minority who refused to be screened at all, and hadn't been screened for, say, 20 years, then the average of once every three years would not truly be representative.

In sum, the argument that frequent screening does not prevent illness or save lives is logically unsound. If the author showed that the populations of Peabody and Orange are similar, that there are no other significant differences between the towns other than the frequency of screening, and that the average frequency of screening in Orange is actually representative, the argument would be much stronger. In the absence of this additional evidence, however, we should be wary about accepting the truth of the argument's conclusion.

Analysis

This essay begins by identifying the conclusion and premises of the argument and taking the position that the argument is flawed because of its shaky assumptions. Remember, this is always our position. The argument is always weak because of its assumptions. Each body paragraph follows the pattern of identifying an assumption made by the argument, and then criticizing that assumption with concrete objections. The argument essay is almost a mechanical exercise once you learn how to find the assumptions, so these essays will sound very much alike. The conclusion restates the main point and recaps the assumptions.

Argument Essay #2

> *A recent study reported that people who own dogs live healthier and longer lives than people who are not dog owners. In particular, people who own dogs have much lower rates of strokes than the general population. Therefore, the city of Weston should create a program that selects dogs from the Weston animal shelter and gives them to stroke patients when they return home to convalesce. Not only will this speed their recovery, but it will save the city money by reducing the number of return visits to the hospital. Furthermore, the stroke patients will tell their friends, which means that more people will become dog owners, reducing the number of people who have strokes in the future.*

Write a response in which you discuss the stated or unstated assumptions of the argument. Be sure to explain how the argument depends on these assumptions and what the implications are if the assumptions are unsupported.

The argument concludes that the city of Weston will save money and reduce the number of people who suffer strokes by creating a program that selects dogs from the local animal shelter and giving them to recently discharged stroke patients as pets. This conclusion is based on the premises that dog owners have lower rates of strokes than the general population does, according to a recent study. The logic of the argument is not convincing, however, because it assumes the truth of many things that have not in fact been demonstrated.

To start with, the argument assumes that dog ownership is in fact the cause of the lower incidence of stroke among dog owners, rather than a mere correlated fact. But noting that people who have dogs also have low rates of stroke does not demonstrate that the former is the cause of the latter. It's quite possible that both of these facts are explained by something the argument does not mention. For example, perhaps energetic people who like to lead active lives are less likely to have strokes because of the exercise they get, and are also more likely to own dogs that they run with and take to the park to play frisbee. If that is the case, then it is the active lifestyle that is the real cause of better health, and giving a dog to an inactive person will do nothing to prevent a stroke.

In addition, the argument assumes that giving dogs to people after they have had strokes will have healing benefits. But the evidence provided by the study does not support that idea. The study says that people who own dogs have lower rates of strokes than most people. It suggests that owning a dog may be a good measure to prevent strokes. But once a person has actually had a stroke, there is no evidence that a dog will help them get better. Brushing your teeth may help prevent cavities, but once you have one, brushing won't do anything to fix it.

Finally, the argument fails to address the possibility that the program will not save money after all. The program itself will cost money to implement and no figures have been presented that show that there will be a net savings to the town of Weston once the program has been put in place. It might turn out to be quite expensive to find the right dog for each stroke patient. The patients might have to be driven to the shelter to see the dogs first. The dogs would have to be transported to their homes. People would have to be hired to make all of this happen. Furthermore, we have no idea how many return visits will be prevented by this program. It could be very few, or even none at all. Without some evidence that allows us to at least estimate these numbers, it's difficult to have any confidence in this claim.

In conclusion, the argument that giving dogs to stroke patients will save money and reduce the number of strokes in Weston is dubious. If the author demonstrated that dog ownership was the actual cause of the lower rate of strokes in dog owners, showed that owning a dog could heal a stroke as well as prevent one, and provided some evidence to back up the claim of saving money, the argument would be substantially stronger. As it currently stands, however, there is little reason to follow its recommendation.

Analysis

The introduction presents the components of the argument and establishes our permanent point of view: The argument is terrible. The first body paragraph identifies a very common assumption, namely that a correlation of two things implies a causal relationship. The second body paragraph criticizes a common unjustified leap of logic and uses a comparison with brushing teeth to make the criticism easier to understand. The third body paragraph addresses a third claim that the argument makes, and gives concrete reasons why that claim might not be true. Finally, the conclusion wraps it all up. The argument has been thoroughly demolished.

Argument Essay #3

> Excelsior Corporation provides subsidized daycare to its employees and is usually ranked among the top 10 companies for employee satisfaction. Excelsior's competitor, Sigma corporation, is hoping to boost its productivity and take some market share from Excelsior. Sigma intends to provide free daycare for its employees as the cornerstone of this strategy. Clearly, Sigma will soon command a bigger piece of market share than Excelsior.

Write a response in which you discuss the stated or unstated assumptions of the argument. Be sure to explain how the argument depends on these assumptions and what the implications are if the assumptions are unsupported.

The argument concludes that Sigma Corporation will soon have a greater share of the market than Excelsior Corporation. The evidence provided for this conclusion is that Excelsior gives subsidized daycare to its employees and is highly ranked in employee satisfaction, and Sigma plans to give its employees free daycare. The argument's logic is faulty, however, since it relies on several unsupported assumptions to bridge the gap between its premises and conclusion.

First of all, the argument does not address the possibility that the high employee satisfaction rating enjoyed by Excelsior is due to factors unrelated to its subsidized daycare. No direct causal relationship has been established between subsidized daycare and employee satisfaction. The author simply mentions the former and assumes a connection to the latter. But the high employee satisfaction rating could be caused by excellent salaries, health benefits, a good working environment, respectful treatment by company management, or a host of other factors. There is no reason to assume that subsidized daycare is the main explanation for employee satisfaction.

Furthermore, the argument fails to take into account that the market share currently possessed by Excelsior may have nothing to do with its high employee satisfaction ranking. We know nothing about Excelsior's business—what it does or how it does it. Excelsior's market share could be caused by patented designs, or excellent branding, or attractive pricing, or exceptional management. Nothing indicates that the satisfaction of the employees is directly responsible for the company's market share, and that Sigma could take some of that market share or boost its productivity by raising the satisfaction level of its employees.

Finally, the argument assumes that giving free daycare to Sigma's employees will increase their level of satisfaction and raise productivity. However, we don't know anything about the current levels of satisfaction of Sigma employees. The employees could be so demoralized by horrible working conditions, low salaries, and other negatives that free daycare won't be nearly enough to satisfy them. Or, alternatively, Sigma's employees might already be extremely satisfied, so much so that adding free daycare won't change things much. Perhaps Sigma is already ranked among the top five companies in employee satisfaction. All of these possibilities remain unexamined by the author.

To sum up, the argument that Sigma will steal market share from Excelsior by giving free daycare to its employees is quite weak. If the author demonstrated that Excelsior's level of employee satisfaction is due to its subsidized daycare, that Excelsior's current market share is caused by the satisfaction of its employees, and that free daycare will raise the level of satisfaction for Sigma employees, the argument would be on much firmer ground. Without additional support, however, there isn't much reason to believe the conclusion.

Analysis

Are you bored yet? Yet again, we have an essay that follows a very clear template. But more important, we have an essay that accomplishes the task, and would receive a high score on the GRE. This is an example of an argument that has a few tricky assumptions because they seem quite natural. For example, you might not have thought at first to criticize the idea that Excelsior's high employee satisfaction is the reason for its current market share, because that idea seems so natural. In other words, you yourself may have made that assumption. It's often difficult to identify the assumptions we ourselves are making. However, this essay did take that into account, and a solid paragraph of criticism resulted. Two other key assumptions were also identified and criticized, and the conclusion ties a bow on the essay, giving it the right tone of completion. Length is good. Transitions and organization are good. Do something similar on your GRE, and you'll score well on the Analytical Writing section.

6

Vocabulary

WORDS, WORDS, WORDS

As we mentioned in the Strategies chapter, one of the most important things you need to do to improve your score on the GRE Verbal section is to improve your vocabulary. There is simply no getting around it. It's also very important that you learn the techniques and apply them on the test, but relying on technique alone is like relying on exercise alone to keep you healthy. Exercise is great, but to be as healthy as possible you also have to focus on nutrition and eating the right things. Likewise, think of words as your GRE verbal nutrition. You need a healthy diet of vocabulary as well as good technique to get your maximum score on the Verbal section.

The best way to learn words is to read good books and magazines and newspapers throughout your life. However, since you presumably can't put off the GRE for a few more years while you beef up your reading, we need to find other ways.

THE HIT PARADE

The Hit Parade is a list of about 300 words that appear with great frequency on the GRE. It was compiled by analyzing every written GRE available, as well as dozens of computer-based GREs. This is the first task in your vocabulary preparation: Learn the Hit Parade cold. We have split the list into four groups, and each group of words is followed by quizzes, drills, and some sample questions that make use of those words. Make sure to spend some time learning each group before you tackle the practice material. Use the drills and questions to see how well you've mastered that particular group. When you have the first group down, move on to the second, and so on.

The Hit Parade also appears in our book *Cracking the New GRE*, but the drills in this book are slightly different. You can use these drills as extra practice if you already own *Cracking*.

BEYOND THE HIT PARADE

The Hit Parade is the beginning, not the end, of your vocabulary workout. Once you've mastered all the words in the Hit Parade, you should move on to the additional vocabulary lists we've provided. Remember, every new word you learn makes it more likely you'll score higher on the GRE Verbal section. Furthermore, learning vocabulary is the only part of your GRE preparation that is actually useful to you in grad school and in life.

HOW TO LEARN NEW WORDS

Before we give you the lists, we're going to talk a bit about how to learn words. There are many different ways because everyone is a little different, and what works well for someone else might not work well for you. In the end, you'll have to find the method that helps you the most. However, there are several things that most people find useful. Here are some suggestions.

- **Write them down.** In order to learn words, you have to make them your own. One of the first ways you do that is by writing them and their definitions down, rather than just reading them on a list. Whether you write them in a notebook or on flash cards or on the palm of your hand is your call, but write them down somewhere.

- **Make flash cards.** In addition to the benefits of writing down vocabulary mentioned above, making flash cards helps in several other ways. Most important is that flash cards are very portable. Many people study vocabulary in the same way they study for everything else: Sit down and stare. Those words are rarely going to end up in your long-term memory that way. Instead, focus on spending a little bit of time with each vocabulary word throughout the day. If you look over your words for a couple minutes before your commute, and then again for a couple minutes after your commute, your brain will have been working on those words in the meantime. By working on them again, you're telling your brain "Hey, these words are important! They keep coming up, so you better remember them." We have a set of fantastic GRE-specific flashcards that were recently released. Check them out at your local bookstore.

- **Connect flash cards and ideas.** Say you're learning words like *panacea* and *nostrum*. A panacea is a cure-all, something that cures everything. A nostrum is a quack medicine that was probably advertised as a panacea, but isn't one. Rather than just keeping those words as abstract concepts, connect them to objects in your life. Tape those flashcards up next to your medicine cabinet. Next time you walk by, your brain will start to connect those words to medicine. If the word nostrum made you think of a particular sham medicine ("Order SuperMagnetPills now and receive a MagicBandage for free!"), then draw or cut out a picture of that medicine and paste it to your flash card. If a word makes you think of a particular person, put a picture of that person or write his or her name on that flashcard. Give your brain multiple ways of remembering a word. Our Princeton Review flashcards are written this way, to help you memorize the meanings using helpful techniques and tricks.

- **Use a dictionary.** You probably have a dictionary, but you might not have a paperback dictionary that you can carry with you easily. Get one. You're much more likely to look up a word and check its definition if you have easy access to a dictionary. A dictionary will also give you secondary meanings of words that you might not have known, as well as information about their history and etymology that may make it easier to remember them.

- **Say them out loud.** This is related to writing them down, because saying them aloud is another way that you make words your own. It also brings another sense into play (hearing) and makes it more likely that you'll remember the meaning of the word. (Just don't say words aloud during your test. The other test takers in the room may hurt you.)

- **Create mnemonic devices.** A mnemonic device is a memory trick that helps you remember something by tying it to a rhyme, story, sentence, song, acronym, or anything that you already know or can remember more easily. A simple example of a mnemonic device that many students are taught is the sentence "My very educated mother just sliced up nine pickles," used to remember the order of the planets from the sun. Making a mnemonic is one of the best ways to nail down those words that keep eluding you no matter how many times you seem to read their definitions.

- **Visualize.** Another great way to remember words is to visualize them—to associate them with some image. One of the more creative visualizations we've heard in our classes involved the word *sycophant*, which is someone who attempts to win advancement by flattering influential people—basically, a brownnoser. This student imagined a psychotic elephant putting its trunk into a giant puddle of mud—brownnosing—and then, every time she saw the word *sycophant*, she thought of her "psycho-elephant." We doubt she'll ever forget the meaning of that word.

- **Look at word roots.** You can also help yourself remember words by learning a little bit about their etymology. Many English words have prefixes and suffixes that come from Latin and Greek. So perhaps you remember the word *anachronism* (something out of its proper time, like an automobile showing up in a movie about the eighteenth century) by remembering that *chron* is a root that means time. For example, think of the words *chronology*, *synchronize*, *chronic*, and others.

- **Make sentences with them.** One of the hard things about learning words from lists is that the words have no context. Writing down a sentence for each word not only ensures that you understand the definition, it gives you context for the meaning of the word, which makes it easier to remember. When you make a sentence like, "My grandfather was from a small, bucolic town in Kansas," it's easier to remember that bucolic means "rustic, pastoral, rural."

- **Use them.** Try to incorporate as many new words as you can into your writing and your conversation. Not only will you impress people with your superior command of language (unless they want to smack you for showing off), you'll truly be internalizing these words and making them part of your permanent vocabulary. Ultimately, it's through constant reinforcement that you expand your vocabulary.

- **Make it a priority.** This is just one final reminder that in order to increase your vocabulary you have to work at it. If you don't put effort into learning words, don't expect to get results. You'll just be wasting your time. Remember, there is no way to get a high score on the GRE Verbal section without a strong vocabulary, and there is no way to get a huge improvement in your score without expanding your vocabulary.

So, bring on the words!

HIT PARADE GROUP 1

aberrant	adjective	deviating from the norm (noun form: *aberration*)
abscond	verb	to depart clandestinely; to steal off and hide
alacrity	noun	eager and enthusiastic willingness
anomaly	noun	deviation from the normal order, form, or rule; abnormality (adj. form: *anomalous*)
approbation	noun	an expression of approval or praise
arduous	adjective	strenuous; taxing; requiring significant effort
assuage	verb	to ease or lessen; to appease or pacify
audacious	adjective	daring and fearless; recklessly bold (noun form: *audacity*)
austere	adjective	without adornment; bare; severely simple; ascetic (noun form: *austerity*)
axiomatic	adjective	taken as a given; possessing self-evident truth (noun form: *axiom*)
canonical	adjective	following or in agreement with accepted, traditional standards (noun form: *canon*)
capricious	adjective	inclined to change one's mind impulsively; erratic; unpredictable
censure	verb	to criticize severely; to officially rebuke
chicanery	noun	trickery or subterfuge
connoisseur	noun	an informed and astute judge in matters of taste; expert
convoluted	adjective	complex or complicated
disabuse	verb	to undeceive; to set right
discordant	adjective	conflicting; dissonant or harsh in sound
disparate	adjective	fundamentally distinct or dissimilar
effrontery	noun	extreme boldness; presumptuousness
eloquent	adjective	well-spoken; expressive; articulate (noun form: *eloquence*)
enervate	verb	to weaken; to reduce in vitality
ennui	noun	dissatisfaction and restlessness resulting from boredom or apathy
equivocate	verb	to use ambiguous language with a deceptive intent (adj. form: *equivocal*)

erudite	adjective	very learned; scholarly (noun form: *erudition*)
exculpate	verb	exonerate; to clear of blame
exigent	adjective	urgent; pressing; requiring immediate action or attention
extemporaneous	adjective	improvised; done without preparation
filibuster	noun	intentional obstruction, esp. using prolonged speechmaking to delay legislative action
fulminate	verb	to loudly attack or denounce
ingenuous	adjective	artless; frank and candid; lacking in sophistication
inured	adjective	accustomed to accepting something undesirable
irascible	adjective	easily angered; prone to temperamental outbursts
laud	verb	to praise highly (adj. form: *laudatory*)
lucid	adjective	clear; easily understood
magnanimity	noun	the quality of being generously noble in mind and heart, esp. in forgiving (adj. form: *magnanimous*)
martial	adjective	associated with war and the armed forces
mundane	adjective	of the world; typical of or concerned with the ordinary
nascent	adjective	coming into being; in early developmental stages
nebulous	adjective	vague; cloudy; lacking clearly defined form
neologism	noun	a new word, expression, or usage; the creation or use of new words or senses
noxious	adjective	harmful; injurious
obtuse	adjective	lacking sharpness of intellect; not clear or precise in thought or expression
obviate	verb	to anticipate and make unnecessary
onerous	adjective	troubling; burdensome
paean	noun	a song or hymn of praise and thanksgiving
parody	noun	a humorous imitation intended for ridicule or comic effect, esp. in literature and art
perennial	adjective	recurrent through the year or many years; happening repeatedly
perfidy	noun	intentional breach of faith; treachery (adj. form: *perfidious*)
perfunctory	adjective	cursory; done without care or interest

perspicacious	adjective	acutely perceptive; having keen discernment (noun form: *perspicacity*)
prattle	verb	to babble meaninglessly; to talk in an empty and idle manner
precipitate	adjective	acting with excessive haste or impulse
precipitate	verb	to cause or happen before anticipated or required
predilection	noun	a disposition in favor of something; preference
prescience	noun	foreknowledge of events; knowing of events prior to their occurring (adj. form: *prescient*)
prevaricate	verb	to deliberately avoid the truth; to mislead
qualms	noun	misgivings; reservations; causes for hesitancy
recant	verb	to retract, esp. a previously held belief
refute	verb	to disprove; to successfully argue against
relegate	verb	to forcibly assign, esp. to a lower place or position
reticent	adjective	quiet; reserved; reluctant to express thoughts and feelings
solicitous	adjective	concerned and attentive; eager
sordid	adjective	characterized by filth, grime, or squalor; foul
sporadic	adjective	occurring only occasionally, or in scattered instances
squander	verb	to waste by spending or using irresponsibly
static	adjective	not moving, active, or in motion; at rest
stupefy	verb	to stun, baffle, or amaze
stymie	verb	to block; thwart
synthesis	noun	the combination of parts to make a whole (verb form: *synthesize*)
torque	noun	a force that causes rotation
tortuous	adjective	winding; twisting; excessively complicated
truculent	adjective	fierce and cruel; eager to fight
veracity	noun	truthfulness; honesty
virulent	adjective	extremely harmful or poisonous; bitterly hostile or antagonistic
voracious	adjective	having an insatiable appetite for an activity or pursuit; ravenous
waver	verb	to move to and fro; to sway; to be unsettled in opinion

QUICK QUIZ #1

Define the following words.

Assuage: _____

_____

Axiomatic: _____

_____

Ennui: _____

_____

Paean: _____

_____

Perspicacious: _____

_____

Voracious: _____

_____

Capricious: _____

_____

Precipitate: _____

_____

Virulent: _____

_____

Prevaricate: _____

_____

Equivocate: _____

_____

Obviate: _____

_____

Tortuous: _____

_____

Laud: _____

_____

Mundane: _____

_____

QUICK QUIZ #2

Match the following words to their definitions. The answers are on page 236.

A. Aberrant   _____ Urgent; pressing

B. Disabuse   _____ To babble meaninglessly

C. Prescience   _____ Truthfulness; honesty

D. Solicitous   _____ Harmful; injurious

E. Veracity   _____ To undeceive; to set right

F. Audacious   _____ Deviating from the norm

G. Noxious   _____ Misgivings; reservations

H. Qualms   _____ Coming into being

I. Nascent   _____ To stun, baffle, or amaze

J. Enervate   _____ Daring and fearless; recklessly bold

K. Exigent   _____ Foreknowledge of events

L. Prattle   _____ To loudly attack or denounce

M. Fulminate   _____ To weaken; to reduce in vitality

N. Stupefy   _____ Concerned and attentive

QUICK QUIZ #3

Try the following questions. The answers are on page 236.

1. While health care reform was being debated in the legislature, the opposition repeatedly _____ to filibuster the bill.

   - ☐ refused
   - ☐ endeavored
   - ☐ consented
   - ☐ strived
   - ☐ declined
   - ☐ hesitated

2. Given the lack of popular protest against the strident and polarized character of modern political discourse, observers must ask whether the American people have become _____ to it or are simply apathetic.

   - ☐ drawn
   - ☐ antipathetic
   - ☐ inured
   - ☐ habituated
   - ☐ averse
   - ☐ committed

3. The nation's recent ill-starred series of foreign entanglements, each undertaken on a more tenuous basis than the last, cautioned the president, a voracious acolyte of history's lessons, against the danger of taking _____ action.

   - ☐ precipitate
   - ☐ prudent
   - ☐ deliberate
   - ☐ compulsory
   - ☐ martial
   - ☐ rash

4. The stainless steel fabrication process requires the machinist to be extremely _____; even a measurement off by less than the width of a hair can make the entire project unusable.

pristine
tenacious
nice
feckless
perfunctory

5. Given that Saturday Night Live has been on the air since the 1970s, it is unsurprising that it has become somewhat (i) _____. For example, since Dan Aykroyd and Chevy Chase's celebrated impersonations of Presidents Nixon and Ford, respectively, it has become (ii) _____ for the program frequently to feature (iii) _____ of the current president.

Blank (i)	Blank (ii)	Blank (iii)
progressive	anomalous	biographies
temporal	perfunctory	analyses
ossified	superfluous	parodies

6. Altruism is thought by some to be a purely human trait, developed during our evolution as a tribal species. However, studies of other animals (i) _____ this notion. Chimps will adopt orphaned infants, and many species of birds will warn others, at the risk of exposing themselves, when a predator approaches the flock. These displays of animal altruism (ii) _____ that animals other than humans also evolved to exhibit this trait.

Blank (i)	Blank (ii)
belie	assuage
confirm	intimate
promote	rescind

7. Books on statistics frequently use the (i) _____ paradox between attitudes about flying and driving as evidence of the public's (ii) _____ understanding of probability. Even though fliers have a much lower risk of injury or death than drivers, people consistently attest to having fewer (iii) _____ about driving than flying.

Blank (i)	Blank (ii)	Blank (iii)
variegated	nebulous	disputes
ostensible	nefarious	antitheses
sibilant	obligatory	qualms

8. During the series between the Hawks and the Bears, the Bears' coach wrongly accused Archer, the Hawks' star player, of using (i) _____ performance enhancing drugs. At the inquiry, despite Archer's eloquent (ii) _____ of his innocence, the tribunal chose to censure him as punishment. A few months later however, Archer was (iii) _____ when another player from the Bears confessed his coach's perfidy.

Blank (i)	Blank (ii)	Blank (iii)
deleterious	attestation	consternated
illicit	repudiation	habituated
irregular	abridgement	exculpated

9. Poverty can be a function not only of absolute wealth, but also of comparison in a community; in an area with _____ income levels, those at the very bottom will suffer cost-of-living increases brought on by those in the middle and top income brackets.

disparate
reticent
arduous
onerous
wavering

10. Though Adam was incredulous upon hearing Madam Sofia's psychic reading, after a few weeks had passed, he was (i) _____ by how remarkably (ii) _____ she had turned out to be.

Blank (i)	Blank (ii)
dubious	prescient
stupefied	exhaustive
blasé	mundane

HIT PARADE GROUP 2

abate	verb	to lessen in intensity or degree
accolade	noun	an expression of praise
adulation	noun	excessive praise; intense adoration
aesthetic	adjective	dealing with, appreciative of, or responsive to art or the beautiful
ameliorate	verb	to make better or more tolerable
ascetic	noun	one who practices rigid self-denial, esp. as an act of religious devotion
avarice	noun	greed, esp. for wealth (adj. form: *avaricious*)
axiom	noun	a universally recognized principle (adj. form; *axiomatic*)
bucolic	adjective	rustic and pastoral; characteristic of rural areas and their inhabitants
burgeon	verb	to grow rapidly or flourish
cacophony	noun	harsh, jarring, discordant sound; dissonance (adj. form: *cacophonous*)
canon	noun	an established set of principles or code of laws, often religious in nature (adj. form: *canonical*)
castigation	noun	severe criticism or punishment (verb form: *castigate*)
catalyst	noun	a substance that accelerates the rate of a chemical reaction without itself changing; a person or thing that causes change
caustic	adjective	burning or stinging; causing corrosion
chary	adjective	wary; cautious; sparing
cogent	adjective	appealing forcibly to the mind or reason; convincing
complaisance	noun	the willingness to comply with the wishes of others (adj. form: *complaisant*)
contentious	adjective	argumentative; quarrelsome; causing controversy or disagreement
contrite	adjective	regretful; penitent; seeking forgiveness (noun form: *contrition*)
culpable	adjective	deserving blame (noun form: *culpability*)

dearth	noun	smallness of quantity or number; scarcity; a lack
demur	verb	to question or oppose
didactic	adjective	intended to teach or instruct
discretion	noun	cautious reserve in speech; ability to make responsible decisions (adj. form: *discreet*)
disinterested	adjective	free of bias or self-interest; impartial
dogmatic	adjective	expressing a rigid opinion based on unproved or unprovable principles (noun form: *dogma*)
ebullience	adjective	the quality of lively or enthusiastic expression of thoughts and feelings (adj. form: *ebullient*)
eclectic	adjective	composed of elements drawn from various sources
elegy	noun	a mournful poem, esp. one lamenting the dead (adj. form: *elegiac*)
emollient	adjective/ noun	soothing, esp. to the skin; making less harsh; mollifying; an agent that softens or smoothes the skin
empirical	adjective	based on observation or experiment
enigmatic	adjective	mysterious; obscure; difficult to understand (noun form: *enigma*)
ephemeral	adjective	brief; fleeting
esoteric	adjective	intended for or understood by a small, specific group
eulogy	noun	a speech honoring the dead (verb form: *eulogize*)
exonerate	verb	to remove blame
facetious	adjective	playful; humorous
fallacy	noun	an invalid or incorrect notion; a mistaken belief (adj. form: *fallacious*)
furtive	adjective	marked by stealth; covert; surreptitious
gregarious	adjective	sociable; outgoing; enjoying the company of other people
harangue	verb/noun	to deliver a pompous speech or tirade; a long, pompous speech
heretical	adjective	violating accepted dogma or convention (noun form: *heresy*)

hyperbole	noun	an exaggerated statement, often used as a figure of speech (adj. form: *hyperbolic*)
impecunious	adjective	lacking funds; without money
incipient	adjective	beginning to come into being or to become apparent
inert	adjective	unmoving; lethargic; sluggish
innocuous	adjective	harmless; causing no damage
intransigent	adjective	refusing to compromise (noun form: *intransigence*)
inveigle	verb	to obtain by deception or flattery
morose	adjective	sad; sullen; melancholy
odious	adjective	evoking intense aversion or dislike
opaque	adjective	impenetrable by light; not reflecting light
oscillation	noun	the act or state of swinging back and forth with a steady, uninterrupted rhythm (verb form: *oscillate*)
penurious	adjective	penny-pinching; excessively thrifty; ungenerous
pernicious	adjective	extremely harmful; potentially causing death
peruse	verb	to examine with great care (noun form: *perusal*)
pious	adjective	extremely reverent or devout; showing strong religious devotion (noun form: *piety*)
precursor	noun	one that precedes and indicates or announces another
preen	verb	to dress up; to primp; to groom oneself with elaborate care
prodigious	adjective	abundant in size, force, or extent; extraordinary
prolific	adjective	producing large volumes or amounts; productive
putrefy	verb	to rot; to decay and give off a foul odor (adj. form: *putrid*)
quaff	verb	to drink deeply
quiescence	noun	stillness; motionlessness; quality of being at rest (adj. form: *quiescent*)
redoubtable	adjective	awe-inspiring; worthy of honor
sanction	noun/verb	authoritative permission or approval; a penalty intended to enforce compliance; to give permission or authority to

satire	noun	a literary work that ridicules or criticizes a human vice through humor or derision (adj. form: *satirical*)
squalid	adjective	sordid; wretched and dirty as from neglect (noun form: *squalor*)
stoic	adjective	indifferent to or unaffected by pleasure or pain; steadfast (noun form: *stoicism*)
supplant	verb	to take the place of; supersede
torpid	adjective	lethargic; sluggish; dormant (noun form: *torpor*)
ubiquitous	adjective	existing everywhere at the same time; constantly encountered; widespread
urbane	adjective	sophisticated; refined; elegant (noun form: *urbanity*)
vilify	verb	to defame; to characterize harshly
viscous	adjective	thick; sticky (noun form: *viscosity*)

QUICK QUIZ #4

Define the following words.

Pernicious: _____

_____

Eulogy: _____

_____

Aesthetic: _____

_____

Castigation: _____

_____

Prodigious: _____

_____

Penurious: _____

_____

Satire: _____

Ebullience: _____

Incipient: _____

Penurious: _____

Quaff: _____

Emollient: _____

Harangue: _____

Inveigle: _____

Facetious: _____

Caustic: _____

Cogent: _____

QUICK QUIZ #5

Match the following words to their definitions. The answers are on page 236.

A. Pious   _____ Drawn from different sources or styles

B. Intransigent   _____ Evoking intense aversion or dislike

C. Torpid   _____ To examine with great care

D. Eclectic   _____ To defame; to characterize harshly

E. Heretical   _____ Unwilling to compromise

F. Peruse   _____ Impenetrable by light

G. Culpable   _____ Lethargic; sluggish

H. Ascetic   _____ Extremely reverent or devout

I. Enigmatic   _____ Argumentative; quarrelsome

J. Supplant   _____ Mysterious; obscure

K. Opaque   _____ Deserving blame

L. Odious   _____ One who practices rigid self-denial

M. Vilify   _____ Violating accepted dogma or convention

N. Contentious   _____ To take the place of

Quick Quiz #6

Try the following questions. The answers are on page 236.

1. The two colleagues made a concerted effort to steer clear of the ongoing argument between their respective supervisors, preferring instead to continue their _____ until the hearing.

☐ neutrality
☐ stoicism
☐ cynicism
☐ skepticism
☐ disinterest
☐ disagreement

2. Roger's personality was described by all of his literary critics as _____, but this description was widely regarded as hyperbole by those who knew him well and ultimately came to appreciate his even-handed and flexible approach to his analyses.

☐ pernicious
☐ facetious
☐ doctrinaire
☐ dogmatic
☐ sarcastic
☐ didactic

3. The naked _____ endemic in our corporate culture was well documented in the criminal trial of the CEO, who confessed to embezzling employee retirement funds in order to purchase his third Italian villa.

☐ opprobrium
☐ magnanimity
☐ avarice
☐ altruism
☐ cupidity
☐ conservatism

4. The retiree's testimonial dinner was a great mixture of (i) _____ that highlighted his many accomplishments as well as some good-natured (ii) _____ that caused everyone to break into laughter.

Blank (i)	Blank (ii)
insults	gravity
accolades	malevolence
inquiries	satire

5. Considering the (i) _____ upbringing he sings about in his ferociously bitter lyrics, it was a total surprise to his fans that Randy's autobiography had such a (ii) _____ tone when describing his childhood.

Blank (i)	Blank (ii)
wretched	unhappy
substantial	innocuous
successful	troubled

6. For some, the power of omens and signs is easy to dismiss as (i) _____ belief, based on (ii) _____ evidence, that the future can be foretold by specific, unrelated events. For others, though, those same omens and signs are clear and reliable markers of (iii) _____ events.

Blank (i)	Blank (ii)	Blank (iii)
a dogmatic	empirical	incipient
an irrational	substantiated	hypothetical
a heretical	circumstantial	erroneous

7. The hostilities between the party's candidates began to (i) _____ once the primary election was over and they no longer had any reason to (ii) _____ each other in their intense fight for the nomination.

Blank (i)	Blank (ii)
reconvene	champion for
escalate	abrogate
abate	vilify

8. At every single public event, the country legend appeared in his (i) _____ boots and cowboy hat. However, those who knew him personally could attest to the fact that his fashion sense was a bit more (ii) _____, with items in his closet ranging from a (iii) _____ old sports jersey to brand-new, hand-tailored suits.

Blank (i)	Blank (ii)	Blank (iii)
customary	garish	bedraggled
profound	staid	pristine
stereotypical	eclectic	imposing

9. After failing to advance to the final round of the state spelling bee for the third year in a row, Heather's mood could only be described as _____.

morose
chary
contrite
impecunious
detestable

10. The success of the espionage mission depended on the ability of the mole to feign (i) _____ in order to ingratiate herself within the company ranks. Otherwise, all the mission plans would be compromised and the spies would have to (ii) _____ the mission.

Blank (i)	Blank (ii)
nescience	actualize
irascibility	truncate
complaisance	execute

HIT PARADE GROUP 3

acumen	noun	keen, accurate judgment or insight
adulterate	verb	to reduce purity by combining with inferior ingredients
amalgamate	verb	to combine several elements into a whole (noun form: *amalgamation*)
archaic	adjective	outdated; associated with an earlier, perhaps more primitive, time
aver	verb	to state as a fact; to declare or assert
bolster	verb	to provide support or reinforcement
bombastic	adjective	pompous; grandiloquent (noun form: *bombast*)
diatribe	noun	a harsh denunciation
dissemble	verb	to disguise or conceal; to mislead
eccentric	adjective	departing from norms or conventions
endemic	adjective	characteristic of or often found in a particular locality, region, or people
evanescent	adjective	tending to disappear like vapor; vanishing
exacerbate	verb	to make worse or more severe
fervent	adjective	greatly emotional or zealous (noun form: *fervor*)
fortuitous	adjective	happening by accident or chance
germane	adjective	relevant to the subject at hand; appropriate in subject matter
grandiloquence	noun	pompous speech or expression (adj. form: *grandiloquent*)
hackneyed	adjective	rendered trite or commonplace by frequent usage
halcyon	adjective	calm and peaceful
hedonism	noun	devotion to pleasurable pursuits, esp. to the pleasures of the senses (a *hedonist* is someone who pursues pleasure)
hegemony	noun	the consistent dominance of one state or ideology over others
iconoclast	noun	one who attacks or undermines traditional conventions or institutions
idolatrous	adjective	given to intense or excessive devotion to something (noun form: *idolatry*)

impassive	adjective	revealing no emotion
imperturbable	adjective	marked by extreme calm, impassivity, and steadiness
implacable	adjective	not capable of being appeased or significantly changed
impunity	noun	immunity from punishment or penalty
inchoate	adjective	in an initial stage; not fully formed
infelicitous	adjective	unfortunate; inappropriate
insipid	adjective	without taste or flavor; lacking in spirit; bland
loquacious	adjective	extremely talkative (noun form: *loquacity*)
luminous	adjective	characterized by brightness and the emission of light
malevolent	adjective	having or showing often vicious ill will, spite, or hatred (noun form: *malevolence*)
malleable	adjective	capable of being shaped or formed; tractable; pliable
mendacity	noun	the condition of being untruthful; dishonesty (adj. form: *mendacious*)
meticulous	adjective	characterized by extreme care and precision; attentive to detail
misanthrope	noun	one who hates all other humans (adj. form: *misanthropic*)
mitigate	verb	to make or become less severe or intense; to moderate
obdurate	adjective	unyielding; hardhearted; intractable
obsequious	adjective	exhibiting a fawning attentiveness
occlude	verb	to obstruct or block
opprobrium	noun	disgrace; contempt; scorn
pedagogy	noun	the profession or principles of teaching, or instructing
pedantic	adjective	the parading of learning; excessive attention to minutiae and formal rules
penury	noun	poverty; destitution
pervasive	adjective	having the tendency to permeate or spread throughout

pine	verb	to yearn intensely; to languish; to lose vigor
pirate	verb	to illegally use or reproduce
pith	noun	the essential or central part
pithy	adjective	precise and brief
placate	verb	to appease; to calm by making concessions
platitude	noun	a superficial remark, esp. one offered as meaningful
plummet	verb	to plunge or drop straight down
polemical	adjective	controversial; argumentative
prodigal	adjective	recklessly wasteful; extravagant; profuse; lavish
profuse	adjective	given or coming forth abundantly; extravagant
proliferate	verb	to grow or increase swiftly and abundantly
queries	noun	questions; inquiries; doubts in the mind; reservations
querulous	adjective	prone to complaining or grumbling; peevish
rancorous	adjective	characterized by bitter, long-lasting resentment (noun form: *rancor*)
recalcitrant	adjective	obstinately defiant of authority; difficult to manage
repudiate	verb	to refuse to have anything to do with; disown
rescind	verb	to invalidate; to repeal; to retract
reverent	adjective	marked by, feeling, or expressing a feeling of profound awe and respect (noun form: *reverance*)
rhetoric	noun	the art or study of effective use of language for communication and persuasion
salubrious	adjective	promoting health or well-being
solvent	adjective	able to meet financial obligations; able to dissolve another substance
specious	adjective	seeming true, but actually being fallacious; misleadingly attractive; plausible but false
spurious	adjective	lacking authenticity or validity; false; counterfeit
subpoena	noun	a court order requiring appearance and/or testimony
succinct	adjective	brief; concise
superfluous	adjective	exceeding what is sufficient or necessary

surfeit	noun/verb	an overabundant supply; excess; to feed or supply to excess
tenacity	noun	the quality of adherence or persistence to something valued; persistent determination (adj. form: *tenacious*)
tenuous	adjective	having little substance or strength; flimsy; weak
tirade	noun	a long and extremely critical speech; a harsh denunciation
transient	adjective	fleeting; passing quickly; brief
zealous	adjective	fervent; ardent; impassioned; devoted to a cause (a *zealot* is a zealous person)

QUICK QUIZ #7

Define the following words.

Tirade: _____

_____

Solvent: _____

_____

Idolatrous: _____

_____

Opprobrium: _____

_____

Obsequious: _____

_____

Luminous: _____

_____

Tenuous: _____

_____

Reverent: _____
_____

Iconoclast: _____
_____

Fervent: _____
_____

Amalgamate: _____
_____

Repudiate: _____
_____

Specious: _____
_____

Pervasive: _____
_____

Surfeit: _____
_____

Hedonism: _____
_____

QUICK QUIZ #8

Match the following words to their definitions. The answers are on page 237.

A. Zealous   _____ The essential or central part

B. Malleable   _____ Tending to disappear like vapor

C. Grandiloquence   _____ Brief; concise

D. Proliferate   _____ Controversial; argumentative

E. Evanescent   _____ Lacking authenticity; false; counterfeit

F. Impassive   _____ Capable of being shaped or formed

G. Misanthrope   _____ Fervent; ardent; devoted to a cause

H. Tenacity   _____ Persistent determination

I. Spurious   _____ One who hates other human beings

J. Pith   _____ Revealing no emotion

K. Querulous   _____ Pompous speech or expression

L. Specious   _____ To grow or increase swiftly

M. Polemical   _____ Prone to complaining; whiny

N. Succinct   _____ Seemingly true, but actually false

QUICK QUIZ #9

Try the following questions. The answers are on page 237.

1. After months of speculation drove it upward, the pharmaceutical company's stock price _____ upon news that its experimental drug did not receive governmental approval.

   - ☐ stymied
   - ☐ assuaged
   - ☐ plummeted
   - ☐ rebounded
   - ☐ retreated
   - ☐ ascended

2. The researcher's colleagues marveled at how he could review income tax law in such a _____ manner at work, yet complete his own tax return is such a careless way at home.

   - ☐ meticulous
   - ☐ plodding
   - ☐ unhurried
   - ☐ lackadaisical
   - ☐ painstaking
   - ☐ efficient

3. Faced with a _____ of subpar therapy choices, the doctor consulted a colleague, who, once she had reviewed all patient records and available research on the subject, helped the doctor wade through the multitude of options and actually suggested a course of action the doctor had not considered.

   - ☐ dearth
   - ☐ potpourri
   - ☐ exiguousness
   - ☐ confusion
   - ☐ surfeit
   - ☐ overabundance

4. The Pashupatinath temple in Nepal contains the most frequently used cremation site in the Kathmandu Valley. Among its attractions are a two-tiered pagoda where the (i) _____ are able to worship. Images of Ganesh, with his huge trunk and regal bearing, (ii) _____ the walls. The temple is not accessible to non-Hindus, but an excellent (iii) _____ can be seen from the opposite riverbank.

Blank (i)	Blank (ii)	Blank (iii)
fortuitous	adorn	vista
reverent	placate	paragon
luminous	bolster	zenith

5. Many car rental companies will not rent vehicles to customers under the age of 25, claiming that these drivers have higher than average rates of accidents, rendering the risk of loss too great. This argument, however, is (i) _____; senior citizens also have higher than average rates of accidents, and yet their rental privileges are not (ii) _____.

Blank (i)	Blank (ii)
eccentric	adulterated
pedantic	restricted
spurious	dissembled

6. It is ironic that Mary Shelley's focus on Victor's passivity renders the reader incapable of sympathizing with the protagonist, much as Dostoyevsky's depiction of the darkest places in the human psyche once caused his empathy for his characters to be _____.

rescinded
commiserated
occluded
disregarded
lambasted

7. Although Marian thought that the oft-repeated tale was (i) _____, Barbara never tired of telling the story, believing that the lessons it contained were timeless and (ii) _____.

Blank (i)	Blank (ii)
hackneyed	archaic
inchoate	immutable
substantial	evanescent

8. While some in the field of psychology believe that intelligence is a purely genetic trait, and that any new research will demonstrate this fact, the current research on the nature versus nurture debate is by no means (i) _____. Studies on race, environment, and other factors have shown that heredity and the environment one grows up in affect intelligence. One's intelligence can be (ii) _____ by a strongly enriching environment, or neglected by an extremely impoverished one. Studies on genetics are also not decisive; there is not one single "intelligence gene," but more likely there is a (iii) _____ of different genetic markers.

Blank (i)	Blank (ii)	Blank (iii)
incipient	exscinded	maladaptive liturgy
incontrovertible	cultivated	refulgent sojourn
indeterminate	descanted	complicated amalgam

9. Ellen and Suzanne had not planned to have lunch together on Friday, and thus running into each other at the sushi restaurant was simply _____ occurrence

an infelicitous
a fortuitous
a profuse
a transient
a suggestive

10. Many critics of Vice President Al Gore point to the (i) _____ claim that he "invented the internet" in an attempt to discredit him. While, at face value, it seems doubtful that a politician could be responsible for a technological breakthrough, an argument can be made that Gore, as an early champion of the power of technology to drive political change, helped create the vision of a world with high-speed computing and communications. In 1991, he crafted the *High Performance and Computing Act* which led to the development of the National Information Infrastructure, which was (ii) _____ the later telecommunications web which came to be called the internet.

Blank (i)	Blank (ii)
dubious	an alternative to
indefatigable	a precursor to
guileless	a surrogate for

HIT PARADE GROUP 4

acerbic	adjective	having a sour or bitter taste or character; sharp; biting
aggrandize	verb	to increase in intensity, power, influence, or prestige
alchemy	noun	a medieval science aimed at the transmutation of metals, esp. base metals into gold (an *alchemist* is one who practices alchemy)
amenable	adjective	agreeable; responsive to suggestion
anachronism	noun	something or someone out of place in terms of historical or chronological context
astringent	adjective/noun	having a tightening effect on living tissue; harsh; severe
bombast	noun	self-important or pompous writing or speech (adj. form: *bombastic*)
contiguous	adjective	sharing a border; touching; adjacent
convention	noun	a generally agreed-upon practice or attitude
credulous	adjective	tending to believe too readily; gullible (noun form: *credulity*)
cynicism	noun	an attitude or quality of belief that all people are motivated by selfishness (adj. form: *cynical*)
decorum	noun	polite or appropriate conduct or behavior (adj. form: *decorous*)
derision	noun	scorn; ridicule; contemptuous treatment (adj. form: *derisive*; verb form: *deride*)
desiccate	verb	to dry out or dehydrate; to make dry or dull
dilettante	noun	one with an amateurish or superficial interest in the arts or a branch of knowledge
disparage	verb	to slight or belittle
divulge	verb	to disclose something secret
fawn	verb	to flatter or praise excessively
flout	verb	to show contempt for, as in a rule or convention
garrulous	adjective	pointlessly talkative, talking too much

glib	adjective	marked by ease or informality; nonchalant; lacking in depth; superficial
hubris	noun	overbearing presumption or pride; arrogance
imminent	adjective	about to happen; impending
immutable	adjective	not capable of change
impetuous	adjective	hastily or rashly energetic; impulsive and vehement
indifferent	adjective	having no interest or concern; showing no bias or prejudice
inimical	adjective	damaging; harmful; injurious
intractable	adjective	not easily managed or directed; stubborn; obstinate
intrepid	adjective	steadfast and courageous
laconic	adjective	using few words; terse
maverick	noun	an independent individual who does not go along with a group or party
mercurial	adjective	characterized by rapid and unpredictable change in mood
mollify	verb	to calm or soothe; to reduce in emotional intensity
neophyte	noun	a recent convert; a beginner; novice
obfuscate	verb	to deliberately obscure; to make confusing
obstinate	adjective	stubborn; hardheaded; uncompromising
ostentatious	adjective	characterized by or given to pretentious display; showy
pervade	verb	to permeate throughout (adj. form: *pervasive*)
phlegmatic	adjective	calm; sluggish; unemotional
plethora	noun	an overabundance; a surplus
pragmatic	adjective	practical rather than idealistic
presumptuous	adjective	overstepping due bounds (as of propriety or courtesy); taking liberties
pristine	adjective	pure; uncorrupted; clean
probity	noun	adherence to highest principles; complete and confirmed integrity; uprightness
proclivity	noun	a natural predisposition or inclination
profligate	adjective	excessively wasteful; recklessly extravagant (noun form: *profligacy*)

propensity	noun	a natural inclination or tendency, penchant
prosaic	adjective	dull; lacking in spirit or imagination
pungent	adjective	characterized by a strong, sharp smell or taste
quixotic	adjective	foolishly impractical; marked by lofty romantic ideals
quotidian	adjective	occurring or recurring daily; commonplace
rarefy	verb	to make or become thin, less dense; to refine
recondite	adjective	hidden; concealed; difficult to understand; obscure
refulgent	adjective	radiant; shiny; brilliant
renege	verb	to fail to honor a commitment; to go back on a promise
sedulous	adjective	diligent; persistent; hardworking
shard	noun	a piece of broken pottery or glass
soporific	adjective	causing drowsiness; tending to induce sleep
sparse	adjective	thin; not dense; arranged at widely spaced intervals
spendthrift	noun	one who spends money wastefully
subtle	adjective	not obvious; elusive; difficult to discern
tacit	adjective	implied; not explicitly stated
terse	adjective	brief and concise in wording
tout	verb	to publicly praise or promote
trenchant	adjective	sharply perceptive; keen; penetrating
unfeigned	adjective	genuine; not false or hypocritical
untenable	adjective	indefensible; not viable; uninhabitable
vacillate	verb	to waver indecisively between one course of action or opinion and another; waver
variegated	adjective	multicolored; characterized by a variety of patches of different color
vexation	noun	annoyance; irritation (noun form: *vex*)
vigilant	adjective	alertly watchful (noun form: *vigilance*)
vituperate	verb	to use harsh condemnatory language; to abuse or censure severely or abusively; berate
volatile	adjective	readily changing to a vapor; changeable; fickle; explosive (noun form: *volatility*)

QUICK QUIZ #10

Define the following words.

Soporific: _____

_____

Rarefy: _____

_____

Ostentatious: _____

_____

Variegated: _____

_____

Unfeigned: _____

_____

Terse: _____

_____

Glib: _____

_____

Disparage: _____

_____

Cynicism: _____

_____

Contiguous: _____

_____

Neophyte: _____

_____

Mercurial: _____

_____

Flout: _____

_____

Volatile: _____

_____

Phlegmatic: _____

_____

Mollify: _____

_____

Vexation : _____

_____

QUICK QUIZ #11

Match the following words to their definitions. The answers are on page 237.

A. Obstinate	_____	To go back on a promise
B. Sedulous	_____	Using few words; terse
C. Pungent	_____	One who spends money wastefully
D. Fawn	_____	To dry out or dehydrate
E. Vigilant	_____	An overabundance; a surplus
F. Shard	_____	Stubborn; uncompromising
G. Trenchant	_____	Alertly watchful
H. Desiccate	_____	Characterized by a strong, sharp smell
I. Spendthrift	_____	To flatter or praise excessively
J. Laconic	_____	To permeate throughout
K. Plethora	_____	Excessively wasteful
L. Renege	_____	A piece of broken pottery or glass
M. Profligate	_____	Diligent; hardworking; persistent
N. Pervade	_____	Sharply perceptive; keen; penetrating

QUICK QUIZ #12

Try the following questions. The answers are on page 237.

1. Because the agreement between the two dueling factions was _____, rather than formal, it was more easily broken.

   - ☐ tacit
   - ☐ contentious
   - ☐ terse
   - ☐ volatile
   - ☐ implied
   - ☐ trivial

2. When my niece came to visit New York City for a weekend, she was in awe of the _____ sights and sounds that I, as a lifelong New Yorker, rarely even notice.

   - ☐ quotidian
   - ☐ eccentric
   - ☐ pragmatic
   - ☐ untenable
   - ☐ garrulous

3. While the poet believed that his recent choice of _____ themes indicated a maturation of his work, the critics lambasted the lack of whimsical subject matter that they had become accustomed to in his verses.

   - ☐ lyrical
   - ☐ laconic
   - ☐ quotidian
   - ☐ pragmatic
   - ☐ quixotic
   - ☐ metaphorical

4. Haile Selassie, the Emperor of Ethiopia for most of the twentieth century, blamed the rise of evil on the _____ of people who, because they were not party to the events, showed no concern for the plight of the downtrodden.

approbation
cognizance
indifference
corruption
vileness

5. It is only because the towns along the river's shore are (i) _____ populated, and therefore generate little pollution, that the river's waters can remain so (ii) _____.

Blank (i)	Blank (ii)
contiguously	pristine
substantially	adulterated
sparsely	hastily

6. A successful moderator must have a soothing personality; (i) _____ any offended parties is an important part of his responsibilities, and (ii) _____ manners will only succeed in exacerbating his clients' indignation.

Blank (i)	Blank (ii)
mollifying	amenable
touting	credulous
coveting	crass

7. The (i) _____ adoration the collectors felt for the current gallery display was evident in the number of paintings purchased, despite the (ii) _____ cost of each piece.

Blank (i)	Blank (ii)
phony	exorbitant
phlegmatic	spendthrift
unfeigned	tawdry

8. The debate between nature and nurture in determining personality traits is a long–standing one. A (i) _____ in the psychology profession may readily defend one particular side of the argument, but the more (ii) _____ professional will acknowledge that there are too many undecided factors, the existence of which precludes taking a firm stance on this (iii) _____ issue.

Blank (i)	Blank (ii)	Blank (iii)
maverick	fledgling	enduring
scholar	cynical	subtle
neophyte	seasoned	transitory

9. Taking a few art classes had convinced Elaine that she was an expert in sculpture, but the museum curators viewed her instead as a mere ____.

bystander
fraud
dilettante
anachronism
maverick

10. The (i) _____ nature of the protagonist is clearly developed in the first few chapters of the book and contributes to the vacillating emotions the author hopes to evince in his readers. The decisions the principal character makes in later chapters, though, are more fitting of a (ii) _____ personality.

Blank (i)	Blank (ii)
exaggerated	bombastic
mercurial	steadfast
glib	acerbic

EXTRA VOCABULARY

The 300 or so words on the Hit Parade are the most important part of your vocabulary building, but they shouldn't be the end. After you've mastered the Hit Parade, learn as many more words as you can. For you hardcore vocabulary students, here are another 200 good GRE words that you should study. Once you've learned them, test yourself with the exercises at the end. Remember, every new word you learn makes it more likely you'll score well on the GRE Verbal section. So keep it up!

abash	verb	to make ashamed; to embarrass
abject	adjective	hopeless; extremely sad and servile; defeated
abnegate	verb	to deny oneself things; to reject; to renounce
abrogate	verb	to abolish or repeal formally; to set aside; to nullify
abstemious	adjective	sparing or moderate, especially in eating and drinking
abstruse	adjective	hard to understand or grasp
abysmal	adjective	extremely hopeless or wretched; bottomless
accede	verb	to give in; to yield; to agree
accrete	verb	to increase by growth or addition
adduce	verb	to bring forward as an example or as proof; to cite
adroit	adjective	skillful; dexterous; clever; socially at ease
advent	noun	arrival; coming; beginning
affable	adjective	easy to talk to; friendly
affectation	noun	unnatural or artificial behavior, usually intended to impress
aggregate	noun	sum total; a collection of separate things mixed together
aghast	adjective	terrified; shocked
allege	verb	to assert without proof
allusion	noun	an indirect reference to something else; a hint
ambience	noun	atmosphere; mood; feeling
ambivalent	adjective	undecided; having opposing feelings simultaneously
amiable	adjective	friendly; agreeable
amorphous	adjective	shapeless; bloblike
anathema	noun	something or someone loathed or detested; a formal ecclesiastical curse and excommunication
ancillary	adjective	subordinate; providing assistance
animosity	noun	resentment; hostility; ill will

antecedent	noun	something that went before; a preceding cause or event
antipathy	noun	firm dislike; a strong feeling of aversion
antithesis	noun	the direct opposite
apex	noun	highest point
aphorism	noun	a brief, witty saying; a proverb
apocryphal	adjective	of dubious authenticity; fictitious
apostasy	noun	abandonment or rejection of faith or loyalty
apposite	adjective	distinctly suitable; pertinent
appropriate	verb	to take without permission; to set aside for a particular use
arbiter	noun	one who decides; a judge
arcane	adjective	mysterious; known only to a select few
archetype	noun	an original model or pattern
arrant	adjective	utter; unmitigated; very bad
astute	adjective	shrewd; keen in judgment
attrition	noun	a gradual wearing away, weakening, or loss; a natural decrease in numbers or size
augment	verb	to make bigger; to add to; to increase
auspicious	adjective	favorable; promising
avow	verb	to claim; to declare boldly; to admit
banal	adjective	unoriginal; ordinary
belabor	verb	to go over repeatedly or to an absurd extent
beleaguer	verb	to surround; to besiege; to harass
belie	verb	to give a false impression of; to contradict
benign	adjective	gentle; not harmful; kind; mild
bereave	verb	to deprive or leave desolate, especially through death
blithe	adjective	carefree; cheerful
broach	verb	to open up a subject for discussion, often a delicate subject
brook	verb	to bear or tolerate; to put up with something
callow	adjective	immature
cardinal	adjective	most important; chief
catholic	adjective	universal; embracing everything

cavil	verb	to quibble; to raise trivial objections
chagrin	noun	humiliation; embarrassed disappointment
choleric	adjective	hot-tempered; quick to anger
circumspect	adjective	cautious
coalesce	verb	to come together as one; to fuse; to unite
coda	noun	a passage concluding a musical composition
cognizant	adjective	fully informed; knowledgeable; aware
collusion	noun	conspiracy; secret cooperation
commensurate	adjective	equal; proportionate
conciliatory	adjective	making peace; attempting to resolve a dispute through goodwill
consecrate	verb	to make or declare sacred
consonant	adjective	harmonious; in agreement
consummate	adjective	perfect; complete; supremely skillful
contumely	noun	rudeness; insolence; arrogance
convivial	adjective	fond of partying; festive
copious	adjective	abundant; plentiful
corroborate	verb	to confirm; to back up with evidence
coterie	noun	a select group of close associates
countenance	noun	face; facial expression
covet	verb	to wish for enviously
cull	verb	to pick out from among many; to select; to collect
cursory	adjective	hasty; superficial
daunt	verb	to make fearful; to intimidate
debacle	noun	a sudden disastrous collapse, downfall, or defeat; a rout
debauchery	noun	corruption by sensuality; intemperance; wild living
decorous	adjective	in good taste; orderly; proper
deleterious	adjective	harmful
deluge	noun	a flood
deprecate	verb	to express disapproval of
dilapidated	adjective	broken-down; fallen into ruin
discomfit	verb	to confuse; to disconcert; to thwart the plans of; to defeat in battle

discourse	noun	to converse; to formally discuss a subject
doggerel	noun	comic, loose verse
egregious	adjective	extremely bad; flagrant
elucidate	verb	to explain; to make understandable
empirical	adjective	relying on experience or observation; not merely theoretical
endemic	adjective	native; belonging to a specific region or people
enormity	noun	extreme evil or wickedness
epicure	noun	a person with refined taste in wine and food
epitome	noun	the perfect example of something; a paradigm
equanimity	noun	composure; calm
eschew	verb	to avoid; to shun
espouse	verb	to support; to advocate
evince	verb	to show or demonstrate clearly; manifest
exhort	verb	to urge strongly
exposition	noun	a setting forth of meaning or intent; a discourse intended to explain
extol	verb	to praise highly
facile	adjective	fluent; skillful in a superficial way; easy
fatuous	adjective	foolish; silly; idiotic
fetter	verb	to restrain; to hamper
flag	verb	to weaken; to slow down
flippant	adjective	frivolously shallow and disrespectful
foment	verb	to stir up; to instigate
forbear	verb	to refrain from; to abstain
founder	verb	to fail; to collapse; to sink
fulsome	adjective	offensively flattering or insincere; repulsive
gainsay	verb	to deny; to speak or act against
gambit	noun	a scheme to gain an advantage; a ploy
genial	adjective	cheerful and pleasant; friendly; helpful
germane	adjective	applicable; pertinent; relevant
gratis	adjective	free of charge
gratuitous	adjective	given freely (said of something bad); unjustified; unprovoked; uncalled for

guile	noun	cunning; duplicity; artfulness
harbinger	noun	a forerunner; a signal of
hermetic	adjective	impervious to external influence; airtight
idyllic	adjective	charming in a rustic way; naturally peaceful
ignominy	noun	deep disgrace
impecunious	adjective	without money; penniless
impromptu	adjective	without preparation; on the spur of the moment
impugn	verb	to attack as false or questionable
incandescent	adjective	brilliant; giving off heat or light
incipient	adjective	beginning; emerging
incorrigible	adjective	incapable of being reformed
indolent	adjective	lazy
indulgent	adjective	lenient; yielding to desire
ineluctable	adjective	inescapable; unavoidable
inept	adjective	clumsy; incompetent
inert	adjective	inactive; sluggish; not reacting chemically
inexorable	adjective	relentless; inevitable; unavoidable
inherent	adjective	part of the essential nature of something; intrinsic
inundate	verb	to flood; to overwhelm
inveterate	adjective	habitual; deeply rooted
itinerant	adjective	moving from place to place
judicious	adjective	exercising sound judgment
lament	verb	to mourn
largess	noun	liberality in giving gifts; money or gifts bestowed; generosity of attitude
lascivious	adjective	lustful; obscene; lewd
latent	adjective	present but not visible or apparent; potential
levee	noun	an embankment designed to prevent the flooding of a river
levity	noun	lightness; frivolity; unseriousness
licentious	adjective	lascivious; lewd; promiscuous; amoral
magnate	noun	a rich, powerful, or very successful businessperson
manifest	adjective	visible; evident
maudlin	adjective	tearfully sentimental; silly or weepy

maxim	noun	a fundamental principle; an old saying
mendicant	noun	a beggar
motility	noun	spontaneous movement
noisome	adjective	offensive or disgusting; stinking; noxious
nominal	adjective	in name only; insignificant
novel	adjective	new; original
oblique	adjective	indirect; at an angle
palliate	verb	to make less severe or intense; to make an offense seem less serious
panacea	noun	something that cures everything
paradigm	noun	a model or example
paradox	noun	a true statement or phenomenon that seems to contradict itself
parsimonious	adjective	stingy; miserly
partisan	adjective	having a bias in support of a party, group, or cause
partisan	noun	one who supports a particular party, group, or cause
patina	noun	surface discoloration caused by age and oxidation
paucity	noun	scarcity
pedestrian	adjective	unoriginal; banal
perturb	verb	to disturb greatly
piquant	adjective	pleasantly pungent or tart
placid	adjective	pleasantly calm; peaceful
plaintive	adjective	expressing sadness or sorrow
plumb	verb	to measure the depth of something
portent	noun	an omen; a sign of something coming in the future
precipitous	adjective	steep
predilection	noun	a natural preference for something
presage	verb	to portend; to foreshadow; to forecast or predict
privation	noun	lack of comforts or necessities; poverty
provincial	adjective	limited in outlook to one's own small corner of the world; narrow
prurient	adjective	having lustful thoughts or desires; causing lust
putative	adjective	commonly accepted; supposed; reputed
quay	noun	a landing on the edge of the water; wharf; pier

queue	noun	a line of waiting people or things
queue	verb	to get in line
quintessential	adjective	being the most perfect example of
rampart	noun	a fortification; a bulwark of defense
redolent	adjective	fragrant; aromatic; suggestive or reminiscent
remonstrate	verb	to argue against; to protest; to raise objections
remuneration	noun	payment; recompense
renaissance	noun	a rebirth or revival
replete	adjective	completely filled; abounding
reproach	verb	to scold, usually in disappointment; to blame; to disgrace
reprobate	noun	a wicked, sinful, depraved person
reprove	verb	to criticize mildly
respite	noun	a period of rest or relief
ribald	adjective	characterized by vulgar, lewd humor
sagacious	adjective	wise
sagacity	noun	wisdom
sage	noun	a wise person
salutary	adjective	healthful; remedial; wholesome
sanguine	adjective	cheerful; optimistic; hopeful
surreptitious	adjective	sneaky; secret
sycophant	noun	one who sucks up to others; a servile, self-seeking flatterer
taciturn	adjective	untalkative by nature
temerity	noun	recklessness; audacity; foolhardy disregard of danger
turpitude	noun	shameful wickedness or depravity
unalloyed	adjective	undiluted; pure
usury	noun	lending money at an extremely high rate of interest
venal	adjective	capable of being bribed; corrupt
verdant	adjective	covered with green plants; leafy; inexperienced
vestige	noun	a remaining bit of something; a last trace
vitiate	verb	to make faulty or defective; impair; to corrupt morally
wizened	adjective	shriveled; withered; shrunken

Quick Quiz #13

Define the following words.

Quintessential: _____

_____

Surreptitious: _____

_____

Apex: _____

_____

Affable: _____

_____

Belie: _____

_____

Inexorable: _____

_____

Debacle: _____

_____

Founder: _____

_____

Gainsay: _____

_____

Largess: _____

_____

Mendicant: _____

_____

Queue: _____

_____

Sycophant: _____

_____

Apostasy: _____

_____

Impugn: _____

_____

QUICK QUIZ #14

Match the following words to their definitions. The answers are on page 238.

A. Panacea   _____ Pleasingly pungent or tart

B. Cavil   _____ Rudeness; insolence; arrogance

C. Itinerant   _____ To explain; to make understandable

D. Aghast   _____ To make ashamed; to embarrass

E. Guile   _____ Moving from place to place

F. Piquant   _____ Extreme evil or wickedness

G. Banal   _____ Terrified; shocked

H. Enormity   _____ Cunning; duplicity

I. Abash   _____ Unoriginal; ordinary

J. Contumely   _____ Something that cures everything

K. Fetter   _____ To quibble; to raise trivial objections

L. Apposite   _____ To argue against; to protest

M. Elucidate   _____ Distinctly suitable; pertinent

N. Remonstrate   _____ To restrain; to hamper

QUICK QUIZ #15

Try the following questions. The answers are on page 238.

1. Though high, the _____ the artisan received for the sale of his wares was commensurate with his skill level and years of experience.

   ☐ remuneration
   ☐ commendation
   ☐ remonstration
   ☐ compensation
   ☐ deprecation
   ☐ renown

2. The _____ of a wise test-taker is one who studies every day, becomes familiar with good test-taking strategies, and gets plenty of sleep the night before the test.

   ☐ nadir
   ☐ debacle
   ☐ archetype
   ☐ epitome
   ☐ harbinger
   ☐ antecedent

3. Despite grandiose hopes that the fall of the Berlin Wall would lead to rapid economic equality and integration of the Eastern and Western German blocs, one still finds that the preponderance of _____ German citizens lives in the east, while the luxury-automobile-driving citizens are more likely to live in the west.

   ☐ arrant
   ☐ indigent
   ☐ hermetic
   ☐ fatuous
   ☐ deleterious
   ☐ impecunious

4. The new task force that was created by the city to deal with the (i) _____ houses that were abandoned long ago due to foreclosure was a (ii) _____ task force only. Though the devoted members had (iii) _____ their commitment to improving the neighborhoods, they had neither a budget nor the influence to affect any true change.

Blank (i)	Blank (ii)	Blank (iii)
flippant	cognizant	avowed
dilapidated	nominal	broached
provincial	impromptu	reproved

5. The director gave the playwright's latest work only (i) _____ reading before dismissing it as superficial. Had he read it more carefully, he would have found the underlying themes quite (ii) _____.

Blank (i)	Blank (ii)
a cursory	glib
a novel	indulgent
an illusory	profound

6. The theory that women are more verbally skilled than men (i) _____ anthropological history. This theory also gives credence to why men might have better spatial analysis skills. In traditional hunter-gatherer groups, the men used spatial skills to figure out puzzling tasks, such as how to catch their food. They needed to remain (ii) _____ during their hunts to avoid scaring off the prey. On the other hand, women spent their days doing (iii) _____ tasks, such as picking berries, while talking to other women and socializing their young.

Blank (i)	Blank (ii)	Blank (iii)
has no basis in	taciturn	simpler
is supported by	strident	culinary
is disputed by	melodic	complicated

7. No one has suggested that the professor is not (i) _____; nonetheless, some have suggested that the affection shown to him by the faculty is more a result of his (ii) _____ nature than his academic skill.

Blank (i)	Blank (ii)
sagacious	prurient
witless	convivial
parsimonious	incipient

8. Benjamin Franklin was born the son of a candle-maker, and his first marriage proposal was rejected due to his lack of financial standing or prospects. Nonetheless, Franklin became, through industry and (i) _____ that made him sometimes appear (ii) _____, quite (iii) _____ during his accomplished lifetime.

Blank (i)	Blank (ii)	Blank (iii)
inimicality	pedantic	squalid
improvidence	penurious	intransigent
frugality	prodigal	affluent

9. Alice was shocked at her brother's _____ when he stood up in class and interrupted the teacher to disagree with her.

equanimity
debauchery
temerity
animosity
countenance

10. According to her later testimony, it was because of his indecorous conduct that the senator chose not to _____ his appointment.

countenance
belabor
remonstrate
ramify
impugn

ADVANCED VOCABULARY

You want more? Wow, you really are a glutton for vocabulary. Congratulations, that's great! Here is a list of about 100 very challenging vocabulary words for your perusal. Enjoy!

abjure	verb	to repudiate; to take back; to refrain from
adumbrate	verb	to foreshadow vaguely; to suggest or outline sketchily; to obscure or overshadow
anodyne	adjective/ noun	soothing; something that assuages or comforts; something that allays pain
apogee	noun	the most distant point in the orbit of the moon or of an artificial satellite
apotheosis	noun	an exalted or glorified example; elevation to divine standard
artful	adjective	crafty; wily; sly
artless	adjective	completely without guile; natural, without artificiality
assay	verb	to examine by trial or experiment; to evaluate or assess
asseverate	verb	to aver; to allege; to assert
augur	verb	to serve as an omen or sign; to predict or foretell
baleful	adjective	sinister; pernicious; ominous
beatify	verb	to bless, make happy, or ascribe a virtue to; to regard as saintly
bilious	adjective	ill-tempered; cranky
calumny	noun	slander; a maliciously false statement
captious	adjective	disposed to point out trivial faults; calculated to confuse or entrap in argument
carapace	noun	a protective shell
celerity	noun	swiftness of action or motion; speed
coeval	adjective	of the same period; coexisting
contretemps	noun	an embarrassing occurrence; a mishap
contumacious	adjective	stubbornly rebellious or disobedient
corrigible	adjective	capable of being set right; correctable; reparable
denouement	noun	an outcome or solution; the unraveling of a plot
descry	verb	to discriminate or discern

desuetude	noun	disuse
desultory	adjective	moving or jumping from one thing to another; disconnected; occurring haphazardly
diaphanous	adjective	of such fine texture as to be transparent or translucent; delicate; insubstantial
diffident	adjective	reserved; shy; unassuming; lacking in self-confidence
diurnal	adjective	occurring every day; occurring during the daytime
dulcet	adjective	melodious; harmonious; mellifluous
egress	noun	exit
encomium	noun	a formal expression of praise; a tribute
essay	verb	to test or try; attempt; experiment
estimable	adjective	worthy; formidable
excoriate	verb	to censure scathingly; to upbraid
execrate	verb	to denounce; to loathe
exegesis	noun	critical examination; explication
expiate	verb	to make amends for; to atone
fecund	adjective	fertile; productive
fell	verb/ adjective	to cause to fall by striking; cruel; lethal; dire; sinister
fractious	adjective	quarrelsome; rebellious; unruly; irritable
hirsute	adjective	hairy; shaggy
hoary	adjective	gray or white with age; ancient; stale
husband	verb	to use sparingly or economically; conserve
imbroglio	noun	difficult or embarrassing situation
importune	verb	to urge with annoying persistence; to trouble
indefatigable	adjective	not easily exhaustible; tireless; dogged
insouciant	adjective	nonchalant; lighthearted; carefree
invidious	adjective	causing envy or resentment; offensively harmful
jejune	adjective	vapid; uninteresting; childish, immature, puerile
lachrymose	adjective	causing tears; tearful
lassitude	noun	exhaustion; weakness
ligneous	adjective	woodlike
limn	verb	to draw; to outline in detail; to delineate; to describe
list	verb	to tilt or lean to one side

loquacious	adjective	very talkative; garrulous
lubricious	adjective	lewd; wanton; greasy; slippery
lugubrious	adjective	exaggeratedly mournful
meet	adjective	fitting, proper
mellifluous	adjective	sweetly flowing
meretricious	adjective	plausible but false or insincere; gaudy; showy; tawdry; flashy
minatory	adjective	menacing; threatening
nadir	noun	low point
nice	adjective	exacting; fastidious; extremely precise
nonplus	verb	to baffle; to bewilder; to perplex
nugatory	adjective	of little or no importance; trifling; inconsequential
obstreperous	adjective	noisily and stubbornly defiant; aggressively boisterous
ossify	verb	to convert into bone; to become rigid
otiose	adjective	lazy; of no use; futile
panegyric	noun	formal or elaborate praise
parry	verb	to deflect or ward off; to evade or avoid
pellucid	adjective	transparent; easy to understand; limpid
peripatetic	adjective	wandering; traveling continually; itinerant
perorate	verb	to speak formally
plangent	adjective	pounding; thundering; resounding
pluck	noun	courage; spunk; fortitude
prize	verb	to pry; to press or force with a lever
prolix	adjective	long-winded; verbose
propinquity	noun	nearness; proximity
propitiate	verb	to appease; to conciliate
propitious	adjective	marked by favorable signs or conditions
puerile	adjective	childish; immature
puissant	adjective	powerful
pulchritude	noun	physical beauty
pusillanimous	adjective	cowardly; craven
salacious	adjective	lustful; lascivious; bawdy
saturnine	adjective	melancholy or sullen; of a gloomy disposition

sententious	adjective	given to pompous moralizing; preachy; self-righteous
sidereal	adjective	astral; relating to stars or constellations
sinecure	noun	a position requiring little or no work and usually providing an income
stentorian	adjective	extremely loud and powerful
stygian	adjective	gloomy; dark
succor	noun	assistance; relief in time of distress
succor	verb	to give assistance in time of need
sundry	adjective	various; miscellaneous; separate
supine	adjective	lying face upward; offering no resistance
tendentious	adjective	argumentative; biased
turbid	adjective	murky; opaque; unclear
tyro	noun	novice; rank amateur
unctuous	adjective	oily, both literally and figuratively; characterized by earnest insincerity
vagary	noun	whim; unpredictable action; wild notion
voluble	adjective	fluent; verbal; having easy use of spoken language
wag	noun	a wit; a joker

ANSWER KEY

HIT PARADE GROUP 1

Quick Quiz #2

K
L
E
G
B
A
H
I
N
F
C
M
J
D

Quick Quiz #3

1. B and D
2. C and D
3. A and F
4. C
5. ossified, perfunctory, parodies
6. belie, intimate
7. ostensible, nebulous, qualms
8. illicit, attestation, exculpated
9. A
10. stupefied, prescient

HIT PARADE GROUP 2

Quick Quiz #5

D
L
F
M
B
K
C
A
N
I
G
H
E
J

Quick Quiz #6

1. A and E
2. C and D
3. C and E
4. accolades, satire
5. wretched, innocuous
6. irrational, circumstantial, incipient
7. abate, vilify
8. customary, eclectic, bedraggled
9. A
10. complaisance, truncate

Hit Parade Group 3

Quick Quiz #8

J
E
N
M
I
B
A
H
G
F
C
D
K
L

Quick Quiz #9

1. C and E
2. A and E
3. E and F
4. reverent, adorn, vista
5. spurious, restricted
6. D
7. hackneyed, immutable
8. incontrovertible, cultivated, complicated amalgamation
9. B
10. dubious, a precursor to

Hit Parade Group 4

Quick Quiz #11

L
J
I
H
K
A
E
C
D
N
M
F
B
G

Quick Quiz #12

1. A and E
2. A and B
3. C and D
4. indifference
5. sparsely, pristine
6. mollify, crass
7. unfeigned, exorbitant
8. neophyte, seasoned, enduring
9. C
10. mercurial, stoic

EXTRA VOCABULARY

Quick Quiz #14

F
J
M
I
C
H
D
E
G
A
B
N
L
K

Quick Quiz #15

1. A and D
2. C and D
3. B and F
4. dilapidated, nominal, avowed
5. a cursory, profound
6. is supported by, taciturn, simpler
7. sagacious, convivial
8. frugality, penurious, affluent
9. C
10. A

7
Mixed Drills

DRILL #1

Try the following questions. The answers are on page 255.

1. One major _____ that some scientists have about the practice of cloning is their fear of the potentially negative outcomes associated with a homogenous population.

gambit
rampart
conviction
qualm
certitude

2. While the life of _____ may appeal to some, others hold interests they believe are more intellectually based than cultivating a discriminating taste in food.

an epicure
a sage
a hedonist
a connoisseur
an ascetic

3. The intentions of the restaurant critic were (i) _____; he accepted the assignment to review the new bistro not as (ii) _____ journalist, but as a private citizen seeking revenge against the owner, who had wronged him in a business deal years before.

Blank (i)	Blank (ii)
squalid	a surreptitious
discreet	a discerning
malevolent	an indifferent

4. It is part of human nature to resist change and (i) _____ new ideas. This fact is evidenced in many teachers' (ii) _____ adherence to archaic methodologies, which makes educational reform difficult to enact. Until some (iii) _____ teachers and administrators begin to welcome new classroom techniques, the attempts of the current administration at modifying the system will be ineffective.

Blank (i)	Blank (ii)	Blank (iii)
eschew	inept	sagacious
aver	partisan	superfluous
covet	dogged	obstinate

5. Near the end of his life, author Leo Tolstoy was increasingly influenced by aspiring communist revolutionaries. Tolstoy came to believe that excessive personal wealth was (i) _____ to the well-being of his Russian countrymen, and was persuaded to bequeath his copyrights and much of his fortune to the Russian state; his wife Sophia, who believed in her right to be an aristocrat, regarded this as (ii) _____ decision.

Blank (i)	Blank (ii)
convivial	a heretical
inimical	an opulent
stupefying	a refulgent

6. Doctors have remained (i) _____ in the face of the incredible news that a Swedish research team has discovered a gene that causes cancer. Their reluctance to show excitement is due to their awareness that transforming the mere identification of this gene into usable medicine is (ii) _____ task and will not (iii) _____ the need for uncomfortable and lengthy treatments any time in the near future.

Blank (i)	Blank (ii)	Blank (iii)
felicitous	a prized	obviate
morose	an arduous	aggrandize
impassive	an austere	effect

A tenured art history professor at a major university recently asserted that **the head of the Art History department is incompetent**, pointing to the decline
(5) in enrollment in art history courses despite an increase in enrollment overall at the university. While one may argue that professors who lash out at department heads are rarely likely
(10) to achieve anything constructive, **in this case the complaint is entirely unwarranted**. It is true that a decrease in enrollment within a department often indicates incompetence on the part of
(15) the department head, but not so here. Rather, the decline in enrollment in art history courses is entirely due to the university's admissions committee's decision to admit far more students who
(20) plan to enroll exclusively in pre-medicine courses.

7. In the argument, the two bold-faced portions play which of the following roles?

○ The first provides evidence intended to support a claim that the argument overall opposes; the second provides information to undermine the strength of that evidence.

○ The first provides evidence intended to support a claim that the argument overall opposes; the second states the conclusion of the argument overall.

○ The first provides evidence intended to support a claim that the argument overall opposes; the second provides evidence to undermine the claim being opposed.

○ The first states a claim that the argument overall opposes; the second provides evidence to undermine the claim being opposed.

○ The first states a claim that the argument overall opposes; the second states the conclusion of the argument overall.

The London Board of Trade limited the quantity of pound sterling banknotes permitted in circulation in the American *Line* colonies, citing fear of devaluation (5) induced by overprinting. The Board also denied the necessity of paper money, considering the ever-increasing colonial exports purchased by foreign nations that rendered payments in gold (10) and silver. However, in 1749, Governor Glen of South Carolina contended that access to more paper currency was essential because there was actually a deficit of gold and silver. This shortfall (15) led to difficulties in exchanging goods for these precious metals, forcing many merchants to earn their success only through continued reliance on the barter system. Such a system limited (20) the colonists' ability to obtain certain goods for which they had no apparently comparable trade, severely hampering widespread economic growth in the colonies.

8. Select the sentence that suggests the final phrase, *severely hampering widespread economic growth in the colonies,* may be an exaggeration.

9. Which of the following statements, if true, would most strengthen Governor Glen's argument in favor of paper currency?

○ It was difficult for the colonists to maintain high levels of foreign exports during the winter months.

○ Although colonists were not always able to find trade partners in their local communities, there were strong domestic trade links among the various colonies.

○ Since the value of a pound sterling banknote was linked directly to that of silver, the two methods of payment were equally acceptable to a merchant.

○ Foreign countries often wanted to barter with colonial exporters, but the value of some foreign goods was difficult to determine.

○ Because some colonies had already developed their own form of legal tender and no longer used the British pound sterling, the Board of Trade should not have been worried about devaluation.

El Niño-Southern Oscillation is a climate pattern that occurs across the tropical Pacific Ocean
Line approximately every five years. The
(5) phenomenon includes a change in ocean temperature—the "El Niño" component—and a change in air surface pressure—the "Southern Oscillation" component. When prolonged, above-
(10) average ocean warming coincides with higher air surface pressure, the phenomenon is popularly called El Niño; when prolonged, above-average ocean cooling coincides with lower air surface
(15) pressure, the phenomenon is popularly called La Niña. El Niño or La Niña events typically last between five and nine months.

El Niño begins with increased surface
(20) pressure over the Indian Ocean and reduced air pressure over the central and eastern Pacific Ocean, a combination which causes trade winds traveling from Peru to the Eastern Pacific to subside.
(25) Under normal conditions, these trade winds blow warm water near the surface away from Peru along the Equatorial Current, leading to an upwelling of cold, nutrient-rich water. During an El Niño,
(30) however, this effect is reduced. Because the Pacific Ocean has a potent impact on climate throughout the world, El Niño disturbs weather patterns more powerfully than does any other known
(35) force. Typical effects include severe droughts in Indonesia, Australia, and the Philippines, and substantially increased rainfall in parts of South America.

The effects of El Niño can be
(40) economically devastating in South America. Because of the increased rainfall, flooding in Peru and Ecuador is common. Moreover, El Niño significantly diminishes the amount of cold water
(45) that usually rises from the deep, depriving local fish populations of the important nutrients brought up with the cold water. In the absence of these nutrients, fish swim deeper, head south,
(50) or die off, causing great harm to the fishing industry. Indeed, during the 1972 El Niño, the world's largest fishery collapsed. In addition, these same fish feed local bird populations; during an
(55) El Niño event, birds, the droppings of which are used in the fertilizer industry, leave to find new food sources.

Although no one knows how long El Niño has existed, evidence suggests
(60) that there may have been El Niño phenomena for thousands of years. Coral records suggest a warming of sea surface temperatures as early as 3,000
(65) B.C.E. Five hundred years ago, fishermen in Peru saw their anchovy catch diminish substantially when water temperatures warmed. The most destructive El Niño
(70) event occurred in 1982-1983, when droughts and associated wildfires killed nearly 2,000 people; this incident sparked intense occupation among
(75) scientists worldwide with the causes of El Niño.

10. In the last sentence of the passage, the word *occupation* most nearly means

- ○ function
- ○ employment
- ○ concern
- ○ affair
- ○ professionalism

11. The passage suggests which of the following about phenomena associated with El Niño?

- ☐ The surface water of the Pacific Ocean near South America is warmer because of reduced trade winds.
- ☐ Severe droughts are seen in some parts of the world, while increased flooding is seen in other parts of the world.
- ☐ Because many fish relocate or die, fewer fish are caught by many people in the South American fishing industry.

12. On the basis of the passage, it can be inferred that

   ◯ In the absence of an El Niño event, drought conditions are rarely present in Indonesia, Australia, or the Philippines.

   ◯ No observable phenomenon influences global weather patterns to a magnitude greater than does an El Niño event.

   ◯ Because of the changes in surface pressure and reduction in trade winds associated with El Niño events, many South American birds are forced to relocate.

   ◯ The El Niño event of 1982-1983 caused more deaths than did any other climate-related event that year.

   ◯ The effects of the 1972 El Niño event were felt most profoundly in Peru and Ecuador.

13. Although we had planned the vacation trip to the sunny spa for weeks, no one could have predicted the _____ onset of rainy weather that spoiled most of our outdoor activities.

   ☐ welcome
   ☐ precipitous
   ☐ unforeseen
   ☐ fortunate
   ☐ fruitless
   ☐ lethargic

14. The _____ outcries from the disgruntled union workers were apparently to no avail; the supervisor decided to reject the enhanced benefits package without any further discussion.

   ☐ pristine
   ☐ fervent
   ☐ quizzical
   ☐ redolent
   ☐ allusive
   ☐ impassioned

15. David's report card stated he is sometimes regarded as a _____ student by his teachers when his narrow-minded interpretations and adamant attitudes dominate his classroom discussions.

   ☐ intransigent
   ☐ assiduous
   ☐ intractable
   ☐ gregarious
   ☐ pensive
   ☐ diligent

16. With the inception of numerous exorbitant tolls throughout the state's major highways, the popularity of long-distance automobile travel _____ while the rate of train travel experienced a concomitant upswing.

   ☐ waned
   ☐ equivocated
   ☐ intensified
   ☐ importuned
   ☐ abated
   ☐ surged

Late Victorian writers obsessed about the relationship between art and the artist—as Basil Hallward lamented in *Line* *The Picture of Dorian Gray*, "We live in *(5)* an age when men treat art as if it were meant to be a form of autobiography." Yet Oscar Wilde, the author of that very novel, himself made fortunes from the rampant speculation about the *(10)* connections between his work and life. The irony inherent in this contradiction seems obvious: only by recognizing and manipulating the public's tendency to impute biographical meaning to *(15)* the aesthetic can the artist maneuver the perception of his art to his own advantage. But if the "art of art" is really all about "the art of the ruse," then what value does any of it have, anyway?

For the following question, consider each of the choices separately and select all that apply:

17. An example of treating "art as if it were meant to be a form of autobiography" would be:

☐ reading a novel about a young girl as an allegory for modern political circumstances.

☐ viewing the bare shoulders in a painting of a well-known society figure as an indication of her seductive nature.

☐ observing that the director of a film had a childhood injury similar to that of one of the characters in the film.

18. Click on the sentence in which the author refers to a creation of an artist to support an assertion about a conundrum that was commonly faced by artists in the time period discussed in the passage.

Recently, scientists studying how the brain interprets expressive gestures that communicate emotional states *Line* undertook a study comparing neural *(5)* activity relating to hand gestures expressing emotions such as "I don't care" to neural activity relating to instrumental gestures intended to change behavior through spoken *(10)* commands such as "sit down." Volunteers undergoing fMRI testing were shown brief videos of both expressive gestures and instrumental gestures and were asked to interpret the import of *(15)* the gestures. As anticipated, expressive gestures activated different neural networks than did instrumental gestures. Expressive gestures activated neurons in the paracingulate cortex and the *(20)* amygdale, both of which are known to be activated during social interaction. Instrumental gestures, by contrast, activated neurons in a region of the brain associated with language.

19. In context, the word *import* most nearly means

○ enticement
○ influx
○ transmission
○ magnitude
○ connotation

Recently, scientists studying how the brain interprets expressive gestures that communicate emotional states
Line undertook a study comparing neural
(5) activity relating to hand gestures expressing emotions such as "I don't care" to neural activity relating to instrumental gestures intended to change behavior through spoken
(10) commands such as "sit down." Volunteers undergoing fMRI testing were shown brief videos of both expressive gestures and instrumental gestures and were asked to interpret the import
(15) of the gestures. Expressive gestures activated different neural networks than did instrumental gestures. Expressive gestures activated neurons in the paracingulate cortex and the amygdale,
(20) both of which are known to be activated during social interaction. Instrumental gestures, by contrast, activated neurons in a region of the brain associated with language.

20. The function of the highlighted portion of the passage is to

   ◯ describe the role that neural networks play in perception
   ◯ refute a hypothesis anticipated at the outset of the study
   ◯ highlight the definitive nature of certain aspects of neurology
   ◯ summarize the conclusion to be drawn from a study
   ◯ explain the appropriateness of a particular methodology

DRILL #2

Try the following questions. The answers are on page 260.

1. Although the Modern Library Board selected Joyce's *Ulysses* as its number one novel of all time, Friendswood Library disagrees and instead chose Fitzgerald's *The Great Gatsby* as its _____ of literature.

antithesis
escutcheon
apotheosis
litigation
demotion

2. Polonius, one of Shakespeare's most _____ characters, speaks some of the bard's classic epigrammatic lines such as, "To thine own self be true," and, "Neither a borrower nor lender be."

obsequious
auriferous
sententious
dysphonic
mellifluous

3. Maggie decided that decorating her denim jacket with rhinestones was an easy way to (i) _____ her look, changing it from a run-of-the-mill outfit to (ii) _____ creation.

Blank (i)	Blank (ii)
regard	an inimitable
isolate	a laughable
personalize	an austere

4. The researcher expected to find only (i) _____ medical tips in the medieval texts and was surprised to find information about things such as lemon balm, cayenne pepper, and onions, items that modern medical experts recommend for their (ii) _____ benefits.

Blank (i)	Blank (ii)
commodious	tenebrious
antediluvian	lugubrious
extant	salubrious

5. (i) _____ debating whether bread should be buttered on the top or the bottom was impossible for the Yooks and the Zooks, who each felt strongly that their own perspective was the correct way and refused to consider any alternative. Instead of recognizing the absurdity of the conflict, they allowed things to (ii) _____, with each side developing bigger and better weapons that ultimately lead them to the threat of (iii) _____ destruction.

Blank (i)	Blank (ii)	Blank (iii)
Tempestuously	confabulate	predisposed
Dogmatically	stagnate	mutual
Rationally	escalate	incongruous

6. Lower taxes would have many
(i) _____ effects on the
nation as a whole. In addition to
encouraging businesspeople to be
more optimistic and (ii) _____
in their investments, tax cuts would
encourage the mass hiring of
employees, which is not
(iii) _____ given the current
payroll tax rate.

Blank (i)	Blank (ii)	Blank (iii)
execrable	bullish	feasible
salutary	bearish	malleable
indeterminate	birdlike	atypical

In *The Great Gatsby,* F. Scott
Fitzgerald created a protagonist
who was a staunch believer in the
Line agrarian myth espoused by Thomas
(5) Jefferson and Benjamin Franklin, yet
was simultaneously entrenched in
the corruption and materialism of
American society during the 1920s.
This dual nature of the title character
(10) has commonly been viewed as a
thinly disguised reflection of Fitzgerald
himself, who, as reviewer Allen claimed,
maintained a "catholic sensibility" his
whole life despite well-known episodes
(15) of public drunkenness and debauchery.
Fitter agreed, perceiving in Fitzgerald a
"deep-seated conservative quietism" not
dissimilar to Jay Gatsby's adherence to
the principles of honorable living dictated
(20) by Benjamin Franklin in *Poor Richard's
Almanack.* The parallels were so
apparent to Mencken that he regarded
the book as little more than a "glorified
anecdote." Other critics have rejected
(25) this narrow, egocentric interpretation and
given far more credence to the novel
as shrewd social commentary. Trask,
for example, considered the eyes of Dr.
T.J. Eckleburg, featured prominently on
(30) a billboard in the novel, not those of
an all-seeing god evaluating Gatsby's
personal shortcomings, but those
of Thomas Jefferson mourning the
collective American abandonment of his
(35) belief in hard work and integrity as the
paths to fortune. Even Trask, though,
conceded that the hedonistic Fitzgerald
spoke clearly through the character of
Nick Carraway in an ironic plea for the
(40) preservation of a more austere way of
life.

7. Select the sentence that best
defines one of the two contradictory
facets of Jay Gatsby's character.

8. According to the passage, which of
the following statements about *The
Great Gatsby* cannot be shown to be
accurate in the estimation of at least
one critic?

○ The novel was merely a
description of an episode
from Fitzgerald's life.
○ The symbolism in the novel
sometimes reflected
Fitzgerald's lack of self-worth.
○ The novel provided insight
into American culture of the
1920s.
○ Fitzgerald used the novel as a
vehicle to voice his opinions
about changes in America.
○ The novel's main character
provided a truthful depiction
of the author.

9. Which of the following situations
is most analogous to Fitter's belief
about the character of Jay Gatsby?

○ A job candidate in an interview
mimics the actions of the
interviewer in an unconscious
effort to establish rapport and
familiarity.
○ A photographer chooses to
repeatedly use a model
who has many of the
same mannerisms and
facial expressions as the
photographer.
○ A character in a movie written
by a health-conscious
playwright has a gym
membership and buys only
organic foods.
○ A college student relates
strongly to a character in a
novel and begins to take an
interest in that character's
hobbies.
○ An actor improvises many of
his character's lines in order
to add depth to the role.

Newton's theory of universal gravitation states that every massive particle in the universe attracts every *Line* other massive particle with a force (5) proportional to the mass of the particles and their proximity to one another. Consequently, cosmologists would expect that calculations based on this theory would yield an accurate measure (10) of the mass in the universe; in fact, though, the total amount of observable matter in the universe does not contain enough mass to account for the organization of the universe into clusters (15) of galaxies. To explain this discrepancy, cosmologists have developed the theory of "dark matter:" they postulate that the missing mass consists of elementary particles too small to be detected by (20) electromagnetic radiation, and that these particles provide the mass necessary to hold the universe together. According to available evidence, these particles can only account for a maximum of (25) 20 percent of the missing mass in the universe, yet their existence brings us one important step closer to solving the mystery of the missing matter.

10. According to the passage, which of the following factors is believed to help account for the missing mass in the universe?

○ Massive particles with a force proportional to the mass of the particles attract additional mass to the universe.

○ Tiny particles that are not currently observable by humans compose some of the missing mass.

○ "Dark matter" adheres to mass and causes it to expand.

○ Galaxies organize themselves into clusters to compensate for the lack of other mass in the universe.

○ The proximity of certain particles to each other forces an attraction that creates mass.

For the following question, consider each of the choices separately and select all that apply:

11. The passage suggests that a massive particle would be most likely to attract another particle:

☐ with a force related to the mass of each particle.

☐ at a distance related to the mass of each particle.

☐ by using an elementary particle as an intermediary.

High tax rates, not the new regulations on carbon emissions, are responsible for the poor industrial production in Country A since its new government was elected. Neighboring Country B imposes the same regulations on carbon emissions, but while industrial production in Country A has been declining, it has been improving in Country B.

12. Which one of the following statements, if true, would most weaken the argument?

   ○ While Country B has a regional airport, Country A has an international airport.
   ○ Country A's newly elected government raised taxes with the goal of guaranteeing a more just distribution of wealth.
   ○ The type of coal always burned in Country A is different from the type of coal always burned in Country B.
   ○ Both Country A and Country B have been in a recession.
   ○ Agricultural production is also falling in Country A.

13. An aspiring pop star should be _____, playing concert after concert and sending out hundreds of demo tapes, even though in the end, fame may depend solely on having the right connections.

   ☐ idolatrous
   ☐ dogged
   ☐ tenuous
   ☐ notorious
   ☐ tenacious
   ☐ advantageous

14. In many Western cultures, the four-leaf clover is easily identified as _____ symbol; in Buddhist cultures, it is the wheel that is widely recognized as a good omen.

   ☐ an auspicious
   ☐ a facetious
   ☐ a pious
   ☐ a pervasive
   ☐ a propitious
   ☐ a prophetic

15. Because he had initially feared public displays of outrage from constituents who felt their taxes were already too high, the governor was shocked to hear so many people _____ his decision to sign the new bill that would generate much needed revenue for the state.

   ☐ effectuate
   ☐ reproach
   ☐ annul
   ☐ laud
   ☐ extol
   ☐ flout

16. After a brief, but vexing, attempt at living in the countryside without the amenities which are readily accessible to the modern urbanite, the young lawyer, who previously had found a certain _____ charm in the lifestyle of the Pennsylvania Dutch, quickly changed his mind.

   ☐ bucolic
   ☐ erudite
   ☐ pedestrian
   ☐ idyllic
   ☐ banal
   ☐ lugubrious

The ubiquity of jeans across social classes in modern America might be surprising given that throughout history
Line jeans have transmitted very specific
(5) cultural messages. Their crude, durable fabric initially made them symbolic of poor, working-class men, but when women hung up their skirts in order to take their turns at the heavy machinery
(10) while their husbands fought fascism in Europe, jeans were transformed into a hallmark of patriotism and early feminism. In the 1950s, after exposure in films as the garments of choice of
(15) brooding icons such as Marlon Brando and James Dean, jeans also served as an emblem of rebellious youth. Ultimately, their rise to dominance over the American wardrobe in the 1970s did
(20) nothing to lessen the ability of jeans to align the wearer with a certain social group, thanks to the scope of brands and styles that became available.

17. The passage implies all of the following about people who have worn jeans throughout history EXCEPT

- ○ their social affiliations are not exclusive to one particular social class
- ○ they found jeans more suitable for some working environments
- ○ the early adopters wore jeans in order to identify with certain social groups
- ○ they progressively gained more control over the symbolism of the jeans they wore
- ○ they were members not only of a variety of economic classes, but age groups as well

18. What is the function of the highlighted portion?

- ○ to provide a specific example of another shift in the symbolism of jeans
- ○ to present a viewpoint that differs from that of the initial premise
- ○ to summarize an argument in favor of the inconsistent historical symbolism of jeans
- ○ to weaken the author's premise by conclusively demonstrating why jeans gained widespread popularity
- ○ to reconcile an apparent contradiction presented in an earlier sentence

Precipitation—in the form of dew in
the warmer months and frost in the
colder ones—often forms on grass
Line and leaves during the night. But since
(5) this precipitation results from a change
between surface and atmospheric
temperatures, how can similar
water droplets also appear on some
houseplants? The answer is that some
(10) globules are the result of guttation.
Occurring only in vascular plants,
guttation begins when water moves
from saturated soil into drier plant roots.
Water accumulation in roots creates
(15) pressure, which, in daytime, is offset
through evaporation. At night, however,
these plants use the pipe-like elements
of their tissue to draw the excess water
upwards and push it out the tips of their
(20) leaves.

Precipitation—in the form of dew in
the warmer months and frost in the
colder ones—often forms on grass and
Line leaves during the night. However, since
(5) this precipitation results from a change
between surface and atmospheric
temperatures, how can similar
water droplets also appear on some
houseplants? The answer is that some
(10) globules are the result of guttation.
Occurring only in vascular plants,
guttation begins when water moves
from saturated soil into drier plant roots.
Water accumulation in roots creates
(15) pressure, which, in daytime, is offset
through evaporation. At night, however,
these plants use the pipe-like elements
of their tissue to draw the excess water
upwards and push it out the tips of their
(20) leaves.

19. Consider each of the choices
separately and select all that apply.

- [ ] There is sufficient evidence in
the passage to support
which of the following
inferences about guttation?
- [ ] Guttation is more likely to occur
in climates that have only
rainy and dry seasons, as
opposed to ones with four
distinct seasons ranging
from winter to summer.
- [ ] Analyzing the quantity of
moisture in the soil and
the type of plant one were
dealing with would be
inadequate to determine
whether certain droplets
were the result of guttation
or were simply dew.
- [ ] In arid climates, guttation is not
likely to occur under natural
conditions.

20. In the passage, *vascular* most nearly
means

- ◯ containing channels
- ◯ needing excessive moisture
- ◯ needing little sunlight
- ◯ absorbent
- ◯ suitable for moderate climates

ANSWERS AND EXPLANATIONS

DRILL #1

1. **D** The clue that you need to fill in the blank is *fear of potentially negative outcomes*. If the scientists are afraid of an outcome, they must have a *problem* with cloning. *Qualm* is the only synonym here for *problem*. *Conviction* and *certitude* may seem like possible answers, but the outcomes are described as *potential*. *Gambit* (tactic) and *rampart* (barrier wall) do not make sense in context.

2. **A** The *others* referred to in the sentence have interests that are not related to food, so the blank must refer to a person whose interest *is* food. Choice (A) is the correct answer. Choice (D) is tempting because *connoisseur* is a word often used in conjunction with fine food or wine. However, a *connoisseur* is a general term for someone who has expertise in subject, which may or may not be food. *Epicure* is a term that necessarily involves food. *Sage* means *wise person*, which is not a match. A *hedonist* is someone who pursues pleasure as a priority, and is the opposite of an *ascetic*.

3. **malevolent** and **an indifferent**

    Given that the critic is seeking *revenge against the owner*, his intentions must be bad. A critic should be *discreet* so that he doesn't ruin his cover, but *malevolent* is the word that matches the clues. *Squalid* means *filthy*, and is irrelevant. In the second blank, you need a word that is dissimilar to vengefulness and conveys impartiality and good intentions. Neither *surreptitious*, which means sneaky, nor *discerning*, which means *discriminating*, has the desired meaning. *Indifferent* is a good synonym for *impartial*, and is the best choice.

4. **eschew**, **dogged**, and **obstinate**

    From the trigger word *and* you know that the first blank has to be similar to *resist change*. *Covet* means to desire greatly and *aver* means to assert, so *eschew* is the correct choice. The next two blanks have to work together. If the *adherence* is strong, then the teachers will be stubborn, and if it is weak, then the teachers will be uncertain. The trigger word *Until* makes it clear that the teachers are preventing changes. Therefore, you need the first situation given above, which would lead to *dogged* and *obstinate*. *Inept* means *unskilled*, and is not a match. *Partisan* may seem plausible for the second blank, but then the teachers would be *biased*, for which there is no available synonym for the third blank. *Sagacious* means *shrewd* and *superfluous* means *unnecessary*, and thus neither one fits the meaning of the third blank.

5.   **inimical** and **a heretical**

The first blank describes Tolstoy's belief regarding *excessive personal wealth* in relation to his *countrymen*; since he was *influenced by aspiring communist revolutionaries*, and relinquished *his copyrights and much of his fortune* to the state, a word like *harmful* would make sense. Of the choices, only *inimical* means harmful. The second blank describes the decision as seen by Sophia; since *she believed in her right to be an aristocrat*, she probably thought it was a *foolish* or *incorrect* decision. Of the choices, only *heretical*, which means contrary to accepted custom, is sufficiently negative.

6.   **impassive**, **arduous**, and **obviate**

Start with the first blank; the clue there is in the second sentence, which says the doctors have a *reluctance to show excitement*. The only choice for the first blank that expresses a suitable lack of emotion is *impassive*. The second blank describes the task of turning the discovery into useful medicine; since the doctors aren't excited, and the end of the passage suggests that significant change is far in the future, you need something like *long and difficult* in the blank. Of the choices, *an arduous* is the best fit. The third blank describes what the new medicine will, hopefully, eventually do to the need for uncomfortable treatments—*eliminate* it. Of the choices, only *obviate* means eliminate. Be careful with *effect*: As a verb, it means to cause, not to have an effect on.

7.   **E**   First, identify the main conclusion of the argument, using the Why Test. The second bold-faced portion is the main conclusion, which is supported by the remainder of the passage. Thus, eliminate choices (A), (C), and (D), which wrongly assert that the second bold-faced portion is information or evidence. Once you have identified the conclusion, you can see that the first bold-faced portion is a claim with which the main conclusion disagrees. Thus, eliminate Choice (B), as the first bold-faced portion is not evidence. Choice (E) is correct.

8.   **"The Board also denied the necessity of paper money, considering the ever-increasing colonial exports purchased by foreign nations that rendered payments in gold and silver."**

Keep in mind that the question says *may* be an exaggeration, but still look for the sentence that provides the strongest support. The correct sentence says that, according to the Board, the colonies were exporting more goods as time went on, and therefore were obtaining more gold and silver. In the face of an increase in gold and silver, the inability to obtain some goods through barter, though limiting, as the text says, likely did not *severely hamper* growth.

9.   **D** Governor Glen's argument relies on the fact that colonists were often forced to barter, but bartering was an unreliable method of doing business. Choice (D) supports that point of view not only by pointing out that the Board was wrong about the colonists' ability to obtain gold and silver from foreign trading partners, but also by giving another example of how barter is a poor system. Choice (A) is incorrect because although trade is low at one point during the year, it may be high enough during the rest of the year for the colonists to save up plenty of gold and silver to last them through the slow months. Choice (B) weakens the argument by widening the range of partners with whom the colonists can barter, thus lessening the need for paper currency. Choice (C) does not address any of the main points of the Governor's argument and neither does choice (E).

10.   **C** Come up with your own word to replace *occupation*, based on the context of the sentence. You might choose a word like *interest* to describe what a destructive El Niño event would likely spark among the world's scientists. Of the choices, only *concern* can mean interest.

11.   **A, B,** and **C**

Each choice is supported. According to the second paragraph, the reduced trade winds during an El Niño fail to bring as much warm water away from South America as is typical. The second paragraph also mentions droughts in places such as Indonesia and flooding in South America. The third paragraph confirms that fish dive deeper, move south, or die off, which negatively affects the fishing industry.

12.   **B** In an inference question, the correct answer must be supported by the text of the passage. Choice (B) is supported: The second paragraph states that *El Niño disturbs weather patterns more powerfully than does any other known force.* Choice (B) is a fair paraphrase of this statement. Choice (A) is not supported: While drought conditions may be severe in these locations during El Niño, the passage offers no information about drought conditions in the absence of El Niño. Choice (C) is wrong because the birds relocate due to reduced food supplies, not the changes in pressure and winds. Choice D is not supported: The 1982–1982 El Niño was the worst El Niño, but the passage does not make a comparison with other climate-related events of that year. Choice (E), finally, is also not supported: While the passage describes some of the effects of the 1972 El Niño event in Peru and Ecuador, no information is provided to make a comparison between those countries and other countries.

13.   **B and C**

The trigger word *although* indicates that the plans for a sunny vacation were overturned unexpectedly in the second half of the sentence, so you need a word that means something like *sudden* or *unexpected* in the blank. Neither *welcome* nor *fortunate* means sudden or unexpected, so eliminate answer choices (A) and (D). Neither *fruitless*, which means useless, nor *lethargic*, which means sluggish, makes sense in the blank; eliminate choices (E) and (F). Both *precipitous* and *unforeseen* can mean sudden and unexpected, so answer choices (B) and (C) give you appropriate, equivalent sentences.

14.   **B and F**

The *disgruntled* workers registered *outcries*, signifying they had intense feelings about their enhanced benefits package that was later rejected; thus, you want a word for the blank that means *passionate* or *emotional*. Neither *pristine*, which means clean, nor *quizzical*, which means puzzling, makes sense in the sentence, so eliminate answer choices (A) and (C). Choices (D) and (E) give roughly synonymous meanings, but nothing in the sentence supports the description of the cries as suggestive. Both *fervent* and *impassioned* can mean passionate, so answer choices (B) and (E) give you appropriate, equivalent sentences.

15.   **A and C**

David is characterized as *narrow-minded* and *adamant*; you can recycle either of those clues into the blank, or you can use a simple word like *stubborn*. Choices (B) and (F) give roughly synonymous meanings, but nothing in the sentence supports the idea that David is hard-working. Neither *gregarious*, which means social, nor *pensive*, which means thoughtful, is supported by the sentence, so eliminate choices (D) and (E). Both *intransigent* and *intractable* mean stubborn, so answer choices (A) and (C) give you appropriate, equivalent sentences.

16.   **A and E**

You have two clues about *the popularity of long-distance automobile travel*: [N]umerous exorbitant tolls indicate that such travel is now more expensive due to excessively high costs, and the *upswing* on the other side of the trigger *while* suggests that the popularity of traveling by car is swinging in the other direction. Hence, you need a word like *decreased* in the blank. Both *intensified* and *surged* are nearly the opposite of what you're looking for, so eliminate choices (C) and (F). Neither *equivocated*, which means spoke in an ambiguous manner, nor *importuned*, which means begged, is supported by the sentence, so eliminate choices (B) and (D). Both *waned* and *abated* mean decreased, so answer choices (A) and (E) give you appropriate, equivalent sentences.

17. **B and C**

In choice (B), the viewer sees the *bare shoulders* as an indication of the woman's character, relating an artistic feature to speculation about the woman's life. In choice (C), the viewer notices a relationship between the life of the director and the life of a character in his film. Both of these choices contain autobiographical observations. In choice (A), the reader sees the novel as an *allegory*, a story about something different from the main plot. In this case, the allegory is about politics, not an autobiography.

18. **"Late Victorian writers obsessed about the relationship between art and the artist—as Basil Hallward lamented in *The Picture of Dorian Gray*, 'We live in an age when men treat art as if it were meant to be a form of autobiography.'"**

In this passage, writers are defined as artists, and as a character in Wilde's novel, Basil Hallward is one of Wilde's creations. The quotation from Hallward is about the autobiographical assumptions that the public makes about art. The problem, or *conundrum*, that the Victorian writers faced concerned the public's inclination to infer information about the artist from his art. Basil Hallward's complaint illustrates their frustration with this tendency.

19. **C** Come up with your own word, based on the context of the sentence. You might come up with something like *meaning*. Of the choices, only *connotation* means meaning. Choice (E) is correct.

20. **D** Begin by considering what role the highlighted portion plays. Before the highlighted portion, the author describes the nature of an experiment. After the highlighted portion, the author describes the details of the results of the experiment. The highlighted portion presents the results in summary form. Thus, Choice (D) is correct. Although the passage discusses neurons and perception, Choice (A) is too broad. Choice (B) is wrong as no hypothesis was offered, let alone refuted. While Choice (C) may seem appealing, the author never commented upon the definitive nature of neurology or any science. Choice (E) is wrong because the author did not attempt to defend the methodology used.

DRILL #2

1. **C** The text tells you that the first novel was *selected as the number one novel*, which means that novel is at the peak and is the *best of all time*. The missing word should mean something that relates to that idea. Eliminate choices (A) and (E) because they both go in the opposite direction of *best of all time*. Choice (D) could be slightly attractive simply because it looks a little like the word *literature*, but it means *engaging in lawsuit* and you can eliminate it. Choice (B) deals with coats of arms and shield and ships, and has nothing to do with books; eliminate it. This leaves you with choice (C), which means *ideal example*.

2. **C** Although several of the answer choices may describe Polonius, you have to use the clues to determine the best answer. The sole clue is that he *speaks epigrammatic lines*, so you're looking for something that means *using maxims* or *pompously moralizing*. Choice (C) means exactly that, so it's your best answer. *Obsequious* means *excessively obedient* and *auriferous* means *containing gold*; neither one has the meaning suggested. Choice (D) and (E) pertain to vocal quality, and are irrelevant.

3. **personalize** and **an inimitable**

    Start with the second blank: The outfit is *changing*, so you know the second blank has to contrast with *run-of-the-mill outfit*. Something like *extraordinary* or *unique* would make sense. Of the choices, only *inimitable* makes sense. Once you have that, it's easy to fill in the first blank: if she's *changing her look* from something *run-of-the-mill* to something *inimitable*, she's *making it her own*. Of the choices, *personalize* is the best fit.

4. **antediluvian** and **salubrious**

    You know that the texts the researcher is working with are *medieval*, so the medical tips are likely to be *old* or *outdated*. Thus, the best word for the first blank would be *antediluvian*, and not *commodious* (comfortable) or *extant* (existing). When the researcher finds the tips, they *surprise* him because they are things that *modern medical experts recommend*. Because of the contrast with *old*, the second blank could mean *current*, or it could mean *healthy* because the medical experts are recommending them. *Salubrious* means *healthful*, and matches one of the possible meanings. Neither *tenebrious* (gloomy) nor *lugubrious* (sad) fits either of the options, so you can eliminate both choices.

5.   **Rationally, escalate, mutual**

From the word *absurdity*, you know the argument was foolish and that each side *felt strongly* about its viewpoint and *refused to consider alternatives*. These clues could make *Tempestuously* attractive for the first blank. However, you have to consider the clue *was impossible for*, which signals that the missing word will contrast with the irrational nature of the argument. Based on the context, *Rationally* is the best choice. For the second blank, the clues tell you that both groups work to *develop bigger and better weapons*, meaning things are getting worse. *Escalate* is the best choice. *Confabulate*, which means *talk over*, and *stagnate*, which means *stop moving*, are irrelevant. Finally, the clues tell you that *each side* is participating, making *mutual* the best choice for the third blank.

6.   **salutary, bullish,** and **feasible**

The author argues that lower taxes would *encourage businesspeople*, so the effects that the lower taxes have must be positive. *Indeterminate* would mean that the effects are *in doubt* and *execrable* would mean they were *negative*. *Salutary* means *positive*, so it's a good fit for the first blank. The second blank must mean that the people's attitude towards investments is *optimistic*. *Bearish* means *cautious*, and *birdlike* means delicate, so those words aren't what you're looking for. *Bullish* means *optimistic*, so it's a good fit for the second blank. The purpose of the tax cuts is to encourage something that is not currently *possible*, so the third blank must mean something like *possible*. *Malleable* means *changeable*, and *atypical* means *unusual*, so those words don't fit here. *Feasible* means *possible*.

7.   **"Trask, for example, considered the eyes of Dr. T.J. Eckleburg, featured prominently on a billboard in the novel, not those of an all-seeing god evaluating Gatsby's personal shortcomings, but those of Thomas Jefferson mourning the collective American abandonment of his belief in hard work and integrity as the paths to fortune."**

The two contradictory aspects of Gatsby's personality are given in the first sentence; he believed in the *agrarian myth* and yet was entrenched in *corruption and materialism*. The passage does not elaborate on the corruption or materialism, so you need to find the sentence that explains what is meant by the *agrarian myth*. You also know from the first sentence that Thomas Jefferson was a proponent of this myth. The correct sentence choice is linked clearly to the myth and gives a solid definition with the phrase *of his belief in hard work and integrity as the paths to fortune*. The sentence that begins *Fitter agreed, perceiving in Fitzgerald...* may seem like a good answer, but there is not enough information to connect *Poor Richard's Almanack* to the *agrarian myth*. Furthermore, the phrase *principles of honorable living* is quite vague and cannot really be considered a definition. The final sentence may also seem like a plausible answer, but, again, there is no direct link to prove the connection between *an austere way of life* and the *agrarian myth*.

8. **B** The question asks which statement can *not* be shown to be accurate for at least one critic, so you can eliminate any answer for which you can find support in the passage. Choice (A) is supported by Mencken's view of the novel, and choice (C) is supported by the phrase *shrewd social commentary*, attributed to *other critics*. Choice (D) is supported by the information in the last sentence on Trask, and choice (E) is supported by the use of the phrase *a thinly disguised reflection of Fitzgerald himself* to describe how Gatsby *has commonly been viewed*. Only choice (B) is not accurate: Although you know that Trask does not think Dr. T.J. Eckleburg's eyes represent god, it cannot be shown that someone else does. Additionally, Gatsby can recognize his *personal shortcomings* without affecting his *self-worth*.

9. **C** Given the placement of the sentence in the paragraph shortly after the phrase *has commonly been viewed as a thinly disguised reflection of Fitzgerald himself*, you know that Fitter believed Fitzgerald intentionally attributed his own personal characteristics to Gatsby. Choice (C) gives the best analogy. Choice (A) is not analogous because the action was unintentional; choice (B) is not analogous because the photographer did not force the model to act as she does. Choice (D) is not analogous because the sequence of events is backwards: The character existed before the student acquired certain habits. And, finally, choice (E) is not analogous because the actor may or may not be expressing himself through the role.

10. **B** According to the passage, cosmologists believe that the missing mass is partially accounted for by *elementary particles too small to be detected by electromagnetic radiation*. Choice (B) rephrases this statement, and so it's the best response. Choices (A) and (E) recycle words from the first sentence of the passage, but they have different meanings; moreover, the first sentence is referring to the problem the cosmologists are trying to solve, whereas the question asks for the solution. Choice (C) is wrong because the passage doesn't say anything about dark matter causing the expansion. Choice (D) also doesn't work: The galaxies are the evidence that shows that Newton's theory has a problem, not the solution.

11. **A** Newton's theory states that massive particles attract each other *with a force proportional to the mass of the particles and their proximity to one another*, so the strength with which the particles attract each other is related to their mass and the distance between them. Choice (B) is tempting, but incorrect: It relates *distance* and *mass* to each other, when it needs to relate them both to *force*. Choice (C) is also incorrect, because it uses the idea of *elementary particles* presented later in the passage out of context—the passage doesn't say that these particles are used as *intermediaries* between massive particles. Choice (A) is supported by the passage: It forms a relationship between *force* and *mass*, which is one of the relationships contained in the theory.

12. **C** This argument contains one of GRE's favorite flaw patterns: The author makes a comparison between Country A and Country B and assumes that those two countries are the same in all relevant respects. Any time you see a comparison flaw, the answer will address whether the comparison is a fair one; in this weaken question, the answer must show that the countries are different in a relevant respect. Choice (C) does so: If the types of coal that the two countries use always differ, it is possible that the regulations on emissions have a negative effect on Country A's industrial production but not on Country B's industrial production. While Choice (A) also provides a difference between the two countries, the link connecting the type of airport, the regulations, and industrial production is less strong than that connecting coal, the regulations, and industrial production in choice (C). Choices (B) and (E) do not establish any difference between the two countries. Choice (D) establishes a similarity between the countries and so does not help explain the differences in industrial production.

13. **B and E**

    The blank should be a word that describes someone who will play lots of concerts and send out many demos of his work. So, the word should be similar to *persistent*. *Dogged* and *tenacious* both are close synonyms for *persistent*. Choices (A), (D), and (F) are detractor answers which you may think are associated with fame, but they do not work with the clue words.

14.   **A and E**

The same-directional semi-colon trigger and the clue words *good omen* are evidence that you need a positive word in the blank. You can recycle the word *good* to describe the symbol. *Prophetic* and *pious* are loosely related to the ideas of symbols and Buddhism, but are not supported by the clues. *Facetious*, meaning *humorous*, and *pervasive*, meaning *spread throughout*, do not fit the context of this sentence. The correct answers are *auspicious* and *propitious*.

15.   **D and E**

The time trigger word *initially*, as well as the clue word *shocked* in the main clause, tells you that the people must not have displayed outrage and were instead happy with the decision. You need a supportive word in the blank, but choices (B), (C), and (F) are all negative words. Choice (A), *effectuate*, means *to bring about*, which is also incorrect.

16.   **A and D**

Although the connection between the first part of the sentence and the Pennsylvania Dutch may not be immediately obvious, the first part must be describing the way these people live, or there would be no reason for the lawyer to change his mind about their lifestyle. So you need to find words that reflect the idea of *living without amenities* and *non-urban*. *Bucolic* and *idyllic* are both used to describe the perfect country setting. *Banal* and *pedestrian* are synonyms that mean *ordinary* or *unimaginative*, so neither of them work. There is no support for *lugubrious*, which means excessively mournful, or *erudite*, which means very learned. The correct answers are choices (A) and (D).

17. **C** You are looking for a choice that is not supported by the passage. Choice (A) is supported by the first sentence, which describes the *ubiquity of jeans across social classes*. You also know the women *hung up their skirts…machinery*, and that action prompted a shift in the symbolism of jeans. The women must have been wearing the jeans and gave up their skirts specifically for factory work; choice (B) is supported and can be eliminated. Choice (D) is supported by the final phrase *the scope of brands and styles that became available*, and choice (E) is supported by the sentence concerning jeans and *rebellious youth*. There is no support for choice (C) because there is no evidence that *poor, working-class men*, or even women a little later on, were actively trying to make a statement. The sequence is backwards; their use of jeans actually created the symbolism.

18. **E** The contradiction referred to in the correct answer is in the first sentence, as indicated by the word *surprising*. Jeans should not be universally popular if they send a narrow message. The highlighted sentence reconciles the contradiction by pointing out that everyone can wear jeans, but the brands and styles still send specific messages. Choice (A) is incorrect because the highlighted sentence is a general comment about the 1970s, not an example. Choice (B) is incorrect because the viewpoint is not different as stated. The highlighted sentence is also not a summary, but rather a continuation of the evolution of the symbolism of jeans, and so choice (C) is incorrect. Finally, the word *conclusively* eliminates choice (D). While the variety of jeans could have been a reason for their increased popularity, there is no evidence that it certainly was the only reason.

19. **B and C**

Choice (A) is incorrect because the passage says that guttation occurs only in vascular plants, and there is no discussion of the difference in the number of vascular plants that exist in the two climates mentioned. Choice (B) is supported because the text says that dew *results from a change between surface and atmospheric temperatures.* Therefore, an analysis that does not factor in those measurements would be *inadequate*, as this answer indicates. The described analysis is also *inadequate* because the passage provides no information on which process is more likely to occur, given that the conditions for both exist. Choice (C) is supported because the passage says that *guttation begins when water moves from saturated soil.* In an arid climate, the soil is not likely to be saturated with moisture. The phrase *under natural conditions* in choice (C) should eliminate exceptions, such as irrigation systems, when considering this choice.

20. **A** In the last sentence, the plants are described as having *pipe-like elements* that enable the process of guttation to take place. *Containing channels* in choice (A) is a good synonym for this description. Choices (C) and (E) may seem plausible, given the reference to houseplants. However, there is no proof that all houseplants are vascular plants, or vice versa. Furthermore, houseplants do not necessarily receive only *little sunlight*, nor do they necessarily have a *moderate climate* in which to grow. Choice (B) is incorrect because you only know the plants *take in* the moisture, not that they *need it*, and choice (D) is incorrect because the plants actually *push out* the moisture, instead of *absorbing* it.